"*Weaving the Paths of Buddhism and Psycho* and wisdom to help the reader deepen int broadening their understanding of what (clarity of the writing will appeal to student: practitioners wanting to integrate the personal, spiritual, — , into life as a practitioner. Helen Carter has contributed a text grounded in both ancient wisdom and contemporary theory but always balanced by humility and humanity. This book is a breath of fresh air."

Greg Madison, PhD, *clinical psychologist and author of* Theory and Practice of Focusing-Oriented Psychotherapy and The End of Belonging

"Helen Carter surveys Buddhist wisdom in light of the deepest psychotherapeutic values. I don't think a book like this has ever been written before. Though her training in both systems is really quite rigorous, what makes this work so special is how personal and immediate it is. *Weaving the Paths of Buddhism and Psychotherapy* is not a treatise on liberation, it is an invitation to discover it for yourself."

Susan Piver, *New York Times bestselling author of* The Four Noble Truths of Love *and* The Buddhist Enneagram

"In *Weaving the Paths of Buddhism and Psychotherapy*, Helen Carter weaves together a very readable blend of biographical experience within an extensive investigation of the relationship between Buddhism and Western counselling and psychotherapy. This book explores in some depth key elements of Buddhist psychology and how they can inform and deepen our understanding and practice of psychotherapy. It is an invaluable resource for anyone embarking upon the journey of bridging these approaches to personal transformation."

Rob Preece, *author of* The Wisdom of Imperfection and The Psychology of Buddhist Tantra

Weaving the Paths of Buddhism and Psychotherapy

Weaving the Paths of Buddhism and Psychotherapy is an empathic guide to integrating Eastern and Western wisdom traditions that share the common goal of easing distress. Following the so-called 'mindfulness revolution' there has been a surge in interest as to how Buddhism's overarching view on suffering may enhance therapeutic practice. This book is not just a clinical text; it is a first-person account of one Buddhist therapist educator's lived experience of bringing Buddhism into the very personal and relational experience of psychotherapy. Western-trained therapists will recognize key concepts: the existential underpinnings of distress, driver behaviour and scripts, modifications to contact such as projection and introjection, relational conditions for healing, ethical considerations, and working with complex presentations and trauma, among others. Through autobiographical vignettes and case-study material, the book offers an invitation to all therapists to consider their own practice of human being.

Helen Carter, PhD, is a UKCP-registered humanistic psychotherapist and practitioner of Tibetan Buddhism. She teaches on the counselling and psychotherapy programmes at the University of Brighton in the UK.

Weaving the Paths of Buddhism and Psychotherapy

The Practice of Human Being

Helen Carter

Routledge
Taylor & Francis Group

NEW YORK AND LONDON

Designed cover image: Internalum (xx) © Nuala Clarke

First published 2024
by Routledge
605 Third Avenue, New York, NY 10158

and by Routledge
4 Park Square, Milton Park, Abingdon, Oxon, OX14 4RN

Routledge is an imprint of the Taylor & Francis Group, an informa business

Library of Congress Cataloging-in-Publication Data
Names: Carter, Helen, 1947– author.
Title: Weaving the paths of Buddhism and psychotherapy : the practice of human being / Helen Carter.
Description: 1. | New York : Routledge, 2023. | Includes bibliographical references and index.
Identifiers: LCCN 2023010213 (print) | LCCN 2023010214 (ebook) | ISBN 9781032464923 (hardback) | ISBN 9781032464930 (paperback) | ISBN 9781003383710 (ebook)
Subjects: LCSH: Psychotherapy—Religious aspects—Buddhism | Buddhism—Psychology. | Psychology and religion.
Classification: LCC BQ4570.P76 C368 2023 (print) | LCC BQ4570.P76 (ebook) | DDC 294.3/36150195—dc23/eng/20230508
LC record available at https://lccn.loc.gov/2023010213
LC ebook record available at https://lccn.loc.gov/2023010214

ISBN: 978-1-032-46492-3 (hbk)
ISBN: 978-1-032-46493-0 (pbk)
ISBN: 978-1-003-38371-0 (ebk)

DOI: 10.4324/9781003383710

Typeset in ITC Galliard
by Apex CoVantage, LLC

For Jamie

Inspiring teacher, dependable colleague, much missed friend.

Without him, this book would not have come into being.

Contents

Acknowledgements

To begin where I began, my mum and dad. How can I ever thank you enough for committing to such an unenviable task, bringing a little human being into the world? This book captures my inheritance: from you Mum, your interest in people; and Dad, your insatiable reading and collecting of knowledge. Your belief in me is unabating – thank you.

To my family and friends who, literally, have kept me sane in the pandemic and while writing this book. Special mentions to Lesley, Ollie, Helen, Andy, and my cousins Sarah and Jo. My one regret is that Eileen, Jamie, Gill, and Louis did not get to see this book. I miss you and think of you often.

Deep appreciation for the teachers who have helped me hone the art of therapy. Thank you, Sue, for giving me such a deep rooting in the humanistic tradition, and for generously proofreading the manuscript. Thank you, Lynne, for modelling the psychotherapist who is first and foremost, human. I forgive you for not putting me back together! Pam, your passion for psychotherapy is contagious; and I continue to bask in your enthusiasm as your colleague. To my supervisor, Julia. I have enjoyed how our relationship has evolved and deeply appreciate your interest in my developing practice frame.

To the therapists I have worked with, learnt from, healed through. Julia, Leanne, Lea, Sue, and Rob. "Thank you" can never be enough, but I hope some of the accounts in this book illustrate your impact on my being.

My therapist peers, Zoe, Liz, and Michelle. As trustworthy sounding boards, you enabled this book to take its final shape; through your friendships, you enable continued exploration of my own shape. Your faith in me is incredibly moving – thank you.

I am indebted to Greg Madison, Susan Piver, and Rob Preece for their touching and gracious endorsements; and to Nuala Clarke whose artwork delivers the container the book so wished for.

To my *Vajra* sangha: Louise, George, Joanne, and my *Ngondro* sisters Blaire, Marybeth, Sandra, and Stephanie. If wisdom and compassion are the two wings of the *Dharma*, you have been the propelling force in the turbulence stirred up by the *Vajrayana*. Deepest bows.

Heart-felt gratitude to my *Dharma* brother and sister. To Christopher, thank you for the nudge into the *Vajrayana* (which I curse and bless each day), but more importantly for helping me experience 'family' as created through love, not just blood. To Crystal, like no other you have known what these past ten years on the path have involved for me. Thank you for your love, humour, and challenge; a combination that clarifies and transmutes any 'spiritual stuttering'. To both of you, thank you for allowing me to adopt La Beau as home. Much of this book has been crafted in this magical landscape: the experiences and the insights, as well as the words themselves.

And finally, to Jeanne, my life companion, my constant. For everything you do for me; whether that is laughing at my jokes, cheerleading whatever crazy commitment this path throws my way, or holding me as I doubt the courage to be. *Merci du fond du coeur.*

Author's note

As coach, teacher, mentor, and therapist I have been working with human beings for over two decades. This book is rooted in the experiences of these relationships in which I have had the privilege to serve.

Wishing to fulfil my desire to explicate a genuine therapeutic process I gave considerable thought as to how best honour these many encounters whilst simultaneously protecting anonymity and confidentiality. Furthermore, I am mindful that any commentary from my side of the relationship is subjective; I wanted to protect clients – past and present – from any side effects of those remarks and interpretations. I made the decision therefore to construct case studies based upon the commonality of human being; favouring the general over the particular. The type of presenting issues that bring people to therapy tend to be few; a common humanity, we share common stories, albeit the individuals behind them are unique. Each case study is a fictionalised composite storying a given theme. I have also fictionalised scenarios and changed biographical details. Nonetheless, the acts of disguise have been carefully considered to ensure the overall aim of conveying authentic therapeutic process (and my experience within) remain genuine and intact.

Furthermore, like all therapists I have been trained to be mindful of self-disclosure, and thus an inherent tension exists writing a book based on personal experience. I cannot fully know what impact the autobiographical material may have on past and current clients, or those coming to work with me in the future. It is my hope that the willingness to bare my vulnerability – of mind, heart, soul, and sprit – not only helps bring being vulnerable out of the shadow but also equalises. All human beings experience pain and suffering; all therapists are human beings. I hope this inspires others to form a different relationship to their own unique way of struggle.

Finally, a note on the conventions of language. Whilst there are arguable philosophical, historical, and theoretical differences between counselling and psychotherapy, this is not the book in which to explore them. Therefore, the word 'therapy' is used inclusively, and likewise a 'therapist' can be a counsellor or psychotherapist.

Chapter 1

Introduction

About me

How I came to find meditation

As a psychotherapist, I have had the privilege to listen to people's life stories in some depth. Furthermore, having run numerous workshops as a coach, meditation instructor, and educator, I have had the opportunity to tell the story of my path. Our worlds are made of stories; we find meaning through our stories. Saying them out loud, sharing them with others. We might even say therapy is the rewriting of story. When I look back at the story of how I came to be here now, the steps along the way seem to make perfect sense. I can assure you it didn't feel like that at the time.

I'll start with some placeholders on my personal timeline. My undergraduate studies were in Sport Science, which led to a specialisation in exercise physiology. After completing my PhD, I was offered a research contract, and from 1998 to 2006 I followed that passion. You'll come to know that one thread that runs through me and therefore my timeline is a thirst for learning and mastery. A full-time research role was therefore my dream. A scientist 'in the lab', I began to develop an intrigue in participating in the very field in which I was researching, endurance exercise. At first, I started running, but a knee injury while training for the London marathon took me to cycling. I will never be able to convey the disbelief: "me, Helen Carter . . . an endurance athlete?"; especially when I became quite good. My full-time research career became the subsidy for living as a semi-professional cyclist and an attempt qualifying for the Commonwealth Games. I didn't reach the levels needed for Melbourne 2006, but as my one-time lecturer Pete Keen pointed out, I "had been close enough to the summit to help others get to the top". Although I kept competing between 2006 and 2008, my passion had become helping others become the best they can be. From researcher to coach, I set up a sport science and consultancy unit, eventually taking this out of the University to become an entrepreneur and business owner. To

DOI: 10.4324/9781003383710-1

this day, I am still struck by what it took to make this move. It allowed me to experience life outside the comfort of the Ivory Tower, and to some extent 'get real' earning my living. I also got to work with some great people – from 'weekend warriors' to Olympians.

Moving out of the lab and into the field opened my eyes to the pressures and stress experienced by athletes. People outside of sport might look at athletes as the prime of the human species – but in my experience, despite obvious physical prowess it is a population with unspoken emotional and psychological pain. It started to dawn on me how unhappy some of the athletes I worked with were: issues of low self-worth, eating disorders, and anxieties that went beyond performance nerves and were more 'existential'. My background as a sport physiologist had prepared me well for writing training programmes, considering nutrition, advising on race strategies, and planning recovery protocols, however, I was finding myself falling short in the 'soft skills'. So, with this in mind I decided to train as a Life Coach.

When I consider my decision to retrain, I can see now there was a seeking force within me to find a solution to my own growing 'angst'. Setting up my own business and the pressure to make enough money for my monthly outgoings was taking its toll. Entering personal coaching was my gateway to the self-development world. I started working with my own 'coach', and this developed into a more therapeutic relationship. I remember a discussion with her in mid-2008 in which I explained how my mind was "full of different voices, like a crackling radio set". Helping me "find the volume dial and tune in to another station", she conveyed I was not on my own after all. I became more cognisant as to the stress of carrying the business, and the anxiety of letting go of my athletic achievements. The growing sense there "must be more to life than this" took me to my GP and to medication. This move helped me get the sleep I needed to gain some clarity and to arrive at some significant life realisations. I needed to re-establish some meaning in my life. Working in sport troubled me: how could I work in an environment that I knew provoked inner demons and created unhappiness?

One evening in February 2009, I found myself sitting in the back row of a meditation class. On the surface, my motivation came from the wish to find another 'tool' to help with my insomnia and anxiety. You can imagine the shock when a maroon-robe clad monk with shaved-head appeared on the chair at the front of the class. Helen, the research scientist with very rational ideas, was not quite sure how she came to be with all these people, hands in the Anjali mudra and reciting mantras! A part of me wanted to run . . . a curious part kept me in the chair. I closed my eyes and began following my breath. I left the class slightly confused, strangely excited and overall, hopeful. By the end of that same year, I was meditating daily and studying Buddhist courses online. Finding the New York-based Interdependence

Project online was the route to finding the Buddhist teachings of Chögyam Trungpa Rinpoche.

The wounded healer

The year I start writing this book is the ten-year anniversary of my meditation path and studying the *Dharma* (the teachings of the *Buddha*). Given the Dalai Lama recommends checking on progress on the path every ten years, perhaps this project is timely. This book is intended 'to help others in helping others', but it is also written as a way of reflecting on my own journey and in celebration of where I have come to be. Like many of my colleagues in the world of psychotherapy, I consider myself a 'wounded healer'. In Jung's words, "The analyst must go on learning endlessly . . . it is [her] hurt that gives the measure of [her] power to heal" (Jung, 2014, pp. 115–116). It took some time to realise my own pain and suffering could be useful. Like many Buddhists – and many clients – I came to meditation and psychotherapy because I wanted to stop suffering: to feel less stressed, to stop feeling so anxious and to (please!) start getting some sleep. If only I had known that both approaches required turning towards the most painful aspects of my life . . . well, it is probably better I didn't know that. I might still be on medication and trying to find a cure for being human.

Therapists often find self-disclosure a difficult territory to navigate. Quite rightly, in counsellor and psychotherapy training there is an emphasis towards non-disclosure so to avoid complications for clients. Increasingly, I have come to share my own experiences of suffering and struggle in client work, but always with the caveat of when it is in the best interest of the client. It was encountering the *Buddha's* central teaching of The Four Noble Truths that I realised my struggles in life were not personal failings but rather the very path of the human being and the only way to 'wake up' to a meaningful life. Over the course of this book, I will share some of these experiences. I start by disclosing that I have encountered many of the obstacles and issues faced by clients. Insomnia at its worst meant that at one point I was getting only four to six hours of sleep per week; patterns of disordered eating and obsessive exercise blighted my PhD years; and still to this day, anxiety is my default emotional backdrop that I have come to know and needed to befriend; in some ways, not to take it so personally. It has taken time to arrive at this place, but in all honesty, these aspects of my suffering co-exist as 'super-powers' in life, in relationships, and in work.

Buddhist, therapist, and educator

As a practitioner on the Buddhist path with its integral teachings on 'non-self', it is interesting to reflect upon labels and the question "who is Helen?"

Without some description, why would someone consider reading my point of view? Who am I to talk about bringing the Buddhist *Dharma* and its practices into therapeutic work?

I took the Refuge Vow[1] back in 2015 but my decision to spend most of 2012 travelling back and forth to New York to train as a meditation teacher demonstrates the heart commitment I had already made. What does being a Buddhist actually mean? To me it means I have made the decision that I want to try and 'wake up' – a term I use in preference to 'enlightenment'. It means I orientate my life towards study of the *Dharma* and to the practices both on and off the cushion. I'll come to more definitions later in this book, but for now I'll describe myself as a practitioner of Tibetan Buddhism and its three 'partitions' of *Hinayana*, *Mahayana*, and *Vajrayana* teachings and practices. For those of you who know (and care) about the details, I practice within the *Kagyu* lineage.

In many respects, being a Buddhist is a full-time vocation; but how I earn my livelihood is through two means. Firstly, I am a psychotherapist in private practice, working with both clients and supervisees in one-to-one and in group situations. My training is as a humanistic therapist, with the specific 'frame' I adopt being the Gestalt approach; no coincidence, given Gestalt and Buddhistic worldviews are incredibly compatible. I started my training as a therapist at the same time I was making transatlantic crossings to New York. A path of integrating the Western and Eastern solutions to suffering was already underway. I was fortunate to have therapy and meditation teachers sympathetic to the other system of thought. My first therapy training was in one way a very natural extension of my training as a Life Coach; and yet it was also a naturally opposing reaction: an about turn on my heels, away from goals and a 'positive mental attitude' on to 'a path without goals' and coming face-to-face with suffering. Certainly, at the time working in competitive sport felt incompatible with training as a therapist and being a meditator. So, I made the decision to sell my coaching business and keep a part-time role teaching exercise physiology whilst completing my therapy training. At that point my intention was to leave academia for good.

Ironically, I was then offered a teaching position upon finishing my master's in psychotherapy and I found myself more deeply embedded in higher education than ever before. However, neither my private practice work nor my teaching of counselling and psychotherapy feel like careers. This isn't because they are not important; the contrary perhaps. It is more that I cannot separate out Helen the Buddhist, the therapist, the educator: they are not roles, merely different vehicles for my practice and commitment to 'waking up'. It is from this perspective that I am writing this book. Work and the relational experiences within help smooth off my rough edges. The people around me are like mirrors, revealing blind spots and uncovering more to learn. Working one-to-one with clients brings a depth of relating; and the group work of teaching brings breadth of angles and differing perspectives of *how* I am in relationships.

About this book

My inspiration

What makes me want to write a book? What makes me want to write about bringing together the Buddhist *Dharma* and therapy? And what makes me think that I have something to say or contribute to that theme? In the words of Gestalt therapist Erving Polster "every person's life is worth a novel" (1987) and I often felt there was a book in me. When I was coaching, my cyclists urged me to write a book covering my philosophy towards training and racing, and specifically an emphasis on bringing out a very 'personal best'. I have always enjoyed writing, but it never came to be. Now feels the right time and the right theme.

Van Manen suggests "to write means to write myself, not in a narcissistic sense but in a deep collective sense. To write phenomenologically is the untiring effort to author a sensitive grasp of being itself" (1990, p. 132). Writing – whether that be journaling or blogging – has come to be the way I find myself and the mastery of new areas. As a Buddhist with a Western psychotherapeutic training, it was down to me to understand the 'what, why, how, and when' of bringing Buddhist ideas into my therapeutic practice, often using my assignments to explore *Dharma* and/or meditation-related themes. In parallel, I was regularly reflecting how the insight gained in personal therapy could be integrated and digested by sitting in meditation.

In this book, I offer my experience of the threefold path of 'Buddhist, therapist, educator' to benefit others. There is a growing interest in using meditation practices in the field of psychological and emotional well-being. It is my view that the emphasis on mindfulness misses out the potential richness offered by Buddhist psychology and philosophy. Furthermore, there is a growing understanding of how the wisdom traditions of psychotherapy and Buddhism offer a synergy optimising and enhancing how to work with suffering. It is therefore understandable that Buddhists who are practising therapists may want to incorporate the two but don't know how; similarly, therapists intrigued by the mindfulness movement are wanting to understand what the practices might bring to their work. Many excellent texts looking at the compatibility of Western and Eastern have been written by very experienced therapists and Buddhist practitioners. I have benefitted by standing on the shoulders of giants such as John Welwood, Judith Blackstone, and Claudio Naranjo, to name but a few. As a trainee, however, I was left feeling inspired but equally frustrated – excellent explications of a synergistic frame, yet little sense of what it looked (and felt) like in the room. What was it to be a 'Buddhism-informed therapist'?

This is the question I asked in my master's research (Carter & Greenwood, 2017). This book deepens that enquiry and is therefore tailored to therapists in counselling and psychotherapy who are training or working in traditional Western therapeutic approaches. Having been one such aspirant, I am inspired to share my story of how I endeavour to bring the two together. I speak of a synergy. In other words, it is a two-way integration and in my experience many Buddhist practitioners would benefit from time working with a therapist. This book may also benefit Buddhists, or those on other spiritual paths, to consider how the sharing of one's story within a therapeutic relationship with an Other brings 'value-added' to the deep relationship with oneself formed in meditation.

My aspiration

When I took the *Bodhisattva* Vow[2] in 2019, I was pledging to help as many people as I could find a similar experience of alleviating their load in life. Writing a book for therapists who can help numerous more people than I can alone is a good economy of effort. The danger is that I appear to be setting myself up as an authority. However, I am not writing this book as an expert – there are far more knowledgeable authorities in psychotherapeutic theory and more senior practitioners of Buddhism; but I do have a story to tell which I hope will be of benefit. The story of how I came to find Buddhism, meditation, and psychotherapy a powerful weave on the journey of healing and 'waking up'.[3]

As the *Buddha* himself said in the *Kalama Sutra*, "Don't go by reports, or by the thought, 'this contemplative is our teacher'" but rather "only when you know for yourselves" if my offerings are helpful. Please read the theories presented not as any kind of truth, but rather as placeholders or 'hooks' that might be useful to help understand your experience(s). If what I write in my experience(s) doesn't fit or help you, please disregard.

My apology

In refusing to take an expert position and instead offer my own experience and interpretations, if I make any factual errors that may mislead, I apologise to the reader. In addition – less apology, more caveat – there are many different psychotherapeutic approaches and as many forms of Buddhism. I am a Westerner practising Tibetan Buddhism outside of its geographical and cultural origin. Likewise, I am a European humanistic psychotherapist practising outside of that frame's geographical home of the West Coast of the United States. This book chronicles how these two particular streams have weaved-through and intersected-in the human being, "Helen". It is not my intention, nor can be, to take the particular into the general and propose one clinical approach.

My arc towards human being

Before proceeding, I wanted to speak a little to the shape of my path, and especially to the process often referred to as 'individuation'. At the very foundation of humanistic psychotherapy is the notion of actualisation. With deepening understanding and practice experience, the processes of integration and symbolisation have taken on greater significance for me: that *integration* requires a full-on experiencing of deeper potentials (Mahrer, 1978); and this experience necessitates the creation of meaning, *symbolisation* (Gendlin, 1997). Both are thus antecedents to actualisation, which in itself cannot therefore be organic. It requires work of the self. I came to this more 'experiential humanistic' view through the 'back door' of Jungian depth psychology. Individuation, the process of becoming whole, sees one's self-identifying shift from 'ego' to a new centre of 'Self' that includes both the unconscious and the conscious ego.[4] Authors who straddle the humanistic/transpersonal approaches consider individuation to be roughly equated with self-actualisation in its complete form (i.e., preceded by integration and symbolisation).

I start here because Jung's individuation process inherently involves the feminine and the masculine; archetypes that refer to energetic patterns of being, both of which are present in all people, at all times. The feminine is characterised by the natural tendency of relating based upon receptivity and openness, feeling and intuition; the masculine is more detached and objective, governed by thinking and concept. Indeed, the qualities of the feminine and masculine are often presented in paired polarities: receiving versus seeking; being versus becoming. Much of my own journey towards individuation has been redressing the balance of these two energies, an assimilation heavily influenced by a developmental model of static and dynamic masculine and feminine aspects detailed in the work of two Jungians, Gareth Hill (2001) and Barbera Stevens-Sullivan (1989). In brief, the static feminine (SF) is undifferentiated being and often depicted as Mother Nature who produces hundreds and thousands of offspring; the dynamic feminine (DF) is a more playful form of creation; an experience that is carefree and responsive, energetically depicted by Eros. It cherishes connection between, rather than continuation of, the species (as in the static form); the static masculine (SM) carries an energy of the king, overseeing organisation, creating rules and regulations through logos; and the dynamic masculine (DM) is symbolised by the phallus, action towards a goal, and thus linear analysis, cause and effects are sought.

According to Jung, the journey of individuation requires access to both sides of consciousness. Hill proposes a developmental move from unity (SF), to differentiation (DM), to integration (SM), and finally individuation (DF); and only then we enable our whole Self. The woman, unable to access her animus (Jung's term for the unconscious masculine principle) will have a tendency for that energy to break out in a negative and destructive manner. In Hill-speak, the static masculine is composed of ready-made opinions, argumentation, and dogmatism; the dynamic masculine, of drive and privileging achievement. This will interfere with her ability to relate and be receptive – a block of her feminine principle. Hill's adapted model also suggests that at any one time in our life cycle, one aspect may dominate, leading to a particular mode of consciousness, and subsequent repression and/or projection of other aspects. As Stevens-Sullivan explains "Women have raged against men in the outer world, unaware of the ways in which their own inner masculine aspects have oppressed them more brutally and consistently than outer men could imagine" (1989, p. 16).

Unexpectedly, my path of human being has taken me into the depths of gender, sexuality, and womanhood. Not just territories I needed to traverse, but the very essence of my individuation. I am a gay woman, but only came to 'know' and live this in the second half of my life. And it has only been in the second half of the relationship with my wife that something else has come to emerge; the relationship as an 'alchemical container' that has nurtured an alternative sense of self. Not simply an identity, but a more congruent expression of who, on some level, I knew I already was.

My childhood self knew. I delighted in being a Tomboy. I belonged with boys, I knew how to be, I didn't feel different to them. I can only have been six or seven when Mum bought me a bag, lavender in colour. On it "Daddy's little girl". A well-intended gift and YET it conveyed a message. I only remembered this childhood event recently, and as Jungian Robert Romanyshyn notes (2007), it was a complete remembering. Stored in my viscera was the felt-confusion of that youngster at that time, "Am I?" Something of my Tomboy innocence was pierced. Self-concept replaced Self. And by puberty, 'innocence' became a sort of naivety and persona. I took on the burden of conforming to societal discourse – what I should be and should do. I lived as a woman and did all the things a 'woman' should. Dutiful daughter, dedicated girlfriend, conscientious student, diligent academic, driven athlete. Head rather than heart.

It is only in the last ten years that I have deeply questioned who I am. Three key events that have stirred my inner knowing are remembered. The first was attending the wedding of my partner's sister. We both wore skirts, and I remember feeling so uncomfortable, and not just because we were a gay couple attending a Catholic family wedding. I came home knowing I would never wear a skirt again. The second, the weekly conversations with the counsellor I was seeing during the early days of my therapy training helped me unravel biology, sexuality, gender: what those words meant to me, and how to live the trajectory of "Helen" congruently. The third memory is being in the Brooklyn apartment of a friend. As she prepared dessert, I saw a little mouse scurry across the kitchen floor to hide. Pointing and humorously exclaiming "ani-mouse!" "Or maybe she's your anima" she provocatively retorted. Coming from someone who knows me so well, this became an invitation to delve into aspects 'hidden': through Jungian psychology, archetypes, shadow, and the feminine.

It is no coincidence that these three events have come during the time I have been meditating. The Western ideas presented here have been a great map. Hill's developmental arc of static feminine, to dynamic masculine, to static masculine have helped me understand my drive, my self-sufficiency, my need for certainty, my fear/distrust of authority yet need for rules as exhibited in my life to date. The model has also pointed out the terrain of what needs to be traversed now I am in mid-life – meeting the dynamic feminine and going into the 'descent'. The three years it has taken to write this book have coincided the Covid-19 pandemic. During this time, I have also stepped into the world of the *Vajrayana*, a form of Buddhism incorporating complex philosophical thought and mystical rituals. The Eastern wisdom view of the Buddhist *Dharma*, and the skilful means of meditation have enabled the conceptual map to move to the experiential terrain. From head to a tenderised (sometimes broken) heart.

The *Vajrayana* concerns itself with the dance and balance of masculine and feminine energies in the phenomenal world. Unlike Western religions, the feminine (equated with the body) is not demonised, nor is it to be transcended. Even Jungian psychology, in attempting correction to the prevailing masculine bias, brings a hierarchy and dichotomy (light masculine conscious, dark feminine unconscious). Gross (1984) in her writing on the feminine principle in *Vajrayana* identifies the most important requirement for balance between feminine and masculine principles as the primordial and elemental co-equality. In a world more sensitive to gender, we might say the two indivisible aspects of the same consciousness before man or woman is the ultimate non-binary; an 'unbinary'! The most basic pairing of the masculine and feminine in Buddhism is space and form. And like with Hill's static feminine making way for the dynamic masculine in the process of separation, in the Buddhist View, if it were not for the feminine element, the masculine could not arise. Compassionate action of the masculine cannot be so without the discriminating awareness wisdom of the feminine.

It is the rituals and practices of the *Vajrayana* that have been the vehicle for my 'descent' towards felt experience, one that is both ineffable and timeless. Visualisation of archetypal deity and *dakini* help the practitioner become more aware of the feminine and its enlightened qualities. Moreover, imagining oneself as embodying the qualities of awakened mind goes some way towards a rebalancing. Again, we only need to talk in terms of a balancing dichotomy because they have been systematically dichotomised. These practices are 'training wheels' to help the meditator understand and appreciate the significance of space, of background, of emptiness. Since I have been practising the *Vajrayana*, my meditation practice has taken on a new quality. As Gross adds from her own experience, we "begin to realise that, if anything, action is the 'easier' part; learning to recognise space, to do nothing, to develop discriminating awareness wisdom is the 'harder' part of meditation training and enlightened activity".

Undoubtedly, over the coming pages and chapters you will see how this all comes to life. To inhabit my body rather than use it; to be receptive to 'what is' rather than stamp 'my way' on life; to live the 'both/and' of the Middle Way. The words of alchemist Catherine MacCoun ring true "To attain a magician's power, one must relinquish the impulse to force and conquer. To change anything in an alchemical way, you must allow IT to change YOU" (2008, p. 32). Was encountering the upside down, inside out world of *Vajrayana* during a pandemic the ideal timing for one's 'dark night of the soul'? It was certainly a perfect and paradoxical storm that felt both a blessing and a curse.

Overview of content and chapter

When considering how to structure this book, I questioned whether shaping the content around an autobiographical timeline would better safeguard my heuristic[5] intention. I felt this to be in tension with the desire to provide the reader with key information for becoming a Buddhism-informed practitioner. I hope the decision to organise the content into themes but embrace autobiographical material therein is effective.

Chapter 2, "East Meets West", provides the reader the context within which this book rests. I present the positions that the ancient system of Buddhism and contemporary Western psychotherapy take on human distress, and what their synergy might offer: namely, a weave of the absolute and relative; being and becoming. There is also a brief history of this East/West meeting before detailing the therapeutic approaches that have been developed as a result. I end this chapter with some reflection on philosophy since any attempt to bring together wisdom traditions must be informed by critical thinking and checked for compatibility.

Chapter 3 focuses on "The Human Condition" starting with my story of what it has been to be a human (to date), how my identity has shifted, and how this relates to my experience of distress. I introduce the Buddhist View, describing the three marks of existence that we humans share. One of our common human experiences is that of 'suffering', one that the *Buddha* placed at the centre of the *Dharma* teachings with The Four Noble Truths. This chapter introduces the first two Truths – the diagnosis and aetiology of *dukkha*[6] (suffering) before moving onto a comparison of this presentation with Western models. Traditional psychoanalytic, humanistic, and Buddhistic frames of human nature (deficiency to overcome, propensity for health, inherent health, respectively) are presented, as are their view on what causes distress and the path to alleviation. The chapter ends with a client case study of "Deena" and her journey from 'doing' to 'being'.

Chapter 4 introduces the reader to the Buddhist alchemical methodology of "Taking suffering as the path". The invite of the first two Noble Truths is to go against our instincts and turn towards our experience of suffering. How our suffering is perpetuated and accumulates is explored through the visual depiction offered by the Wheel of Life; how it is then stored in the body is presented, and the client case study of "Claire" is used to illustrate how the Buddhist lens might help loosen some of the patterns that keep us bound. This case study also allows us to visit the teachings on *karma* – perhaps the most well-known yet most misunderstood teaching from Buddhism.

Chapter 5 follows on with the Third and Fourth Noble Truths where the *Buddha* proposes his prognosis and suggested treatment plan for the "Alleviation of distress". I share some of my experiences of meeting meditation, and how the practice opens a gap between 'stimulus-response' in which we find choice. The Eightfold Path is introduced; a very practical teaching that offers enactment of choice and responsibility, and thereby a way to well-being. Anxiety is a common human experience that can be softened from opening up the gap, and I offer my work with "Carol" as an illustration at the end of the chapter.

The next two chapters cover parameters that therapists know bring healing and growth: relationship and interventions. Chapter 6 deals with "The role of the therapist-client relationship" and introduces some aspects where Buddhism may offer 'value-added' to the relational vehicle. My relationship with "Penelope" offers a case study to demonstrate how therapeutic presence scaffolds a sense of an interdependent self. Chapter 7 offers some thoughts and illustrations as to "The role of meditation practices" as interventions for second-order change. I offer the reader my experiences as a practitioner and as a teacher of meditation before detailing my work with "Sebastian" to show how the practice can assist the journey towards wholeness and alleviation of distress in therapy.

Chapter 8 delves into the "Practical implications and applications" of a Buddhism-informed therapy. A range of topics and themes are covered. I explain how Buddhism has formed a container for my work: as the ground upon which I form my being, and as an ethical code within which I situate my doing. The chapter then turns to consideration of working in the spiritual and transpersonal, a theme I felt important to address given main-stream psychotherapy tends not to honour this wider dimension of our being. Furthermore, I would argue that humanistic therapists need to know the upper 'cusp' of the paradigm. The case study of "Jacob" exemplifies working with Buddhists, and justifies tracing the arc of human being, from the personal through to the transpersonal. This chapter also considers the applicability of Buddhism-informed work with non-Buddhists.

Chapter 9 continues with an emphasis on the practice of a Buddhism-informed therapy and is a chapter deliberately dense with client case work. Firstly, this felt the best way to convey how Buddhist principles might help with complex presentations (Borderline, Narcissistic, and Schizoid personality adaptations are covered). Secondly, it has been my experience – especially as a trainee – to lament a lack of published case material when traversing such demanding terrain. The chapter brings forth some of my experiences in synthesising classical psychoanalytic theory, contemporary theory from the humanistic paradigm, and integration of Buddhist ideas.

Chapter 10 attempts to bring together the themes in the book so far and postulate the "Benefits of an integrated path". Again, visiting themes from the transpersonal approach, the very nature of self and its composites are explored, inviting the therapist to ponder: how does 'self' incorporate the aspects of spirit and soul? To aid this consideration, the Buddhist model of mind and consciousness are outlined. We revisit the arc of human being, this time considering when spiritual paths are pursued without sufficient developmental maturity, endangering 'spiritual bypassing', in the chapter's case study of "Jim".

We reach the end of our journey together with Chapter 11, "Ground, Path, Fruition". As this 'threefold logic' suggests, we look at the beginning, middle, and end of the journey of becoming a Buddhism-informed practitioner. I offer my own experience as a path aspirant and now as someone who assists others on this path to reflect on the training needs and development of a wannabe Buddhism-informed therapist. I also offer some personal reflection on how all of "this" (the material in the book) manifests in human being, both on and off the meditation cushion. We also revisit how *karma* becomes a central aspect of the path.

To emphasise an experiential lead, within each of the themes covered in this book I aim to convey how the combined journey of therapy and Buddhism have changed me and my life over the past ten years. At the beginning of each chapter there is an autobiographical 'vignette'. Insights from the *Dharma* are provided to help understand the processes at play from a Buddhist view. To complement this, relevant psychotherapeutic theory proposes consideration of the implications within the therapeutic setting and facilitation of the relationship between therapist and client. To come full circle, each chapter ends with a client case study to illustrate how transformation comes through being and being-with-other.

Notes

1 The official point of becoming a Buddhist.
2 *Bodhisattva* refers to the practitioner who is motivated to attain *Buddha*hood for the benefit of all sentient beings, and in doing so to bring all beings to their own awakening.
3 Gabor Maté, physician and expert on addiction, stresses healing is not an end point but rather a process towards wholeness (Maté & Maté, 2022).
4 A useful analogy is considering the shift Copernicus invited from an Earth- to a Sun-centred solar system. In other words, ego still exists – it is simply put back in its place!
5 A search for the discovery of meanings and essence in significant human experiences.
6 Sanskrit terms are italicised throughout the book and defined on their first use. The reader can also cross reference using the glossary in the Appendix.

References

Carter, H., & Greenwood, D. (2017). The Experience of Therapists Using the Buddhist Dharma and Meditation in Their Psychotherapy Practice. *Journal of Transpersonal Research, 2*, 105–118.

Gendlin, E.T. (1997). *Experiencing and the Creation of Meaning: A Philosophical and Psychological Approach to the Subjective.* Evanston, IL: Northwestern University Press.

Gross, R.M. (1984). The Feminine Principle in Tibetan Vajrayana Buddhism: Reflections of a Buddhist Feminist. *The Journal of Transpersonal Psychology, 16*(2), 179–192.

Hill, G. (2001). *Masculine and Feminine: The Natural Flow of Opposites in the Psyche.* Boulder, CO: Shambhala.

Jung, C. (2014). *Collected Works of C.G. Jung, Volume 17: Development of Personality.* Princeton, NJ: Princeton University Press.

MacCoun, C. (2008). *On Becoming an Alchemist: A Guide for the Modern Magician.* Boulder, CO: Shambhala.

Mahrer, A. (1978). *Experiencing: A Humanistic Theory of Psychology and Psychiatry.* New York, NY: Brunner/Mazel.

Maté, G., & Maté, D. (2022). *The Myth of Normal: Trauma, Illness, and Healing in a Toxic Culture.* London: Ebury Publishing.

Polster, E. (1987). *Every Person's Life Is Worth a Novel.* Highland, NY: Gestalt Journal Press.

Romanyshyn, R. (2007). *The Wounded Researcher: Research with Soul in Mind.* New Orleans, LA: Spring Journal Books.

Stevens-Sullivan, B. (1989). *Psychotherapy Grounded in the Feminine Principle.* Asheville, NC: Chiron Publications.

Van Manen, M. (1990). *Researching Lived Experience: Human Science for An Action Sensitive Pedagogy.* New York: Routledge.

Chapter 2

East meets West

As I sit down to write this chapter, I come into contact with a hesitation and doubt – a recognition of how different it feels compared to the experience of writing the opening section. I am now moving from the autobiographical to the 'factual', and I notice the impact upon me: I feel a contraction and a pressure to deliver.

The awareness of such an experiential process provides a snapshot of how my practice has shaped my being: I have become more able to recognise my reaction to interacting with the phenomenal world; I take a pause, and in that 'gap' I am able to shape a response. I come back to my intention for this book, and I open. I gain confidence and start writing.

At the beginning of my career as a therapist, I might have asked "what do I need to know about Buddhism in order to consider using it in my therapeutic work with people?" I may want to take an even more preliminary step and ask, "Why would I even want/need to look at an integration?" You the reader might have similar questions, so perhaps we can start there.

Why bring together Western psychotherapy and Eastern wisdom traditions?

Both psychotherapy and Buddhism can be said to share the same goal – to alleviate the suffering and distress of being a human. However, the level at which the 'methods' are pitched differs. Buddhism points to "the ubiquitous human striving for security and stability" (Young-Eisendrath, 2003, p. 303) or in other words, there is a general human suffering that comes with an inability to accept impermanence and change. Psychotherapy on the other hand works with the particular; the personal ways in which we come to experience distress.

A teaching from Buddhism that provides a useful frame is that of the two levels of 'truth': the absolute and the relative. Allow me to describe my experience this morning as I meditated on the beach. Sitting looking out

DOI: 10.4324/9781003383710-2

across the sea, I could get in touch with the timelessness and vastness of life; the bigger picture of reality that goes beyond the mere human being. Nature often has this effect. We can 'lose' ourselves. In these transcendental or transpersonal experiences, we realise we are no different to everything around us. Buddhism uses an expression called 'emptiness' to describe this experience, and this is the 'absolute' level of truth. When my wife arrived with breakfast and a coffee, we each had our own way of experiencing that moment and therefore, of experiencing our relationship. Any experience in a given moment is dependent on all the moments leading up to that point including our overall life histories. Psychological work deals with this individual or relative truth. As psychotherapists, we might understand any intra- and inter-personal dynamics (such as splits, conflicts, projections, scripts) as examples of relative truth. We are each unique beings with our own patterns of conditioning and personal meaning.

Do we really need another therapy? What can an ancient wisdom tradition offer to contemporary Western society? Freud gave us a clue in *Studies in Hysteria*, exclaiming "much will be gained [in psychoanalysis] if we succeed in transforming hysterical misery into common unhappiness" (Freud & Breuer 2004, p. 306). Is a manageable unhappiness our best-case scenario, or can the Buddhist view offer something beyond that? Both Freud and later Carl Rogers emphasised a dependence on others, whether that be societal approval suppressing our drives or our caregivers laying down 'conditions' for love and attention. In earlier times, there was arguably a greater contribution of 'others' to an optimal 'holding environment'. Children were brought up in nuclear families often with the support of community or 'elders'; there was more connection to nature; and religion provided a framework for living that people generally adhered to through common consensus. It is generally considered that the Western malaise – one of speed and insatiable need for accomplishment to feel a sense of worth – is explainable through childhood environments not being, in Donald Winnicott's language, 'good enough'. If we receive love and attention when young, we are likely to develop 'secure attachment' and a trust in our sense-of-self. Attachment patterns are known to dictate how our brains form, how well our endocrine and immune systems function, how we handle emotions, how subject we are to depression, how our nervous system functions and handles stress, and how we relate to others. Symptoms of 'insecure attachment' might include disembodiment, lack of grounding, ongoing insecurity and anxiety, overactive minds, self-hatred, and an inability to deeply trust. To overcome a deep sense of inner deficiency, we seek comfort through the external world; our sense of worth is in what we do rather than who we are. Contemporary suffering can be said to be a disconnect from one's own humanity.

Spiritual traditions like Buddhism explain the cause of suffering in general terms as the result of ignorance, faulty perception, or disconnection from our true nature.[1] Western psychology and psychotherapy provide a more specific developmental understanding: how suffering stems from childhood conditioning; and how this creates a rigid and distorted image of self and other. We carry this 'baggage' of our past around with us. Thus, a Buddhism-informed psychotherapy might be thought of as a way towards a system of complete well-being; an expression of absolute true nature in a thoroughly personal, human form (Welwood, 2002).

Wholeness: human being and becoming

In *The Matrix*, Neo is invited by Morpheus to take the red pill and see "how deep the rabbit hole goes". Many people, however, choose the blue pill, remaining trapped in the illusion that happiness is attainable by achieving and having more. For others, a part of them sees through the illusion and wants to 'wake up' and live another way; to choose wholeness rather than perfection. For many, the decision to pursue a different way happens around mid-life. Some people even come to discover that the red pill comes in two doses – as well as actualisation or individuation (the Western notions of growth), there is a possibility of realisation (we will return to this idea when we look at the arc from the humanistic through the transpersonal in Chapter 8's case study of "Jacob").

Attempts thus far to bring the Buddhist and Western psychotherapeutic traditions together range from being complimentary, a meld, or an integration. Buddhist psychologist John Welwood (1984) prefers to see the two as separate albeit synergistic. Horizontal unfolding is facilitated in Western psychotherapy through the therapist-client dialogue, the client's presentation of life issues and sharing of stories, and the therapist's witnessing and response. Psychological work brings understanding and insight; for example, recognising a turbulent childhood that lay behind patterns still seen in relationships of today. The horizontal is the process of 'becoming'. In contrast, Welwood describes spiritual work as a vertical dimension. When on retreat with John in the US a few years ago, I had a first-hand experience in one meditation session of 'dropping in' to a state of being, as if taking an elevator down and meeting the flow of experience directly, no concepts or categories. Being able to tune back into that state is not always easy, but I know now it is there for me. The basic premise of this work is to learn how to rest in that being more completely and more often.

In this description, we see the ideas of relative and absolute again. The horizontal unfolding is *becoming* in the world; whilst the vertical is *being* in each moment 'as it is'. This is one of the times that Buddhism asks us to hold two seemingly contradictory notions together, like two sides of the same coin. Obviously, Helen IS writing these words; but if I rest in experience and try to find her, where is she? "Helen" isn't a solid, fixed thing.

What I think of as "Helen" is actually movement, process, change, flow; a conglomeration of sensations and thoughts coming from those experiences. This mode of experiencing is accessible on retreat, but hard to stay in contact with on re-entry to everyday life. In fact, spiritual realisation is easier than actualising and integrating it fully into one's everyday life. Wholeness might be considered therefore the continual shuttling between being and becoming, the absolute and the relative aspects of reality.

The trap of spiritual bypassing

The *Buddha*, his teachings and his practices go back 2,600 years. Freud first presented his psychoanalysis in the late 1800s. The fact the two traditions have existed independently begs the question why would we need to integrate them in some way. What are the traps of actualising without realisation? And similarly, wouldn't a sole pursuit of realisation be enough?

There is a thesis that spiritual practice like Buddhism might help us to connect to something bigger and offer us complete liberation from suffering by working through an imprisoning self-structure that is the fixed and solid "I". There is a paradox however: the work towards 'being' presupposes a stable self-structure. We've already touched on the contemporary Western society malaise, and how without appropriately well-attuned parenting, children become adults without achieving key developmental stages. 'Unfinished business' from childhood brings unresolved emotional material and problems in relating to the world. One such presentation we might meet in the therapy room is Narcissistic personality adaptation. Imagine someone with the 'thick-skinned' variant coming to the spiritual path to counter the suffering they are experiencing in life. There is a risk of 'spiritual bypassing' – the tendency to avoid or prematurely transcend basic human needs, feelings, and developmental tasks (Welwood, 1984). The spiritual practitioner with Narcissistic adaptation might use progress along the path to inflate and defend the incomplete sense of self that lies underneath. There is also the opposite aspect of Narcissistic presentations, the fragile or 'thin-skinned'.[2] The Buddhist path and its absolute view of egolessness is an attractive, yet dangerous, proposition for people who don't carry self-worth. We will explore this important concept more deeply later in the book with the case study of "Simon" in Chapter 9.

The pitfalls of introspection

As a psychotherapist, I absolutely attest to Socrates' defiant statement that "the unexamined life is not worth living" – I vote for the red pill! However, it is also interesting to consider the ways in which such examination might narrow rather than widen experience in life. One doesn't have to be in psychoanalysis five times a week to risk being overly introspective to the point of solipsism, or "I am the only mind that exists". I remember going for a walk one Sunday during my therapy training and it was only on my return I realised I hadn't looked up and taken in the countryside and seascape – I was so invested in my internal world that I had ignored the world around me. We can become so involved in self-critique and analysis that we risk entangling ourselves. I've also been in therapist social circles where everyone is so busy wanting to 'process' that it stifles any sense of ease or spontaneity in relationship. Whilst some might view meditation as 'navel gazing', the Buddhist view offers the antidote of 'raising the gaze' and with it, an equalisation of mental activity as just another of the senses. Another protection offered by the absolute view in Buddhism is that we are not separate from others nor the phenomenal world. The path of Buddhism offers transit through the complete developmental continuum: dependence to independence, and on to interdependence.

My experience

When I finished the first two years of my training, I had a decision to make regarding my next steps. As a qualified 'counsellor' in the humanistic tradition, one option was to stay at the same training institution for the MSc programme and become a psychotherapist in the same modality. Or I could seek training in line with my growing curiosity of Buddhism's healing power. I had been meditating and studying Buddhism for four years at that point and was feeling the benefit of being on both paths. Yet there was still a separation between the spiritual and the psychological. My Buddhist path was for me: it provided support for my life, and the meditation practices help me ground and bring self-care. In the room with clients, however, I was strictly a humanistic practitioner in the classic existential-phenomenological working view and method. My therapy room was also my office and where I meditated each morning, but my Buddhist being was kept discrete. My shrine was out of sight in the corner, as were my Buddhist texts. Clients might deduce my spiritual path by linking my Gestalt priority on 'awareness as restorative' within the zeitgeist of 'mindfulness'. Clients would be curious about my mindfulness teaching and ask me how I had benefitted from meditation. With some clients, there would come a request I teach them meditation as part of the work together.

Given I had found a benefit of meditating while being a client, it wasn't too surprising to me that clients who were meditating were often able to better digest and assimilate experiences in therapy. Indeed, Eugene Gendlin, the founder of 'Focusing', found this to be the case in his clinical and research work. Those people more successful in therapy come to an inner knowing and bodily sense of meaning that goes beyond what the conscious mind can articulate. Whether we help clients tap this through the steps of Focusing in the therapy room, or they develop a meditation practice that helps them become more present and embodied, awareness of direct experience is fostered. I will return to this later in more detail (see 'Shuttling between insight and experience, p. 171). In brief: sitting with a therapist who attends and listens to the story provides support in development of insight and can bring attention to what is being experienced. Thoughts, feelings, and emotions might arise through the dialogue; all of which can be sat with, witnessed, and held whilst sitting in meditation – whether in the therapy room, or at home in between sessions. This was my experience as a client and continues to be my experience as a therapist facilitating clients' unfolding journeys. I would add that very often, a client who meditates often comes to a session with experiences 'on the cushion' that they want to understand through exploration with me. It sets up something of a cyclical process: insight, awareness, resting with, processing.

All this is to say in my early days of being in practice, my faith in simultaneous therapy and meditation grew. In the end I continued with a more 'classic' mainstream Western psychotherapeutic training, but this decision was in service of taking a 'both/and' approach to my work. Whilst few and far between, there were 'contemplative' psychotherapy trainings in the UK back then, but I felt training more deeply in Western psychotherapy would allow me to go more deeply with the Buddhist application too. In effect, I wasn't having to choose one or the other, I simply had to attend to a balance. A balance in the Jungian sense I detail in the introductory chapter and for which John Welwood (1984, p. 72) provides a beautiful metaphor of a large tent, "like one of those circus tents with a high roof. There is life going on inside the tent, lots of activities and energy. And I can feel that I am this life inside the tent, as well as the structure that contains it – the poles and awning and the high ceiling". Welwood explains this structure keeps out the rain and protects the life within; this is therapy, the firm grounding of the tent, as well as addressing the leaks! He continues

> the sides of the tent remain open, so that the fresh air and breezes can keep blowing through. So, though I am this structure that is tied to the earth, I can still expand out all around. This seems to be the nature of our awareness as human beings: we need earthly structures and frameworks in which to live, yet we are also permeated and surrounded by vast reaches of openness offered by a spiritual discipline.

I greatly appreciate this metaphor, as it conveys the alchemy of the open space and structure, emptiness and form, that allows change to happen.

Since retiring as a competitive athlete and changing gears from being a career-focused academic, I have worked to counter the predominant masculine energy of structure and 'push', surrendering more to the feminine of open space. Letting go of 'project identity' as pursued through accomplishment is not easy. For many of us, this developmental stage rears up in mid-life. For me, this coincided with retraining as a psychotherapist – giving me the ideal vehicle to move from perpetual 'becoming' to 'being'. We will touch on this a bit later when we consider the move from self to Self (p. 162) through the process of individuation.

Existing systems of Buddhism-informed therapy

It was in the early 19th century that Western curiosity in Buddhism gained momentum. The Colonial period took many Europeans to Asia at a time when archaeology was a growing pursuit, and the first 'Buddhologists' came to be. The first translations of Sanskrit manuscripts were made in the mid-1800s. At the same time, there was something of a Buddhist romanticism with its ideas appearing in popular culture through the writing of Arthur Schopenhauer, Herman Hesse, Walt Whitman, and Henry Thoreau. However, it was with the mass exodus of Buddhist teachers from Tibet fleeing the Chinese invasion in the 1950s that shifted an intrigue to adoption of Buddhism in the West. It always strikes me that Tibet's tragic loss of independence has been the West's gain. Many commentators believe the arrival of these teachers mixed with the spirit of experimentation in the 1960s and 70s fuelled an existential engagement with Buddhism. It was after all the same era of the humanistic movement. Young people travelled to Asia in search of teachers and gurus formed the first generation of Western teachers: including the likes of Joseph Goldstein, Jack Kornfield, and Jon Kabat-Zinn.

Mindfulness-based therapies

Kabat-Zinn is considered by many as a pioneer in 'the Mindfulness Revolution'. His work with cancer patients and sufferers of chronic pain gave birth to the first clinical application of meditation: Mindfulness-Based Stress Reduction. 'MBSR' moves patients through an eight-week progression of exercises to build attention and non-judgemental awareness in order to work with habitual patterns and reactivity. A whole range of mindfulness-based interventions have since developed, all seeking to alter the relationship people have with physical symptoms and/or mental phenomena: Acceptance and Commitment Therapy, Dialectical Behaviour Therapy, and Mindfulness-based Cognitive Therapy, to name a few. Research has shown these programmes to have a significant effect on pain, anxiety, depression, and other medical symptoms. So effective is MBCT in reducing relapse/recurrence of clinical depression, it is now a 'treatment of choice' (alongside CBT) in the UK. As well as the health benefits of the practice, neurobiologists are identifying changes in brain function and structure after periods of mindfulness practice that appear to enhance cognitive function and shifts in emotional processing. Applications outside of the medical field are being found in the domains of education, business and leadership, the creative arts, and sporting performance.

The practice of mindfulness-meditation is being sold as an antidote to the speed and stresses of contemporary life. With some synchronicity, this is at a time when organised systems of religion are on the decline and people are thinking of other ways to develop their spiritual selves. Buddhism, its practices no longer marginalised, might provide the container in which the search for meaning can be held. In my role as a trainer of counsellors and psychotherapists, at least four or five students a year ask about Buddhism and where they can go to get the basics. Some have attended a mindfulness course and have a curiosity about the roots of the practice; others' curiosity comes from the existential search that arise in one's therapy training: "Who am I?", "How did I come to be this person?", and "What kind of person do I want to be?"

When I was finishing my psychotherapy training and completing my research, I ran a Google Scholar search and found around 14,000 published books and articles positing an integration of Eastern and Western psychologies up to 2010. At the time of writing, it is now over 20,000! The majority focus on mindfulness interventions; but there is an also growing concern that 'technique' orientation towards mindfulness omits the ethical and philosophical aspects of the Buddhist path (we will explore the 'threefold trainings' in Chapter 5). Plucking mindfulness meditation from its context jeopardises the healthy integration of meditation experiences and prevents taking the full benefits offered by a system with its own comprehensive psychological theory.

Mainstream Western psychology's relationship to Buddhism

The momentum of the 'Mindfulness Revolution' in part might come from a convergence in how neuroscience, cognitive psychology, and even artificial intelligence are conceiving the mind. However, the West also seems to have a growing openness to paradigms outside of positivist science: Buddhist understanding overlaps with existential and phenomenological views such as Heidegger's being-in-the-world and Merleau-Ponty's lived-body; in his later years Carl Rogers, a lead protagonist of the humanistic movement, began alluding to a spiritual characteristic of 'presence'; and the various 'person-centred' approaches to counselling hold a positive view of human nature that has attracted much commentary by Buddhist writers (Brazier, 2001; Bazzano, 2011). Nevertheless, of all the humanistic approaches it is Gestalt psychotherapy that forms the easiest of synergies in view and practice, to the extent it has been described as a modern-day Buddhism (Naranjo, 1978). One can read *Excitement and Growth in the Human Personality* (Perls et al., 1951), the foundational text of Gestalt, and immediately see how both Fritz and Laura Perls were influenced by Zen. Fritz had close friendships with Zen practitioner Paul Weisz as well as Alan Watts, a populariser of Eastern philosophy. Laura was also widely read in spiritual traditions including Taoism, as well as studying theology under Martin Buber and Paul Tillich (names that humanistic practitioners are likely to know).

'The Perls' (as it refers to both Fritz and Laura) aspired for Gestalt to offer a Zen-like self-transformation for Westerners, and there are several Gestalt concepts that clearly take from Buddhist ideas. The first and most obvious is that "awareness of and by itself can be curative" if directed across the differing domains of the somatic, cognitive, and emotional in the present moment. By cultivating presence, identification of wants and needs – at the same time as identifying how needs are blocked – is facilitated. In the Buddhist view it is such presence that helps break the chain of habitual activity that causes suffering. Secondly, Gestalt and Buddhism advocate openness 'to what is' arising in the present moment in an intentional and non-judgemental way. A third aspect is the encouragement to living our life from an attitude of surrendering. In Gestalt, the surrender takes us to the 'fertile void' or place of 'creative indifference' where meaning-making ceases and being begins. Perls likened experiences of acting from this place as 'mini-Satoris', a term that refers to individual enlightenment in Zen Buddhism. Further ideas of commonality include: the simple act of noticing what is in your awareness leads to change, adopted in Gestalt parlance as 'the paradox of change'; being with 'what is' is known to produce feelings of compassion giving rise to what Naranjo calls a "virtuous relationship" (1978, p. 80); and finally, Gestalt's horizontalism and Buddhist interdependence can be seen as similar notions of equalising.

I am intrigued as to why the majority of attempts for integration come predominantly from psychoanalytic writers, given the humanistic and Buddhistic paradigms are arguably more complimentary (as we will come to in the next chapter). Freud personally considered religion and spirituality to be no more than a "universal obsessional neurosis" that was simply an attempt to master the Oedipus complex. Perhaps it was Carl Jung's fascination with the classic texts from the East that encouraged later psychoanalytic writers to explore what a more optimistic lens could offer. Jung's vision of a psychology would eventually encompass both the personal and transpersonal aspects of the psyche. Across the Atlantic, Erich Fromm and Karen Horney were developing their ideas with esteemed Zen teacher Suzuki Roshi.

Fast forward to the present day and there is resurgent interest in Buddhism within psychoanalysis and its offspring, psychodynamics. In the comprehensive text *Psychoanalysis and Buddhism: An Unfolding Dialogue*

(2003), Jeremy Safran suggests this is in part to answer the call for the construction of personal meaning in a growing culture of individualism. Freud's original goal might have been to develop a science based upon rational understanding and control over conflictual impulses, but today the goal is most often the search for a more authentic sense of identity. Buddhism's arrival in the West in the 1960s offered a secular potential for meaning-making, yet its emphasis on interdependence complimented the relational developments in psychoanalysis. It is not surprising to note that the key writers on the dialogue between Buddhism and psychotherapy are orientated within a relational, psychoanalytic practice such as object relations (Epstein, 2009), interpersonal psychoanalysis (Rubin, 2013), and self-psychology (Magid, 2012). We will return to these authors, among others, in later chapters as we explore how Buddhism can inform psychotherapeutic work.

Development of contemplative approaches

As well as serving as a corrective to an excessive Western individualism, Buddhism offers a complimentary philosophy to that of psychotherapy following the postmodern turn: namely its constructivist epistemology and viewing self as multiple rather than unitary. Full integration of the Eastern and Western approaches has culminated in 'contemplative psychotherapies', which are distinguished from the mindfulness-based interventions introduced earlier (MBSR, MBCT, ACT, DBT) by their inclusion of the teachings as well as the practices of Buddhism.

Since there are many psychotherapies and many Buddhisms from which to integrate, there is currently no single formalised clinical approach to the practice of contemplative psychotherapy. At the time of writing, established contemplative psychotherapy programmes based on the Tibetan *Vajrayana* Buddhist teachings include: the Nalanda Institute four-year programme (developed by Buddhist scholar and psychiatrist Dr. Joseph Loizzo) that integrates mindfulness and compassion-based systems of Buddhist psychology and meditation with contemporary psychoanalysis, neuroscience, and health psychology; the Karuna training programmes (based on the teachings from Tibetan Buddhist master Chögyam Trungpa Rinpoche) at Naropa Institute in Colorado with a European faculty in Holland; and Tara Rokpa therapy (developed by the Akong-Rinpoche, who along with Chögyam Trungpa set up Samye Ling, the first retreat centre in the UK), a six-year programme commencing with a Western psychotherapeutic base before deepening into the more esoteric *Vajrayana* meditation practices.

Buddhist-based therapy trainings in the UK include 'Core Process psychotherapy', a four-year master's programme established in 1982 by Franklyn and Maura Sills bringing together a range of Buddhist teachings across lineages alongside Western personality theory and psychodynamics;

'Zen Therapy' founded by David Brazier (a student of Carl Rogers) and grounded first and foremost in the Buddhist psychological system of the *abhidharma*; 'Other-centred therapy' developed by Caroline Brazier with a focus on the mindful engagement with others, both in human relationships and in contact with one's surroundings. Mention should also be made of another Buddhism-influenced training, the Hakomi Method. Developed by Ron Kurtz, this approach integrates general systems theory and modern body-centred therapies (including Gestalt and Focusing) with the core Buddhist concepts of gentleness, non-violence, compassion, and mindfulness.

A note on philosophy

As I sit down to write today, this quote from Bazzano (2011) feels like a good placeholder: "Buddhist meditation – as I understand it – is not 'spirituality' but instead phenomenological and existential enquiry, being aware of the wider organismic field, actively and creatively adapting to the fluid nature of the world", I feel a distinct sense of the intention I have set for this book – to write from experience. I can almost feel my words onto the page. Using the language of Gestalt there are multiple things in the field, and the way in which they are interrelating allows a clear sense of a figure to emerge. For one, I am in the middle of a teaching block that helps our trainee therapists at the university consider a research question they would like to explore: I am thus immersed in the language of 'ontology, epistemology and methodology'. Secondly, I am about to take a major step on the Buddhist path and enter the *Vajrayana*,[3] which signifies a shift in worldview. Not so long ago, a friend of mine commented how synchronous it was to be starting out on the writing of this book as I begin *Ngondro*, the preliminary practices that an initiate to the *Vajrayana* undertakes to 'prepare the vessel' for the teachings to come.

Even though the Buddhist teachings and practices have become increasingly integral to how I practice psychotherapy, I would not change the training path taken. There is deep appreciation of my Western roots and the exposure to many very useful theories of mind, human growth and development, the intersubjectivity of relationship, and various interventions to alleviate distress. It is perhaps an immersion in philosophy that I am most grateful. In contrast to my wife who was born and raised in France where the Baccalaureate includes philosophy, in my secondary school education philosophy was not on the curriculum, not even as an 'option'. My training as a counsellor was the first invitation to consider how I saw the world, how I saw the nature of knowledge, and the question "who am I?" Not even my PhD asked me to deeply reflect on these things – odd given the 'Ph' refers to philosophy!

Ask my parents what I was like as a child and they would probably conjure up the image of a 'little professor', loving all things 'science' and all things 'nature'. A born 'seeker', my formal education through GCSEs, A-levels, and first degree has a consistent thread of science with all its quantitative and positivist view. Positivism carries with it an epistemological assumption that empirical knowledge is the foundation of all authentic knowledge: something discovered rather than constructed. And as a researcher in sport and exercise physiology, my PhD days were spent in the laboratory running experiments designed to test hypotheses. Like all quantitative research, it was deterministic in nature, looking to statistically represent observable phenomena in a reductionist fashion and serving to objectively verify or nullify theory. The data I was studying was exterior to me, the researcher, and the research sought to establish what was 'true'.

Starting my therapy training jolted my worldview from the positivist perspective towards understanding the diversity of views and realities. Exposure to the existential and phenomenological literature shifted me from *explanation* towards *meaning*, and recognition that I brought my own experience and assumptions to an interpretation of others' worlds. My training asked me to consider my ontology – the inquiry into the nature of things; and my epistemology – a study of knowledge and how we come to know what we know. At that point in time, I felt most comfortable with what might be termed a 'critical realist' position: there remained a difference between the 'real' world and the 'observable' world. This position rests upon two facets. Firstly, an ontological 'realism' – things exist independently of awareness or knowledge of it. Secondly, an epistemic 'relativism' – our knowledge of reality is context-, concept-, and activity-dependent. What I experience is based on perception. The house might be burning down, but if I am in the back garden when the fire starts at the front of the house, I won't perceive anything wrong. As therapists, we are often reminded of the need to 'bracket', because perception is impacted by our filters and past experiences – we try to describe rather than explain experience.

The existential-phenomenological position was reinforced at the time by my emerging Buddhist practice and understanding. I originally turned to Buddhism to find 'the truth', 'the way' to be. As I deepened my meditation, I became aware, however, of how the perception of my present-moment experience was dependent on my filters. This is very much consistent with the start of the Buddhist path, which in the Tibetan tradition of Buddhism starts with the *Hinayana* and a focuses on realising the 'egolessness of self'. In meditation, thoughts, sounds, and feelings all appear and there comes a development of a 'watcher' observing these appearances with a somewhat detached and passionless view. We begin to realise these appearances arise and fall without any help from us, or an "I" or self. With the *Mahayana*, there comes a deepening understanding of how our filters exist and operate, and the so-called 'egolessness of phenomena' is realised. Having established what we took to be a 'self' doesn't exist in the way we thought, we begin to see that this is the case with all phenomena. In other words, we come to see how much we project on the world. Buddhist teachings refer to this as 'emptiness', but in phenomenological terms we can equate this to experience in its own terms rather than fixing abstract categories and labels.

The philosophy underpinning the *Mahayana* has much in common with Husserlian phenomenology: that we can distinguish the act of consciousness and the content or object of consciousness; that there is the knowing and the known. Yet it is with Heidegger's hermeneutic phenomenology that the conception of the human moved away from theory and towards an emphasis on the interaction with society and the environment. As a practitioner follows the natural progression of experience in meditation, attention is moved from the known and turned 'back' towards the knowing. It is realised that there is not a 'knower', and this enters the realm of the *Vajrayana*. To simply rest in experiencing itself. It becomes apparent, in glimpses, that 'mind' only arises simultaneously with its contents, that mind and its appearances are of the 'same taste' or essence. Stephen Batchelor, a Buddhist teacher who writes in the existential and Buddhist philosophy domain, contrasts our normal experience of "a mind inside a body inside a world" (Stone, 2018, p. 213) with what we come to experience – world and body exist INSIDE the mind – as we deepen the inquiry of mind in meditation. As the *Buddha* said "We are what we think. All that we are arises with our thoughts. With our thoughts we make the world". We could say that in the *Vajrayana*, ontology and epistemology are indivisible. Certainly, for me at this gateway, I can already see the change to a 'constructivism' position – through experiences, we construct our own understanding of the world we live in. Each morning as I sit in meditation, I see the construction of a reality that is not separate from mind. To reference a Zen teaching, the tree only exists because I am there to hear it has fallen.

As I have come to appreciate, there is much compatibility between humanistic and Buddhistic philosophies. Both share the existential ground of death awareness and responsibility, and the phenomenological tenets of a process view of life and the intentionality of consciousness. Both orientate towards the lived experience; the 'how' rather than the 'why'. I would recommend readers look at Stephen Batchelor's *Alone with Others* (Batchelor, 1983) and Paul Tillich's *The Courage to Be* (1954) for a deeper immersion in how Buddhist and existential ideas meet, particularly in navigating the nature of 'self' in the context of Heidegger's being and being-in-the-world. For now, we can hold in mind that the self and the world are not two separate entities but rather what we consider the subject as co-emergence of self and other, subject and object. Our error in the Western world, according to many scholars and teachers of the Eastern view, is that we forget this non-duality. We make the potentialities of what Heidegger came to call 'Dasein' in to a solid, single, and unchanging "I".

What I hope this section can communicate is the importance of philosophy within psychotherapy. Much of what is written here has only been possible because of the critical reflexivity offered by my training. The danger of some therapy courses and programmes is that theories are merely translated to interventions and skills – what to do in the room rather than who or how to 'be'. The best way to avoid eclecticism is to be able to consider one's worldview; to know how ontology, epistemology naturally and consistently flow into methodology in the room. Of relevance here is the trap of adding mindfulness as a kind of 'bolt-on' rather than from a place of consistent view or frame. The study of philosophy helps us as therapists engage with questions (which open up our world) rather than answers (which reduce possibilities). I appreciate this is a place of groundlessness and potentially much anxiety – but as therapists, this is exactly the terrain if we are to help our clients also bear the uncertainty of what it is to be human.

Notes

1 Known as *the fall* in many spiritual traditions.
2 Whether the thick- or thin-skinned variant, both sub-types of narcissism are characterised by a feeling of fragility of the self that endeavours to maintain its self-perception as someone exceptional. The reader might pursue the work of authors such as Rosenfeld and Kernberg.
3 Entering the *Vajrayana* requires taking the *Samaya* Vow, the third after the Refuge and *Bodhisattva* Vows.

References

Batchelor, S. (1983). *Alone with Others. An Existential Approach to Buddhism*. New York: Grove Press.
Bazzano, M. (2011). The Buddha as a Fully Functioning Person. Toward a Person-Centered Perspective on Mindfulness. *Person-Centered & Experiential Psychotherapies, 10*(2), 116–128.
Brazier, D. (2001). *Zen Therapy*. London: Robinson.
Epstein, M. (2009). *Going on Being: Life at the Crossroads of Buddhism and Psychotherapy*. Boston, MA: Wisdom Publications.
Freud, S., & Breuer, J. (2004). *Studies in Hysteria*. London: Penguin.
Magid, B. (2012). *Ordinary Mind: Exploring the Common Ground of Zen and Psychoanalysis*. Boston, MA: Wisdom Publications.
Naranjo, C. (1978). Gestalt Therapy as a Transpersonal Approach. *Gestalt Journal, 1*(2), 75–81.
Perls, F., Hefferline, R., & Goodman, P. (1951). *Gestalt Therapy. Excitement and Growth in the Human Personality*. New York: Delta Book.

Rubin, J.B. (2013). *Psychotherapy and Buddhism: Toward an Integration*. New York, NY: Springer Science & Business Media.

Safran, J.D. (2003). *Psychoanalysis and Buddhism: An Unfolding Dialogue*. Somerville, MA: Wisdom Publications.

Stone, M. (2018). *The Inner Tradition of Yoga: A Guide to Yoga Philosophy for the Contemporary Practitioner*. Boulder, CO: Shambhala Publications.

Tillich, P. (1954). *The Courage to Be*. London: Yale University Press.

Welwood, J. (1984). Principles of Inner Work. *Journal of Transpersonal Psychology*, *16*(1), 63–73.

Welwood, J. (2002). *Toward a Psychology of Awakening: Buddhism, Psychotherapy, and the Path of Personal and Spiritual Transformation*. Boston, MA: Shambhala.

Young-Eisendrath, P. (2003). Transference and Transformation in Buddhism and Psychoanalysis. In J. Safran (Ed.), *Psychoanalysis and Buddhism: An Unfolding Dialogue* (pp. 301–317). Somerville, MA: Wisdom Publications.

Chapter 3

The human condition

My story of changing identity

"Who am I? What makes me, 'me'"? I imagine you have asked yourself similar questions. And how would you have answered these questions 30 years ago, 20 years ago, 10 years ago, or even last week?

Depending on your belief system, you will have different ideas as to whether we are born with a blank slate or predetermined character (to lesser or greater extents). We would probably all agree that our early life shapes who we become. Carl Rogers used the phrase 'conditions of worth' to explain this shaping. From a very young age we get a sense of who we need to be in order to get love, security, and praise. We note behaviour that safeguards our needs being met and behaviour that doesn't, cementing the former into ways of being. What started as 'one-off' states over time become habits and traits.

My story is probably as good an example as any. Little Helen learned that she could use her thinking and endeavour to get noticed, perhaps even confusing praise for love. She therefore worked hard at being a 'good girl'. Little Helen became a 'little professor', fuelled by curiosity and exploration. This identity got reinforced when her teachers lavished more praise. These relationships became more and more important as her intellect got stronger. By the time she reached Secondary school, Little Helen's intellect and conscientiousness made her feel different – from other school friends and from her family. I hadn't realised until recently just how lonely I felt at school; and how much more at home I was with adults. I longed to be seen and understood; teachers became my point of reference, and books became my friends. There is something very significant about my early teenage years, as it set the habit of allegiance to authority and trusting others' wisdom more than my own.

I was blessed with a broad range of capabilities and skills as a child. I was strong in the sciences at school, I played many sports to a good level, and I was a capable musician. Again, only recently have I come to understand

DOI: 10.4324/9781003383710-3

how often I was thrown in at the deep end. People saw my capability and gave me responsibility. As therapists, we see this in our clients, the child who grew up too quickly; even becoming responsible for the emotional climate of the family. This is prevalent in many of my therapist colleagues too. I never questioned all the accolades when young because they made me feel okay about myself.

Good at sport, fascinated by science. Whilst I didn't know that sport science existed at this time, when it came to selecting my GCSEs I knew who I wanted to be – a copy of my PE teacher! With my typical determination (and some would say stubbornness), I set out to become who I wanted to be, who I knew "I was". A-Levels, degree, PhD, research scientist. I had made it. The Little Helen aged eight who took her telescope in to school to show her teachers was now in a real-life lab (sometimes even wearing a white coat as dreamed). It would be an exaggeration to say everything was planned, but there was a trajectory that felt very clear, and the next step was always straightforward to me. I now have the words to describe my view of the world – there was an answer as to who Helen needed to be, I just needed to keep searching and working hard. One day I would 'make it' and life would be sorted.

Back in 1998, to my knowledge I was the first sport scientist in the country to have a full-time research position: a female physiologist at that, rare in a male dominated field. I really had arrived, well nearly. I was set on my career, and never questioned that I would get married and have a family. A year into my new job and it looked like that part of the equation was also accomplished. I fell in love. My boyfriend and I bought a semi-detached house, a four-door car, and adopted two cats. In one of those pivotal moments in life, my boyfriend introduced me to the wonders of being on two wheels. And when the mid-week commute bike rides became leisure rides at the weekend, I was hooked. From 2000–2008, I invested much of my time and energies in competitive cycling. It was the start of realising my career was not enough anymore.

Helen the scientist became Helen the cyclist. Both identities had much in common. Drive, determination, attention to detail, single-mindedness. These masculine energies have brought me much success in life; but without the balance of the feminine, I was curating a very big fall . . . or a series of big falls. My PhD years were blighted with an eating disorder. The feeling of being different and misunderstood borne out of very early life experiences came back in my isolation of independent study. A PhD is a lonely pursuit. A loneliness exaggerated by staying on in the university department and town where I was once surrounded by friends as an undergraduate. Time on my own became an experience of a void, and I filled that void with plans and control that often involved food and exercise. Entering elite sport perpetuated this dynamic. Exercising hard, after all, was a great disguise for control and punishment. For all my accomplishments, I felt empty. And the only way I knew to keep those feelings at bay was to drive for more success. I needed praise to feel loved, to feel I was somebody, to feel I existed. Having reflected deeply on this time in my life, I have come to query my 'capacity to be alone' (Winnicott, 1958).

Helen the cyclist became Helen the coach. This was a slow relinquishing of my need to perform and be successful. We might say my ego was beginning to soften. Come 2008, I didn't need to race anymore, finding fulfilment in helping others attain their goals. However, I still needed to be the best coach I could be, and in setting up my own business I took on more and more strain. Yet again, my body and health suffered. The same drive that took me to disordered eating led me to sleepless nights, depression, and anxiety. I was unravelling. For the first time in my life, I didn't know what I wanted, but I knew I didn't want 'this' anymore. Meeting meditation and starting my training as a therapist was a salvation of sorts. While I may have entered this dual path with a familiar search for completion outside of myself, they have led me to very different territory, exploring my 'doing' as a surrogate for 'being'.

Go to a dinner party or other social gathering, and introductions will often start with "So, what do you do?" I try not to answer this question with "I am a psychotherapist", firstly because people take a step back and avoid me all evening! More significantly, Helen is so much more than the job. If anything, my priority in life is as an 'awake-ist': someone who wants to see reality of life 'as it is' and not my projections. In everyday parlance, this is the identity of being a Buddhist – but as we will come to see, this is an oxymoron. I aspire to be consistent across my job(s), with friends, and with family: to be open and present, even if the Helen that manifests in any given moment differs. In Gestalt psychotherapy, this idea is often presented as 'selfing', where the self isn't a fixed thing, but rather a verb. The Self that arises and falls depends on the environment, the situation, and the others present. So, Helen might still present as 'strong', but it is a strength predicated upon vulnerability.

For all my shifts in the past ten years, I don't think anything prepared me for the experience of mid-life and the challenges to who I thought I was. It is a transition I am still making – but at least I know what is happening to "me". Furthermore, whilst painful, I know it is a valuable type of pain which means I resist less and therefore suffer less. The same is true of my recent diagnosis of chronic fatigue, and with embarking on the next stage of the Buddhist path as a *Vajrayana* student. The first half of life is said to be focused on 'the identity project'; but when we reach the top of the mountain, the view isn't what we imagined it might be. No doubt for me, the summit did disappoint but the climb served a purpose. As well as gaining some incredible formative experiences and skills, I have come to know the ground of what it is to have 'a healthy sense of self' – an ego that is strong and functional. I would add life until now has allowed me to set up a reliable container for my practice – I have good life circumstances, no immediate threats in my environment, and a good support network. The second half becomes a letting go of who I thought I was and what I need to do to be 'okay'. Buddhism provides good terminology for all of this, and I hope this chapter on the human condition explains how helpful this frame can be for our work supporting clients in their life transitions.

The view

We could see identity, the fact of being who or what a person or thing is, as a reaction to the uncertainty of being a human. Within groundlessness, we attempt to find ground – things all around us might be changing but at least we know who we are. Associating ourselves with a role or a label brings stability and a reference point; it also helps us know how to react and behave. However, is this how things really are? The *Buddha* didn't think so, and he attempted to describe the human condition (and indeed, the existence of all phenomena) in a different way. According to Buddhism, all phenomena – including living beings, the physical world, and psychological experience – are marked with three characteristics: suffering; non-self; and impermanence. Let us look at these in a little more detail and consider how they might be useful in the therapeutic situation.

Suffering

"All I teach is suffering and the end of suffering" might not be the catchiest marketing phrase the *Buddha* could have uttered. In contemporary society people do their best to avoid and deny any kind of discomfort or dissatisfaction. Yet the genius of the *Buddha* was to see that it is only in acknowledging the pain inherent in life, and changing our relationship to it, can we find contentment. He therefore placed 'The Four Noble Truths' at the foundation of the *Dharma*. This list, one of many,[1] is the *Buddha's* method for pointing out and working with suffering. The First Noble Truth, "there is suffering", sets out the basic characteristic of human life as one of dissatisfaction or *dukkha*. The human condition always contains the 'givens', the pains of birth, old age, sickness, and death. The existentialists arrived at a similar conclusion a couple of millennia later. Presented in this way, the *Buddha* wanted to equalise what it is to be human, acknowledging and accepting all of humankind's predicament.

The *Buddha* identified three types of suffering, and as you read them you might recognise the roots of distress presented by clients. The first kind is the 'suffering of suffering'. On some level we know we cannot

not escape the aforementioned 'givens', but they very often happen at the 'wrong' time! We fall ill when we are just about to go on holiday, we feel less able to do the things we used to enjoy when younger, or our loved ones die when it "wasn't their time yet". Consistent with the growing acceptance of transmarginal trauma in therapeutic literature, you'll see being born is on this list. The second kind of suffering is the 'suffering of change'. Even when we do get what we want, we can't hold onto it. It might be that we are enjoying a relaxing massage, but we become aware it will not last forever and anticipate the pleasure ending. Finally on this sub-list of a list there is 'all-pervasive suffering', the type of suffering that floats just below our radar most of the time. It's the general background of anxiety and insecurity that exists even in our happiest experiences. Deep down, we know that life doesn't offer us solid ground and that our very existence is fragile.

The First Noble Truth teaches individuals to accept those things that cannot be changed. In the Second Noble Truth, "there is a cause of suffering", the *Buddha* addressed self-created distress. In the *Sallatha Sutra*, there is the story of a man shot by an arrow who "when touched with a feeling of pain", rather than immediately removing it, effectively shoots himself again by "lamenting and grieving". We know this tendency to obsess rather than address the situation "Who did this, why did it happen to me, wait until I find them, I will get my revenge". Our man's first error is to think that this should not happen to him, that he somehow feels he is impervious (ignorance). Depending on his disposition, he might then lament as to how things were before the arrow (grasping or craving) or might try to deny the pain of the wounding by seeking who is to blame (rejecting or aversion). These three ways in which we tend to relate to our experience – with ignorance, by attachment, and through aversion – are the three poisons or *kleshas*. Later in this chapter we will look at the Buddhist view of seeing humans as inherently whole. Any departure from this wholesomeness and basic sanity is caused by the obscuration of *kleshas* or afflictive emotions. If you are like me, you will have experienced how quickly the states such as anxiety, anger, jealousy, desire, depression surge up and cloud the mind in such a way that we are not able to connect to the situation or to others in a clear or authentic way. Welwood (2002) uses the more experiential phrasing of desensitising, grasping, and rejecting to convey how the three *kleshas* contaminate experience.

We want more of what we want; less of what we don't want. Our clients come each week with stories exemplifying this, and we as therapists are no different – we fail to see life as a process of ups and downs, constantly rejecting and grasping and trying to control our world to regulate our experience. How can we begin to look at the stories we tell ourselves – about what we deserve/don't deserve and instead, be with what is? Jon Kabat-Zinn uses the example of Zorba the Greek, who

> embodies a supreme appreciation for the richness of life and the inevitability of all its dilemmas, sorrows, tragedies, and ironies. His way is to "dance" in the gale of the full catastrophe, to celebrate life, to laugh with it and at himself, even in the face of personal failure and defeat.
>
> (2013, p. xlv)

If you are trained in the humanistic tradition of psychotherapy, you might have used the drama triangle (Karpman, 2014) to explore the conflicting roles of persecutor, victim, and rescuer in client relationships. I believe this can transpose onto the *kleshas*. The client who places themselves in the victim role and believes things should be a certain way; the persecutor is rejecting their experience and pushing that on to others in order to cause distance; and the rescuer who wants to be needed and brings others closer. The drama triangle obviously speaks to relationships with others; but we could just as easily apply it to our relationship to the phenomenal world. In Gestalt language, where do our clients retroflect (turn the discomfort of experiencing life back onto themselves), project (find it hard to hold their own pain and place it elsewhere), or remain confluent (need others to assuage discomfort)?

We therapists too might have a tendency towards one of the *kleshas*. This is not to say that we will *always* grasp or reject, but as with the 'modifications to contact' (of Gestalt) or 'driver behaviour' (of Transactional Analysis), we might find under conditions of stress or threat-to-self we tend towards a particular relating style. When I first started my training, I found it very hard to avoid the need to be liked – so rather than provide clients with challenge or give honest feedback as to my real experience of being in relationship with them, I would shy away and be 'nice'. This was a particularly challenging aspect of development for someone who felt resonance with the ideas of Gestalt, the humanistic approach most reliant on client challenge. I confused the relational attitude of empathy with a fear of separation. As Fritz Perls, would say "there can be no true contact in empathy. At its worst it becomes confluence" (Perls, 1973, p. 106), the tendency towards merger and enmeshment. With growing confidence in experience, expression of our difference in the therapy room emerges. This allows us to be alongside the client (from the Latin root '*com*', *with*; '*passion*', *suffering*) rather than merged and therefore unable to offer environmental and relational support. We cannot assist somebody in quicksand if we are in it too! On the other hand, therapists who tend towards aversion might notice a sense of frustration in their client work and might risk pushing clients towards an action rather than trusting that the client will find a way (but maybe in their own time). When we become too challenging, there is also the risk of activating a shame response in our clients. Hopefully, we can see the need to become aware of such mind states so we can remain present and compassionate.

Whilst the *abhidharma* or psychological branch of the Buddhist teachings was developed over 2,000 years ago, ideas such as the three *kleshas* still speak to our experience of the contemporary Western setting. Clients bring to us their experiences of desensitising with addictions to food, alcohol and drugs, all behaviours that serve to numb the rawness of underlying affect. Similarly, we might notice how many people are glued to their smartphones accessing email or social media and wonder if there is an avoidance of difficult feelings or unpleasant situations – even if that is simply boredom. Finally, the *klesha* of grasping might conjure up those endlessly absorbed in working things out or always obsessed with a new project or 'self-development'. This can even become a trap of psychotherapy or the spiritual path (as we will explore with case study "Jim", Chapter 10). I know when my Amazon spending increases, I am stressed: the searcher in me relying on books to give the answers, and I know the risk of running to an egocentric dead end. As Freud once said (allegedly), we can never drain the swamp.

The pain of the first arrow, and the suffering of the second. The Buddhist *Dharma* draws out how suffering is optional IF we can accept the inevitable painful aspects of our human existence.

Impermanence

The second of the three marks helps us contemplate not only impermanence as death, but also the 'mini-deaths' always in operation. You might read in the original *Dharma* that "all compounded phenomena disintegrate": all things are made of parts, and all things fall apart. As with death, we do appreciate change when it is on a visible scale. As I write now it is autumn, and the tree outside my window is turning yellow and orange. In a few weeks the tree will be bare. We know and expect things to change with the seasons. But change is happening on imperceptible levels. As I look down at my hands typing, I can appreciate (because science tells me so) that the skin cells existing now won't exist in a few months. Even the coffee cup I am drinking from – apparently solid – is breaking down on some level.

I work a lot with clients undergoing change and through 'transitions', though such words may be misnomers, given "change is the only constant", as said Heraclitus. Labelling it a 'transition' is just to sharpen the change. The experience appears 'step-like' because we haven't attended to the gradual change. Looking back over my life story to date, "Helen" was always changing even when she stayed in the same role. Take, for example, my decision to leave academia and become a cycling coach. Yes, there was a transition from one to the next, but in the period leading up to the decision to leave my research role there was already upheaval and discontent. My inner experience of the job was changing, and that led me to impose external change. Clients might convey an outgrowing of the current situation, and much of transition work is acknowledging that change is already happening, and that change/loss needs to be mourned – turning towards the fact that we have expected the job, the role, or the relationship to stay the same and in fact, nothing is solid and long lasting. As the Zen teaching says, "the cup is already broken".

All phenomena are constantly coming into being and ceasing to be – and this is one of the most powerful messages when we learn to meditate and get a chance to view appearances and disappearances within experience – the rise and fall of the breath, the coming and going of sounds, and how thoughts appear from no-where and go back to no-where . . . if we let them! Commentators on the East/West synergy have pointed to a convergence of the Western scientific view with Buddhism being 'process philosophy'. Quantum theory on particles and waveforms are compatible with Buddhist ideas on being and becoming.

Non-self

Regarding all phenomena as process is the crux of the third mark of existence, egolessness, which (like *karma*) is a terribly misunderstood Buddhist teaching. From a Buddhist perspective, the 'self' is not a separate entity but rather an interdependent process that is in constant change and flux. 'Non-self' is perhaps a better term to use, as ego in the Freudian sense is not something we are trying to remove or go beyond. What the Buddhist teachings and practices are looking to deconstruct is the inherently solid experience of "I" and to replace that with a meeting of experience directly that reveals 'self' to be little more than rising and falling of bodily and mental events.

As therapists, we are probably within touching distance of appreciating this. Each week we witness how our clients have been shaped by their experience, and how 'self' comes into being through interaction with others and the environment, 'selfing'. However, there remains a sense that there is a 'core' to a person that simply needs revealing. Buddhism looks to undercut even that by attending directly to experience and notice there is no solid, separate, single self. We have no core, and instead are simply the product of multiple causes and conditions, we are being born and ceasing-to-be moment-by-moment. If you study the *Dharma* to a deeper level both impermanence and non-self can be thought of in terms of emptiness: impermanence is emptiness in terms of time; non-self is emptiness in terms of space.

My understanding and experiencing of non-self has been supported enormously by the writing of Rupert Spira, a teacher in the Advaita Vedanta.[2]

Spira (2012) describes 'three possibilities of self' that conveys an understanding of the mistake we make in considering ourselves separate. These three possibilities are the Known, the Knower, and Knowing.

The Known: considers "me" as a separate self, born in and free to move around a world out 'there'. Me is therefore a KNOWN object that knows other objects, whether that be feelings, sensations, perceptions of others and other things in the world.

The Knower: if we sit down and spend time experiencing (as we do in meditation), we get a taste of "I know the bodymind" just as "I know the world". In other words, "I am the Knower" of experience, and the bodymind is known. Meditation teachers often describe this step as 'developing the watcher'. I know thoughts, feelings, sensations, and perceptions but am not myself made of those thoughts, feelings, sensations, and perceptions. Because we become a mere witness to appearances, we can allow those appearances unconditionally and impartially. We reduce our suffering because we are no longer attached to our thinking, feeling, sensing, perceiving. We get a first sense of our nature being empty space in which all appearances arise. As Spira says "The body and mind are always on a journey, but 'I' never undertakes the journey with them. They journey through 'Me', but 'I' never journey in them. 'I am' the unchanging and ever-present Knower of all that is known".

Knowing: there is a subtle trap to identifying with the Knower. By thinking of Me as the Knower, thought is imagining Me being separate from all that appears. Meditation-teaching metaphors refer to a cinema audience watching appearances play out on the screen. However, we are more like the screen itself – image and screen are one. Likewise, all that is known of the body, mind, and world is the *knowing* of them. Close your eyes for a moment – how do you know you have a body? See if you can forget concepts and instead rest with the experience directly; perhaps tune in to the Knowing of sensations first, and then drop any idea of sensations and just tune in to the Knowing. The third possibility of self is only Knowing. Spira says "it is thought that superimposes a subject and an object upon the seamless intimacy of experience thereby seemingly veiling the peace and happiness that lie ever-present and always available". Across the many spiritual and wisdom traditions the absence of a subject/object split, distance, otherness or separation is described as non-dual.

It is often said that experience is the only teacher we need. Looking back at the various identity shifts in my life, I can see how much of the distress I encountered along the way was self-created: from not appreciating the truth of the three marks, and the arising reactive patterns of the three *kleshas*. Ignorance is said to be the most fundamental since we mistake all phenomena to be independent and separate, permanent, and fixed, thus denying the three marks of existence. In reaction to that mistake, we tend to either cling to experiences that are pleasant or seek to avoid experiences that are unpleasant. A very 'young' part of me, if we think developmentally, had an idea of who I needed to be to ensure survival. Each time that my life situation didn't allow that identity to be expressed – or, using the terminology of Carl Rogers, my 'external locus of evaluation' couldn't be met – I suffered. One season as a cyclist I developed a bad knee injury. That spring, it felt like my world was falling apart because I couldn't train. That summer, I couldn't compete, and I therefore stopped feeling like "Helen". I was so attached to that "Helen the cyclist" persona and I tried very hard to deny my body needed rest and healing.

Ignoring my human fragility, I have a pattern of 'pressing on regardless', so attached to the identity I needed for my survival. Well, it has at times felt like life or death. It is no wonder I ended up with the diagnosis of chronic fatigue. Unlike the days of my cycling injury, however, the practice and study of the *Dharma* allowed me to accept and work with my condition. As a humanistic practitioner, I have an ambivalent relationship to any kind of diagnosis or label, but I do think they can give people a useful map of the terrain – and I found this to be true of CFS. I learnt to navigate a Middle Way between the solidity and rigidity of this 'condition' with the moment-by-moment of how my symptoms manifested. Through the frame of the three marks of existence: Firstly, I had to learn to accept this diagnosis, that this was happening to me, rather than keep going at 100 miles an hour. I needed to let go of the "Helen" I identified with and my expectations of who I was and what I can do. CFS can bring pain, but I don't have to suffer – that IS optional. Secondly, I had to accept that this body is impermanent – it will age, get sick, and eventually die. But impermanence is also good news – the symptoms I experience will end. Finally, my meditation practice offers me the opportunity to sit with the sensations that arise and open to them. I am not saying I like the tension headaches, the deep pervasive fatigue, but when I stop taking these and other symptoms so personally (and shift to the Knowing) rather than identifying with the Known, sitting outside of time and space means symptoms take on a different texture, helping me recognise the awareness always present.

Vignette

I wanted to share a quote coming from my reflective journal written in the first few months as a trainee counsellor. I was attending the first training weekend of the Shambhala Buddhist path, one that introduces the Buddhist teachings on *buddhanature* or 'basic goodness'.

> Last weekend whilst on retreat, I sat on the mediation cushion and became aware of the conflict. The practice was to rest in 'Basic Goodness', and at

the same time I felt huge resistance, I wanted to be at home working on my essay – my childhood conditions of worth around achievement and perfectionism. I was struck by some parallels on these two paths I now tread – the 'actualising tendency vs self-concept of perfectionism'- with 'basic-goodness vs solidification of self''. The meditation path is helping me hold both 'a natural unfolding', and the contrasting 'drive to be better'.

Travelling home on the train from London that Sunday evening, I realised I had experienced something significant. Sitting in meditation over that weekend I had been exposed to the very depth of my being, contacting what the *Dharma* teaches as our true nature, basic goodness. 'Basic' as indicating the primordial, self-existing nature; and 'goodness' as faultless. Our fundamental nature is 'awake' and trustworthy. Sitting and resting in that depth, I could see the suffering as wave-like; I could witness the stories I was telling myself and feel the sensations of restlessness and agitation, yet those waves did not disturb the ocean-like depth. A quote from Chögyam Trungpa: "If we are willing to take an unbiased look, we will find that, in spite of all our problems and confusion, all our emotional and psychological ups and downs, there is something basically good about our existence as human beings" (1994).

This experience offered me a new view that everything is workable; that no matter how painful a situation we find ourselves in, if we can trust in the depth of our being and not associate with the waves; we can begin to respond rather than react to life. That is the difference between pain and suffering. It was also my first insight into what I later learned to be 'co-emergence' – life presents a continuous, unnerving oscillation between clarity and confusion, bewilderment and insight, certainty and uncertainty, sanity and insanity. The Buddhist teaching on co-emergence reminds us that in our minds, wisdom and confusion arise simultaneously. This was true as I sat meditating in London wanting to be home working on my essay. Co-emergence helps us honour and not dismiss any of our experience. There was both wisdom and confusion in wanting to jump up from my cushion, run to the train and get reading and writing again – this type of drive possessed an intelligence: it had kept me safe and seen for many, many years, yet it was a behaviour that often didn't serve me.

These views, when held in the therapeutic relationship, provide some very powerful alternatives for our clients. Co-emergence helps us explore with clients how the same behaviour can be viewed as coming from a confused *and* a wise root. For example, there is a great benefit in helping others, but it can also mask a worth based on giving service. Or, getting up early to check emails before work can be helpful if it helps manage stress but less so if it perpetuates stress by inviting more responses. This helps move clients away from a 'right/wrong' dichotomy and bring attention to 'choice and consequence'.

"You are perfect . . . and you could use a little work"

The ability to hold the two seemingly conflicting aspects of basic goodness and suffering was one of the most helpful findings to come from my research work during my psychotherapy training. In the interviews with several contemplative psychotherapists, all of them remarked that being able to hold this tension was important for clients to depersonalise their suffering, and to see it as distinct from who they are. As described earlier, it is stepping towards identifying with the awareness (Knowing) rather than what is being experienced (Known). It is for us therapists to hold that view. As the section heading's quote from Shunryu Suzuki suggests, each client is perfect and whole as they are; and suffering will lessen when they stop trying to change things as they are. Non-attachment is not resignation: freedom, agency, and responsibility still apply but we stop attaching to an outcome. When in 1955 a 600-year-old plaster *Buddha* was moved across Thailand to a new temple, it cracked as it was lifted to its new pedestal. On inspection, the chip in the plaster revealed a glint of gold. Work embarked on removing all the plaster and all nine feet of the statue was found to be 18 karat gold. This is a perfect analogy – we too are made of gold AND need to work on removing the outer layers of obscuration.

Comparing the Buddhist view with Western models

It is probably helpful at this point to look at how Buddhism's fruitional view[3] – our basic sanity is already ripe and present – compares to Western models of well-being as traditionally taught on counselling and psychotherapy trainings. It is important, particularly for those trained in humanistic psychotherapy, to get a sense of how it might differ to the human potential movement that gave rise to ideas such as the 'actualising tendency'. In my teaching and training role, I prompt students to consider three things in a psychotherapeutic model: what is the understanding of human nature, how is psychological distress set up, and therefore, how do people resolve distress and heal?

Human nature

The perspectives on psychological and emotional health can be placed along a continuum. At one end, we have traditional psychoanalytic theory and its structural 'drive model', a view of human nature based upon individual pleasure-seeking and drive discharge. Moving towards the middle of the continuum we meet the relational model of the various psychodynamic schools of thought. This view highlights the importance of our early years as children and the influence of the relationships with primary caregivers. Whilst the drive and relational schools are considered irreconcilable, their underpinning theories posit some basic motivational force[4] and contain the language of instinct, conflict, and defence. Also, a developmental model, the humanistic approach is considered a more optimistic view than its psychoanalytic predecessor and psychodynamic cousins. The 'fourth wave', as it is known, arose in the 1950s arguably as an emotional protest rather than conceptual critique of its ancestry. According to the founders of the human potential movement, such as Rogers and Maslow, humans are orientated around 'growth' and motivated by a need for enhancement and continuing development, an actualisation of a potential rather than 'deficiency'. However, the process (and ultimate success of the development) is vulnerable to the environment. At the far end of the continuum, we come to a Buddhist view of human nature. It might be more accurate to use 'essence' rather than nature since the Buddhist view holds that on a fundamental level, there is a being that is whole and healthy. This 'goodness' or 'sanity' is 'basic' or inherent. Due to certain causes and conditions, we tend to lose access to this wholeness, but this obscuration is temporary, and our fundamental intelligence remains available for us to reclaim. Thus, we might see the traditional psychoanalytic view of human nature as a deficiency to overcome, the humanistic as a propensity for health, and finally the Buddhistic frame as inherent health.

Psychological distress

In the developmental models of Western psychotherapy, by the age of four to six, our course has been set. In psychoanalytic/psychodynamic models, fragments of self and/or experience are repressed and pushed out of consciousness. Compartmentalising of distress comes with a price tag – strategies for survival persist even when no longer serving. The extent of the price paid varies. If the functioning of the ego is deemed adequate and personality structures are stable, a person might be considered having a 'neurotic level of organisation'; if they are less damaged but still extremely unstable, personality disorders would follow; and at the extreme, complete impairment of ego functions leads to a condition of psychosis (see 'Working with complex presentations', p. 136).

The humanistic view similarly contends an individual develops distress if inadequate relational conditions are present during infanthood into childhood. However, rather than repression into an unconscious, growth of self is compromised through fixed patterns of behaviour that remain out of awareness. As a 'being-in-the-world' a person may receive only conditional positive regard, developing an 'ideal-self'. In the terminology of Gestalt, an individual living under the rule of 'Top Dog' is unable to fully contact their immediate experience and develops 'fixed gestalts' rather than acting spontaneously. The language of Transactional Analysis (TA) similarly speaks of 'scripts'.

There is a prevalent discomfort with discomfort. The Buddhist view of distress offers a paradigm shift; rather than transcend suffering the task is to intimately know its nature. The Four Noble Truths point to suffering as a reaction to the 'givens' of being human. Always wanting different to 'what is' impels individuals towards repeatedly experiencing disappointment. The *Buddha* located the origin of *dukkha* as self-involvement or a solidification of the 'experience of I', creating mental anguish through our distortions and internal commentary rather than being with things as they are.

Healing goal

Again, at the extreme of the continuum, Freud postulated that the analyst's interpretations helped bring material into consciousness, enabling individuals to control their impulses and behaviours. However, in that 'civilizing' trade-off between impulse indulgence and social acceptance, individuals are resigned to "ordinary human misery". In the relational models of psychodynamics, however, the therapist does not remain outside of the process unfolding in the mind but rather engages and participates in it through the vehicle of the transferential relationship, transforming "pathogenic patterns" (Greenberg & Mitchell, 1983, p. 390).

The humanistic tradition moves beyond a remedial goal with its trust in a person's inherent movement towards wholeness. A core tenet is the laying down of certain relationship conditions by the therapist to align the client's self-concept and experience, thus moving them from incongruence to congruence. In Gestalt therapy, the relationship is seen to offer environmental support in which client and therapist explore the 'contact-boundary' i.e., where 'self' and 'other' meet. Dialogue and therapeutic tasks serve to increase both cognitive and somatic awareness to all aspects of self, leaving no part unclaimed. 'Health' is obtained not by deliberate attempts to change, but rather to fully know what is and becoming more spontaneous in thought, feeling and action: 'the paradoxical theory of change' (Beisser, 1970).

With the fundamental view of *buddhanature* the therapeutic work in a Buddhism-informed psychotherapy shifts towards the rediscovering of what is always present but simply obscured. For instance, one way to do this is to help a client construct a history of their sanity through an embodied awareness with no interpretation, no attribution of cause, and no explanation.

One rather simple description of well-being might be "confidence in experience". Buddhist healing starts with seeing the neurosis as arising not out of pathology, but instead out of clarity and vulnerability. This requires being able to recognize brilliant sanity when it manifests in a straightforward way, and critically, to hold it with equanimity and compassion when it arises in confusion or distorted ways. The ultimate goal of the Buddhist path is complete liberation from suffering, a goal seen as every individual's potential and life purpose.

Client case study "Deena": working with identity

"Deena" came to psychotherapy wanting a "better work-life balance". She spoke of herself as a "workaholic" and shared her difficulty in leaving the office at the end of the day. The daughter of an Officer in the Gurkha Brigade, Deena grew up in a home with a strict work ethic and her parents' aspirations resting heavily on her shoulders. Deena often spoke of feeling "morally bound" to do the right thing. Evoking her childhood in Hong Kong, Deena likened it to being on a "runaway tram" with very little choice to choose a different line.

Deena's drive had brought much success in her career as an entrepreneur and business owner. When I asked what brought her to therapy now, she explained that the "near-miss" of breast cancer scare five years ago was now sinking in, given her 50th birthday was on the horizon. Her husband David, whom she married whilst still living in Hong Kong, had recently retired and he was encouraging Deena to do the same. Pulling back from her career was easier said than done. Although running a slightly smaller business now, she still found it hard to hand work over to her assistants. Deena was feeling more stressed than ever.

As our work got under way, I increasingly noticed Deena's ambivalence and my bodily agitation. There became a pattern for Deena to come to a session with "a new plan" on how to achieve the Holy Grail of a "better work-life balance". But week after week, the plan was failing her. The enthusiasm and clarity of what she wanted kept stalling. Each failed plan to help her feel more stimulated/less stressed at work, to leave work on time, or to set up time for a new hobby left her deflated and confused. She knew what she wanted, but she also knew she was sabotaging her own efforts. We worked on separating out the two opposing parts of her experience – a very critical and dominating voice, and a much younger part that seemed scared and vulnerable. All the while, I noticed a pattern in my own experience – each week after the session with Deena I was left with a headache that took a few hours to subside. At first, I didn't think much of it, putting it down to the mental gymnastics in following Deena's plan-stall process.

Much of Deena's story is a common one to encounter with clients. Finding a way to be significant in her family, she grew up very quickly and became a 'parentified child': a process of role reversal whereby a child is obliged to act as parent to their own parent or sibling. In Deena's case there was also a cultural magnifier. With an ancestry deeply rooted in Nepalese-Gurkha, neither of Deena's parents had learned to speak English even when they were living in Hong Kong. From a young age, Deena had to translate and converse with others on her parents' behalf. The day she told me that aged 12 years old she was made responsible for choosing the school for her younger brother Richard I felt the deep ache of sadness and disbelief in my chest: what I would come to know later as relating to loss and grief. For Deena, however, this was simply part of her remit given the responsibility she had for her family's well-being – practically, financially, and emotionally. It was also down to Deena to organise the onward migration of the entire extended family to the UK. The critical voice made sure she stayed on "on the tramline". This voice is often developed when a child creates a parental support not experienced in real life – and being a child's creation, the grown-up voice tends to be very extreme. Deena's internalised critical voice insisted on her success, but now Deena's marker of "success" began to shift. Mid-life often throws up a deep questioning of "what do I really want"; but that, for Deena, became even harder when the "I" wasn't known authentically.

Deena already knew about meditation and Buddhism before starting work with me – her parents' own childhoods were embedded in a culture of its rituals and ideas. Deena's business had also trialled a mindfulness-based stress reduction course the year before. That too became another thing for Deena's ambivalence, liking the theory but not making the time to sit and practice. This mimicked Deena's difficulty – a very able cognitive function dominating over any contact with her feeling and emotional world. And this was playing out in our relationship too. I was starting to make sense of my weekly headaches, realising their emergence at the base of my skull whenever sessions started to touch into emotional territory. For Deena to connect to this realm would have been "too overwhelming" and was feared as something she "couldn't survive". Her 'doing' at work and the inability to leave at the end of the day held at bay her fear of 'being' and an emptiness that would "swallow up" her existence. I was starting to lean into my bodily sense of doing some of the emotional lifting that Deena couldn't bear.

Deena's case can be viewed through the frame of the 'three marks of existence' that we have looked at in this chapter. One of the first times Deena released some emotional energy was when I normalised her experience of suffering. Using my bodily sense of things, I offered it was no wonder she was facing distress in her adult life given what she had shared with me – her family role, an identity and existence that depended on 'doing', and coming to a stage in life where that identity was no longer feeling "right" nor sustainable. Of the three types of suffering, Deena's experience of the 'suffering of suffering' came through turning 50 combining with her health scare to bring awareness of mortality. Furthermore, whilst she recognised the need to slow down, in practice it brought 'suffering of change', challenging the very core of her strategies to provide value and fulfil her duty. Countering the frenetic 'doing' brought Deena to face a void and a deep emptiness that lurks for many of us when we are invited to 'simply be'. This 'all pervasive suffering' is very similar to the existential angst when we recognise non-existence. Through the lens of the three marks, we can perhaps understand how Deena's coming to therapy was a "perfect storm" – her ageing parents and Deena's fear of them dying (impermanence) alongside the threatened death of her identity (non-self).

Deena's weekly attempt to formulate a new plan was a fleeing from the pain in her life and generating a cycle of grasping for a new project (and identity) that would save her. "I know I am running away again" she would often share with me. For now, it was for me to hold the hope that there was a way out of this cycle – but asked of Deena to do things differently. One week she came to the session looking so tired and wrought that I asked her "What if you are never able to out-run your shadow?" She saw that if she did stop, so would her shadow.

Interventions in the therapy

Each week, Deena would keep running in the therapy room too. Whilst important to build the therapeutic relationship in which clients feel heard and feel safe enough to start allowing their vulnerability, as therapists we need to help clients move beyond the 'aboutism' of their stories to experience. Whilst recounting the difficult situations (past and present) and the confidence that I was feeling what Deena couldn't, I would gently invite Deena to 'lean in' to the feeling tone underneath. Using my own body process as a guide, I shared with Deena how painful I found her story and imagined she too might find that in her experience. Speaking to the teary sensation in my eyes and the dull ache in my heart helped Deena recognise her own felt-sense and allow her own tears to come. At times, her critical voice would attempt to discount her pain and add a layer of 'should'. "My life looks perfect on paper, I should be happy" she lamented. It took some time for Deena to acknowledge that her distress was valid, but that required asking the critical voice to step aside for a while. I knew that could only happen when that voice trusted I was a safe pair of hands: after all, this critical voice meant no harm, it was created by Deena when very young to keep the vulnerable part safe. My compassion for the Critical Parent allowed Deena to develop that same compassionate awareness towards her own experience and vulnerability.

It was important we found a way to help Deena integrate what was being learned in the therapy room with life at work, when with her family, and when at home with David. We had practised noticing her story telling, slowing down, and bringing more space between words and sentences. I introduced the acronym 'RAIN' (a practice we will look at in more detail with the case study of "Carol", p. 76). Outside in the real world, this allowed Deena to 'Recognise' the moments of being activated. Deena also began using her breath as an anchor to 'Allow' the experience of the situation without the need to change or run away from it. Once she had connected to the felt-sense of the situation, she learnt to gently 'Investigate' what the feeling was telling her, sometimes prompted by me asking "and what does that part of you need from you right now?" In the beginning, I represented the compassionate presence to provide the 'Nurture' Deena needed, but with time she was able to bring this to herself. Some clients naturally bring a hand to the heart or stomach in times of self-soothing or discover that a gentle 'sigh' on the out-breath helps a release.

In her everyday life, Deena began to spot with more regularity when she was activated at work and how that felt in her body. She would then be able to describe those sensations to me in the room days later. Stories about "who, what, when" became "how" descriptions of her experience. The more she practised, the more familiar she became with the Critical Parent and the vulnerable Child, and how often these voices were pulling her in two opposing directions, setting up a no-win dilemma.

Outcomes of the therapy

Deena and I worked together over her period of mid-life transition. In those five years, she was able to gradually let go of the career-driven identity. The more she was able to drop below the storyline and access her experience in the body and her feelings, Deena saw there was no-one to be or no-where to get to: it was her own beliefs that kept her on the "tramway". This took off the pressure and brought a sense of relief. However, she didn't expect part of the work was also grieving. One week, my post session headache increased in intensity to a level of migraine. It was incredibly fast and potent. As soon as she left the therapy room, I felt a 'whoosh' up my spine and into my head. I was able to make sense of it as a rapid retreat from feeling into cognition, away from heartache and into concepts and stories. I became curious about loss in Deena's childhood. Gently probing the impact of her "time lost" to being "too serious too young", Deena came to realise the grief associated with choices she had not been able to make such as going to art school in Hong Kong, leaving her childhood friends behind, and not having children herself. Our sessions became a process of mourning those losses and a softening towards that little girl that made those choices and traded certainty for freedom. In one of our last exchanges, Deena revealed "in Hindu, my name means 'god-like'. It feels like part of the pact with my parents". Reflections such as this demonstrate Deena's softening towards her own being: A compassion through which she digested the guilt that she would not be able to save her parents. By the time she left therapy, Deena felt better prepared for their death knowing that the grief would not swallow and destroy her.

How this work shaped my human being

Working with Deena gave me my first real taste of how important working with the body is in psychotherapy. More than that: to trust what I am feeling as absolutely relevant to client process. Deena came to therapy with an understanding, like many, that therapy was 'talking about' problems. At first, I was unable to side-step that 'aboutism', but eventually bodily wisdom stepped up with a less than subtle reminder to get out of my head. It was the migraine experience that really astounded, however – my first experience of what the psychodynamic literature would class as 'projective identification'. In Gestalt theory, we often use the term 'projection'; a modification to contact where one person attributes disallowed parts of the self into the other. However, projective identification requires the person who receives the projection to take it in as part of their own psyche. My migraine was Deena's disallowed grief felt as my own. This story will grow in significance as we move into the next chapter and will find a particular resonance with my own story of grief touched upon in Chapter 9.

Notes

1 The numerous lists can be daunting, but it was an imperative 'skilful means' at a time when wisdom traditions were oral traditions.
2 Like Buddhism, a so called 'non-dual' tradition that comes out of Hindu philosophy.
3 'Basic sanity' is a distinguishing feature of a Buddhism-informed psychotherapy.
4 I appreciate there are many branches of psychoanalytic and psychodynamic theory, so apologise for the reductive stance which I make in service of brevity. I recommend the excellent text of Greenberg and Mitchell (1983) if the reader wishes to explore this further.

References

Beisser, A. (1970). The Paradoxical Theory of Change. *Gestalt Therapy Now*, *1*(1), 77–80.
Greenberg, J., & Mitchell, S. (1983). *Object Relations in Psychoanalytic Theory*. Cambridge, MA: Harvard University Press.

Kabat-Zinn, J. (2013). *Full Catastrophe Living: How to Cope with Stress, Pain and Illness Using Mindfulness Meditation.* London: Piatkus.

Karpman, S. (2014). *A Game Free Life. The Definitive Book on the Drama Triangle and the Compassion Triangle by the Originator and Author.* San Francisco, CA: Drama Triangle Productions.

Perls, F. (1973). *The Gestalt Approach and Eye Witness to Therapy.* Ben Lomond, CA: Science & Behavior Books.

Spira, R. (2012). *From the Known, to the Knower, to Knowing.* Retrieved from https://rupertspira.com/non-duality/blog/philosophy/three_possibilities_of_my_self.

Trungpa Rinpoche, C. (1994). *The Ground of Basic Goodness.* Retrieved from www.lionsroar.com www.lionsroar.com/the-ground-of-basic-goodness/.

Welwood, J. (2002). *Toward a Psychology of Awakening: Buddhism, Psychotherapy, and the Path of Personal and Spiritual Transformation.* Boston, MA: Shambhala.

Winnicott, D.W. (1958). The Capacity to Be Alone. *International Journal of Psycho-Analysis, 39,* 416–420.

Chapter 4

Taking suffering as the path
The First and Second Noble Truths

Vignette

Meditation and Buddhism felt like a culmination of the attempts to rid myself of suffering. In the first decade of my life, I focused on 'being a good girl' doing well at school and pleasing my teachers; in the second, I took up the guitar (studying to grade 8) and started excelling at sport (representing my county at tennis and owning a single figure handicap on the golf course); in my twenties I profited from my early years as a 'little professor' (gaining a first class degree and completing my PhD). Having settled with my boyfriend, I remember distinctly on my 27th birthday thinking "I've got it all". But the disordered eating that first surfaced in my teens became increasingly centre-stage as my achievements no longer appeased the inner tyrant who demanded more and more of me. When I took up cycling just as I was entering my fourth decade, the hard training and 'conscious eating' provided the ideal cover for the need to control my body weight in the face of my binge eating. To the outside world, I DID have it all – but there was a growing dissonance with my internal state: I knew I wasn't happy, and I knew things HAD to change.

In the space of 2 years, I left my long-time boyfriend for a woman, and I gave up my secure career at the university in favour of creating a small start-up. I would joke with my friends that it was a classic mid-life crisis – I even bought a GTi with leather seats and alloy wheels!

It was an attempt to reinvent myself, but it only treated the symptoms, not the cause of my deep, deep distress. Even this didn't help beyond the few months of buzz I got from shocking myself and others (although it did bring me a beautiful wife . . . and I got custody of the cats!).

It was when I developed a serious case of insomnia that I realised something had to change. A period of working with a Life Coach helped me understand the nature of my wounding, but as with the first 30 years of my life, I was relying on my intellect and thinking mind to set goals to move towards the life I wanted. A classic example of the Cartesian split – where

DOI: 10.4324/9781003383710-4

body and mind are seen as distinct. Yet the wisdom contained in the sleep-lessness was the 'body keeping score' of all my repeated effort to stay afloat. A visit to the GP got me a prescription of anti-anxiety and anti-depressant medication, but also the introduction to Cognitive Behavioural Therapy. This eight-week CBT 'boot camp' examined my 'be perfect' driver and pro-vided enough clarity to see what needed to be done. From the dark of this period came my decision to retrain as a therapist, and the sense I needed to explore a more spiritual aspect that, to this point, had been neglected in my life. I have so much gratitude to the therapist I was seeing at the time, as it was her gentle containment that first allowed my intuitive and felt wisdom to come forth, including the decision to start meditation.

From my naïve position, I met Buddhist meditation with a "phew, finally! I can rid myself of this". Life to date had been looking outside myself for answers, goal-setting, and essentially turning away from my suffering and distress. Despite its capacity, I had been captive in my thinking mind. I could not think myself out of stress and anxiety. The Buddhist teachings slowly revealed that the only way to work with my suffering was to stop run-ning. To stop on the spot, about turn, and go IN to the very places I had been avoiding. I am still learning what being with 'what is' as experienced through my body and sense perceptions entails; and in a way, the fact it's a lifelong task of more and greater unfolding is a relief. There is no-where to get to other than 'here'.

Our body keeps the score

Aspects of my life I have shared here – the persistent insomnia, disordered eating, exercise addiction, and chronic fatigue – have necessitated I look at how lived experience is expressed through and stored in the bodily tis-sues. To explore this yourself, I invite a little experiment: as you are reading this, bring attention to your mood. How is it to be you today, in this very moment? Take your time to reflect upon this. Feel a little more into that mood whether it be unpleasant, pleasant, or maybe indifferent. Now, move your attention to your body: can you feel your mood in your body? How is it influencing your posture, how you are sitting, standing, or lying down? It is probably no surprise that there is reflection of your mood in your body, an 'embodied cognition'.

In the Western psychological model 'state' refers to a temporary way of being. A situation arises and we respond with thinking, feeling, behaving, relating; for instance, anger at being teased as the youngest in the family. A 'trait' on the other hand is a more stable and enduring characteristic or pattern of behaviour. After continually being teased, the child gives up and turns the anger inward or suppresses it. This in turn might contribute to a personality, a combination of qualities, attitudes and behaviour that are experienced as distinctly "you" by others: a quiet and passive adult who explodes with occasional unexplained rage. Through the Gestalt frame lens, this is a creative adjustment (a response made in a moment to make a situation more tolerable) becoming a fixed gestalt (a response pattern solidified into something more habitual). This applies in body and in mind – in fact, if we stopped seeing the mind and body as split (merci Monsieur Descartes) we wouldn't need to emphasise the union.

Our life impacts our whole being. Our personality, temperament, and indeed our entire life until now has left an imprint. Wilhelm Reich, a student of Freud, coined the phrase 'character armour' to describe this imprinting. He took Freud's notion of libido, or life force, beyond the psyche and towards an energy lived in and through the body. The use of the word 'armour' is a metaphor referring to how muscular contraction and decreased motility lead to postural misalignments. Reich believed that an individual develops these bodily attitudes by way of defending against the breakthrough of intolerable feelings, sensations, or experience. Emotional rigidity arising from a need to 'lock down' and stay safe.

Karen Horney, the German-born/US-based psychoanalyst, reflected on Reich's work, noting how people may arrange their lives to fit their character armour. For instance, I have worked with clients who have needed to eat alone, such was their felt need to protect their 'territory'; and this then grew to become disordered eating, which perpetuated secrecy and the aloneness. It is in these types of examples that we see how life happens, people are impacted, and how that impact lives on to create more of (a similar) impact. The person taking themselves away from interaction might feel the loneliness (whether neglect, or not being seen/heard) without seeing how they invite it; the person with stooped shoulders doesn't see how their posture deters the approach from others; the ever-smiling worker doesn't understand why their colleagues take them for granted. For years, I couldn't fathom my need to lie on my stomach to fall asleep. It was only when I became aware of an ever-present holding in of my stomach – a character armour of keeping myself 'pulled together' – that it made sense. I needed the pressure of the bed to take over the 'holding', or sleep remained elusive.

The field of contemporary therapy is increasingly aware of one particular type of relationship between life history and the body: that of trauma. The seminal text *The Body Keeps the Score* (Van der Kolk, 2015) transformed my thinking, especially conveying how extreme a disconnection from the body trauma history can elicit. Memories completely erased from the mind live on in the bodily tissues and nervous system without any awareness for years. In many cases the only hint of abuse, neglect, or other traumatic episode comes from an individual's development of poor health or disease later in life. Another pioneer in this field, Peter Levine (2012), has described why trauma gets locked down in the body. Like all animals, humans have three responses to perceived life threats. The 'fight' and 'flight' responses to danger are commonly known; the third is 'like a rabbit caught in headlights' experience – when we 'freeze'. This tonic immobility is the most primitive system, and it's the one we (and all mammals) fall back on when the danger seems inescapable – we essentially 'play dead' and hope the danger moves on.

One way we differ to animals is what happens in behaviour AFTER the danger has passed. The massive spike in energy that our bodily functions make available during danger isn't given an outlet in 'freeze' like it is with fighting or fleeing. In the animal kingdom, after the 'freeze' response we see examples of shaking and trembling behaviour to discharge. In humans, temporary immobility (we can perhaps think of how judgement of our physicality, including rage, gets shut down) risks becoming more chronic – the energetic charge gets trapped, and this has a cost. As Van Der Kolk explains it takes tremendous energy to keep functioning while carrying the memory of terror. A second way we humans differ to animals is how we layer the experience of danger with a layer of narrative. A gazelle surviving a lion attack at the watering hole doesn't point the hoof at their family for not being a good enough look out! Conceptual mind is always looking for an explanation, including how not to take responsibility and displace it to another. Shame of utter weakness and vulnerability is another energy cost of trauma; and many of our clients bring this to the therapy room.

Repeated exposure to perceived threat leads to a continual state of 'high alert' even when the threat has passed. The slightest sign of danger (real or perceived) activates an acute stress response with the consequent overwhelming physical and emotional sensations. More and more energy is required, keeping up the alert state whilst simultaneously holding back the (normally discharged) energy. It is a bit like pedalling hard on a bike when applying the brakes; or trying to empty a bath with the tap still on full flow.

Some of the more intuitive of us can read another person's friendliness or hostility based on body language cues. People who have experienced trauma and remain hyper-vigilant are incredibly attuned to even the subtlest emotional shifts in those around them, such as brow tension and even lip curvature. With the most pernicious effects of trauma, there is a disruption in reading others, rendering the trauma survivor either less able to detect danger or more likely to misperceive danger where there is none. It is perhaps in this way we can start to get a sense that trauma stored out of awareness may 'invite' further danger and threat.

Client case study "Claire": working with bodily held narrative

"Claire", a 62-year-old widow suffering from fibromyalgia, originally came for support during a time of isolation. Prior to her symptoms worsening eight years ago, Claire and her husband Tom had attended the same Buddhist community. Health deteriorating, Claire withdrew, and her Buddhist path continued in Tom's sole companionship. When Tom died two years ago, Claire reached out to me to work through her grief, but also hoping I might provide a sense of *sangha*. She believed my understanding of the body would help management of her symptoms. On paper therefore we looked a good fit. Yet in our first few meetings, I experienced some confusion and bodily dis-ease. We interacted with apparent comfort, she keenly expressing her thoughts on the *Dharma* and I listening attentively. However, I was experiencing something of a tentativeness, and left unable to express my distancing. It was if I was holding back from a force not in keeping with Claire's diminutive stature. The result, I felt disconnected whilst playing at being connected.

Just weeks before starting work with Claire I had finished reading *The Divided Mind* by John Sarno. His theory on chronic health conditions (2011) having a psychological/emotional root rather than an organic one remains controversial but struck a chord with me. Rather than risk the emergence of painful psychological material into consciousness, he suggests the mind triggers the brain to start a cascade of biochemical events that reduce oxygen flow to certain tissues, causing inflammation and triggering the pain response. Physical examination and tests reveal no organic cause underlying the symptoms being reported. Sarno lists several physical conditions – ME, CFS, thyroid issues, and many auto-immune conditions – as having a psychosomatic[1] origin. Given my own recent emergence of chronic fatigue without experience of viral infection (e.g., Epstein-Barr) I had been very excited by these ideas of a psychological/emotional aetiology. With optimism for her prognosis, and an assumption she would be equally excited, I shared the ideas of a psychosomatic root with Claire. I witnessed an anger that I had long felt in the room. "It was one thing for the doctors not to believe me, but I didn't expect this from you. This is not all in my head!" I felt the blood drain away to my feet with the shock of her explosion, and yet oddly, the blood pressure dropping felt like relief. Something buried was now revealed.

Claire nearly didn't come back to therapy, such was her sense of being let down. She only returned because she felt some relief in her symptoms in the week following the rupture in our relationship, mirroring my relief at the end of that session. She also told me that my being a Buddhist allowed her to trust my intention. "I know you didn't mean to hurt me; you just weren't very sensitive". I had been guilty of bringing my own agenda into the room. It took several weeks and a shared commitment to use this experience to understand what had been co-created in our relating and had activated Claire's anger. We were able to gain incredible insight into how our relationship had been mimicking the one with her mother, a critical woman.

It was perhaps what had led Claire to the Buddhist path – a code by which to be a "good girl".

Interventions in the therapy

Claire, like most of us, found it very hard to look at the underpinnings of her health history without feeling at fault or casting the blame on others. I could see how she was tangled up in her past story about her present experience – the work needed to start with a disentangling. This is the invitation of the Four Noble Truths. These 'truths' are not meant to be adopted as beliefs but rather practical tasks. Moffitt (2012) describes 12 insights derived from three distinct ways of engaging with each of the Noble Truths: reflecting, experiencing, and finally, knowing.

The first task of *reflecting* was important to help Claire explore and gain insight as to how she came to be so angry and how this gets projected in the present. I knew we needed a way to somehow shift Claire's belief in a personal deficit ("I am not loveable") towards an understanding of the relational deficit ("I was not provided with the love I needed from my Mum"); and to accept how the resulting held-back rage towards her mother was now a residue in the bodymind as inflammation. Claire enjoyed discussing how the *Dharma* might help the understanding of her story; and I see this enjoyment as fundamental to our bonding and the creation of the trusted and holding space of our relationship. Only then could Claire overcome the counter-intuitive turn towards and embrace the very pain she had been wanting rid of.

The second task of 'experiencing' was hard for Claire; understandably, given the magnitude of pain she often felt. We co-created meditation practices that might provide the opportunity to safely lean in to and give space to her experience of the retroflected (inward-turned) anger. The holding of an internal deficit had led Claire to view the symptoms that were "spoiling" meditation as her failing. Like many meditators, she sought a calm mind. The aching limbs, stiff back and shoulders, and extreme tension headaches got in the way. To help, we broke down the constituent parts – to bring attention to the sensations in the body, her feeling towards those sensations, how she labelled them, and how she then treated them. In other words, we removed the label of diagnosis and worked more directly with the experience. "Headache" became "pulsing and tightness". "Anxiety" became "fluttering in the chest". We looked at her reaction to these experiences, even highlighting the subtle aversion that "meditation to achieve peace" demonstrated. Instead, Claire learnt how to be with each moment: to notice the gaps between sensations, that they came, and they went; and importantly, how the story "this will never go away . . . I can't bear it" was neither helpful nor actually true.

Integral to our work together was the offering of my presence to Claire: both in exploratory dialogue (top-down) and while meditating in sessions (bottom-up). Presence, Attunement, Resonance, and Trust are four stages described by Siegel (2010) that can help the client shift away from a disorganised and fearful state; essentially, I was offering Claire a safe neural network on which to attach and through which she could learn to 'accelerate' or 'brake' as she leaned in to experience. We could see this as a soothing mechanism for her hot and inflamed nervous system. I would encourage readers with an interest in neuroscience's input into psychotherapy to look at the work from the field of interpersonal neurobiology (Siegel, 2010; Van der Kolk, 2015; Cozolino, 2016; Porges, 2011).

In the opening chapter I referenced the balancing of the masculine and feminine energies. We might see these combinations of methods as processing 'top-down' accompanied by 'bottom-up' as a blend of the masculine conceptualisation (form) with the feminine being and self-acceptance (space). Harmonising both, a given Noble Truth offers a conceptual description of a general truth in life (top-down or cognitive) and then encourages seeking direct experience in life through mindful, compassionate awareness (bottom-up or experiential). We arrive at the final task of 'knowing', the mindful integration of what has been learned and felt within daily life (Moffitt, 2012). Only then is a client ready to leave therapy, like Claire was two years later.

Outcomes of the therapy

By therapy's end, Claire still struggled with her health but was able to get out of the house at least twice a week. Having a sense of how the trajectory of her life lives on in the body helped her become more accepting (when over-doing things), and patient (in her family relationships). She began to notice the bodily affect when trying to control the pace of life around her and the impatience when others didn't share her agenda. Claire came to know a deeply held anger and became less scared of it erupting. Feeling the anger coming on, she found ways to communicate how she felt rather than holding it in.

How this work shaped my human being

My time with Claire helped me reinforce the different relationship I was trialling with my own body and ailments. When I received my CFS diagnosis, and indeed at other times when I have sensed something is 'wrong' in the body, I lost faith in 'it'. Carel (2016) has called this 'bodily doubt', a loss in the tacit underlying sense of bodily certainty we ordinarily carry. A loss in continuity, transparency, and faith in the body at times of illness can set up a split: self is separated from body, or "my body is causing me pain". Without care, body awareness practices might reinforce this split rather than re-integrate or re-synchronise bodymind. It is critical to inhabit, rather than watch experience in a detached manner.

There was also an outcome for my therapy practice. Although my clumsiness did allow the healing opportunity that we therapists know as 'rupture and repair', it afforded consideration as to the communication of ideas and experiences of being-with clients. Power and language are inseparable. Care is needed in using terms such as 'psychosomatic' when they are so laden with meaning. How do we say things in a way that our clients are able to hear them? Buddhism calls this art *upaya* or 'skilful means'. All clients need our kindness, but for some this means being permissive, for others fiercer; some need our listening, some need our challenge. If I had been more attuned to Claire's inner critic, I might have avoided joining the queue of perceived critics in her life. However, remembering there is never a 'right or wrong' in psychotherapy, my intervention did offer a challenge that moved Claire's process forward towards wholeness.

Language was also a feature in the behind the scenes 'working out' as I reflected on the Buddhist teachings of *karma* between our sessions, and whether introducing it would help or hinder the work. Perhaps the most well-known (and the most misappropriated) of Buddhist ideas, *karma* is likened to sowing seeds that create the next plant to bear fruit with their own seeds. With its focus on cause and effect, it can be a tricky territory to navigate in the domain of psychotherapy. Phrases such as "what goes around, comes around" are misleading at best. To those individuals who already struggle and then take on an added dimension of blame they can be inflammatory. *Upaya* is to move from blame to responsibility; and in Claire's case, the invitation to consider one's personal contribution to the suffering being experienced.

Dis-ease and unravelling karma

In Dante's *Divine Comedy*, Virgil is escorting the protagonist through the Inferno, the first part of his journey through Hell, Purgatory, and Heaven. They arrive at the gates of hell where Dante sees the great horrors within. Gripped with great fear, Dante asks Virgil how they can get out of the terrible situation. Virgil's reply "the only way out is through" is a sentiment adopted by psychotherapy theorists, poets, and songwriters alike; the need to turn towards the painful aspects of life to access the freedom beyond. The *Divine Comedy* is said to be allegorical, the poem representing the soul's journey towards God and the invitation to consider our human being as products of time, place, and circumstance. Similarly in Buddhism, the beautiful iconography of The Wheel of Life depicts the circumstances of *samsara*, and the underlying causes and conditions that perpetuate cyclical existence.

Often presented on *tangka*, the Wheel of Life illustrates how states (the three *kleshas* we met earlier) become habitual patterns of relating to the phenomenal world, or *karma*. The wrathful deity Mara is seen to be holding the whole universe in their teeth. At the centre of the wheel, we find a pig, a bird, and a snake (representing the three *kleshas* of ignorance, attachment, and aversion, respectively). Around this hub, six realms illustrate existence in *samsara*. In the traditional texts, these six realms would be literal – where we take rebirth in a next life dependent on our wholesome or unwholesome actions. A more contemporary view is to see the six realms reflecting patterns in consciousness, we could say the Buddhist equivalent of traits.[2]

Inner shifts of psychological and emotional landscapes mean we are always 'becoming' in each moment, in every day. There are three 'favourable' realms found at the top of the wheel. In the God realm, we find ourselves in a contented and blissful state, but simultaneously cut off from the suffering of others. You might recall a time of accomplishment, how you felt on top of the world and were revelling in the experience. However, this can solidify into a life of carelessness which ignores; thus, we fall into the next realm – the Jealous God realm. This mind state is one of ego and aggression. The fear of losing everything is avoided by seeking more power and position; next is the Human realm, considered the most favourable position because it is the most opportune realm for developing awareness and to be free from suffering. However, there is a more subtle form of aggression which can see us pushing away experience as it is. In the bottom half of the wheel, we see the Animal realm which like the God realm is based on ignorance but this time with a sense of dullness and comfort seeking. Next comes the realm of the Hungry Ghosts. Again, mirroring a realm in the top half there is a grasping for more as with the Jealous Gods, but here the greed is unsatisfiable. Finally, the Hell realm where aversion reigns, but with an aggression more intense than in the human realm and hatred is expressed.

The *upaya* of the Wheel of Life is its powerful iconography, mimicking the use of metaphor and other creative methods that help clients in therapy not just reach insight and understanding, but also get a real visceral sense of their everyday life predicament. For the realm of the Hungry Ghost, the beings with tiny mouths, long necks, and huge bellies really conveys the desperate reaching out, frenetic consuming, and the inability to quell the need. It is a psychological and emotional patterning that I very much relate to. Similarly, I have worked with many clients presenting disordered eating who have related to this imagery and the huge void within that cannot be met from a source without (the case study of "Charlotte" in Chapter 9 illustrates this).

The Wheel of Life describes how we are perpetually creating 'self'; from a moment of being, on to an instance of becoming, and so-on. The momentum that keeps us moving through the realms is that of *karma*. The law of *karma* describes how each volitional act brings about a certain result. Just like planting an apple seed we would expect an apple tree, planting seeds where the motivation is wholeness and benevolence will bring a life of harmony and ease. If we plant seeds from a place of greed or hatred, we will bear a fruit of a similar quality. As I once heard a Buddhist teacher remark "it is hard to meditate or sleep if you have killed someone".

The *Dharma* sees an understanding of *karma* as necessary if we are to be completely alleviated from suffering; and key is understanding the combination of intention and action across body, speech, and mind as determining the *karmic* fruit. Take the example of 'giving'. We are walking through the town centre and notice a homeless woman. Our decision to give some money to her might depend upon thought processes like "what will she do with it?", or upon the circumstances, like "are there people around to witness my act?" Can we simply give some money with the intention to help without a need for it to be the right thing, or being seen to do the right thing? Good *karma* (which sees us elevated into the higher realms) comes from actions with virtuous intentions; bad *karma* comes from actions with non-virtuous intentions (and we enter the lower realms).

Karma has different scopes. On one level, *karma* is the fruit of an action over time. We buy a present for our friend, and sometime later we receive the warm glow of that friend's appreciation for us. Another dimension is the development of the personality. On experiencing the pleasure of the warm glow in ourselves and our friend, we might be encouraged to perform similar deeds for others, and we develop a kindness in personality that magnetises more people of a similar ilk into our lives. Similarly, if an angry thought is not brought into awareness, and there is a reaction imbued with aggression, this is the start of laying down habitual patterns, which if repeated get harder to overturn. In other words, experiences leave a residue even when they pass – and this explains why we might end up experiencing one of the six realms as the prevalent backdrop of our life. Our life trajectory is therefore completely explainable[3] (even if in practice this would be impossible to unravel); *karma* is seen in both the short term and long term.

The value-added of karma

Like gravity, being a natural law, *karma* will keep operating even if we are not aware of it or do not believe in it! Nonetheless when writing this section, I wanted to offer more constructive reasons as to why *karma* brings a 'value-added' to my therapeutic work, specifically appropriate to "the only way out is through". After all, Western psychology has similar descriptions and explanations of patterns (typically those that aided survival when young) becoming rigid and showing up as obstacles, again and again: the 'state to trait' and Gestalt theories describing 'creative adjustments' and 'fixed gestalts' as mentioned in the previous chapter; and in psychoanalysis, the 'repetition-compulsion' that describes the reenactment of the original wounding in the relational field.

Freud first detailed his ideas on repetition-compulsion in his 1914 work *Remembering, repeating, and working-through*. From my experience, Buddhism offers a throughline to these three processes. If *karma* is the compulsion to repeat patterns outside of our awareness, *remembering* the pattern is the foundation to working it through. Whilst Freud emphasised *repeating* of relational patterns (in the transference), Epstein (2013) precedes this with a quality of remembering in the present – not merely of the past – as offered by a meditative quality. It is no coincidence that the Sanskrit *smrti* means 'that which is remembered'. With this, the "working it through" that follows is realised in "the gradual knowing of the disaffected material as *coming from one's own being*" (Epstein, 2013). As a therapist holding an existential position, I already hold conviction in the power of agency, choice, and responsibility. Taking the view as being active participants in the creation of our *karma*, "working-through" requires any consequential suffering to be fully felt. As explored in the chapter's earlier section 'Our body keeps the score', (p. 50) our actions and their results are deeply encoded in the viscera, with gut-wrenching and overwhelming emotions, or manifesting as autoimmune disorders and skeletal/muscular problems. Within bodymind communication is thus the royal road to emotion regulation and therefore healing. Practitioners such as Van Der Kolk and Levine suggest this demands a radical shift in our therapeutic assumptions. More than reclaiming memories or changing our thoughts and beliefs about how we feel, we need to look at the sensations that lie underneath our feelings and uncover our habitual responses to them. Agency, through the lens of *karma*, comes alive when we throw awareness on our bodily and mental activity. With this 'interoception' (which we will return to in the case study of "Sebastian" in Chapter 7) a gap opens, and we can make a choice to respond rather than keep on reacting. Furthermore, our ability to *know* what we feel can be greatly enhanced through meditative practice.

Facilitating Claire's remembering in the present (awareness of moment-by-moment experiencing) helped her identify, on some level, that she was choosing the held-rage underneath. I would add that the lens of *karma* has given me a deepened and nuanced understanding of responsibility in my work with survivors of trauma; how complicated a web is woven through interpersonal connections; how decisions lead us to be in a certain time, space, place. Every choice has a consequence – and *karma* allows us to penetrate these experiences with compassion, without the need for the apportioning of blame nor the taking on of guilt.

Admitting to ourselves and others that we have erred is not an easy task; and yet it is also the key to liberation. It is said that if we want to learn about our past, we should look at our present circumstances, for they are the result of our past actions, the *'karma of result'*. If on the other hand we want to learn about our future, we should look at what we're doing now: the *'karma of causes'*. In her book *Welcoming the Unwelcome*, Pema Chödrön points out "the latter is the more helpful aspect of *karma*. There's nothing we can do to change the past and present, but the future is unwritten" (Chödrön, 2020, p. 13). *Karma* developed from past actions takes a while to exhaust. This was a useful frame to discuss with "Deena", the client case study in Chapter 3, as she began to understand how taking on the role of emotional and financial adult in her family set up her pattern of being dutiful. Whilst these "tramway tracks" were hard to re-route, finding the courage to let go of the impulse to respond to the 'shoulds' she was able to create new possibilities for the future. And this point is critical: understanding and insight will not change our past *karma*. We can only look at what is reflected, and how it may shape our life ahead. Rather than a rear-view mirror, *karma* is best brought into service as a telescope facing forward.

The wide-angle lens of *karma* distinguishes the habits from our being. Our inherent brilliance is simply obscured by layers of protective patterns. Furthermore, understood correctly there is nothing inherently wrong about *karma*; in fact, it is neutral. The traditional texts explain "facing the Mirror, the soul is exposed to truth". As with all natural laws (gravity, evolution) *karma* describes how our world responds to our actions without an opinion, without subjectivity. You could say the mirror of *karma* is a trustworthy one, reflecting our true nature AND the shadow that needs integrating. Subjectivity is our response to seeing the reflection – and a Buddhism-informed psychotherapy views this reflection with compassion. The *karma* of results came about for a reason, probably in service of protection from the wisdom inherent to our essence. Again, we could see the *'karma* of causes' simply as repetition-compulsion; but rather than trying to eradicate the pattern, releasing the wisdom in the confusion is the path.

What is that wisdom? Wisdom is not conceptual knowledge. Wisdom is experiential. The View according to the *Dharma* is to recognise and experience the three marks of our existence: suffering, non-self, and impermanence. If we live in ignorance of these, we continue to sow *karmic* seeds. Later in the book I will present the *Dharma's* model of the mind, and how the seeds sown by our *karma* are stored in our consciousness (the eighth layer, or *alaya-vijnana*). For now, we just need to know that the potential for *samsara* (suffering) and *nirvana* (liberation) co-exist in a storehouse consciousness. Which realm of existence arises in any one moment depends on the View we hold in that moment. If we ignore the three marks (thereby thinking of ourselves as separate, permanent, and above suffering) we continue to sow *karmic* seeds. Even positive actions sow new seeds – giving a gift to Other creates *karma*, as it perpetuates the separateness of the subject-object illusion. Ultimately, the Buddhist path practices take us to a position of 'threefold purity', where there is no self as giver, no action of giving, no other to receive. This might seem beyond us, but if we consider Martin Buber's proposition within the 'I-Thou' attitude of relating, and not submit to the 'I-it', we recognise our commonality. Therapy, at least the relational models, relies on this intersubjectivity to alleviate distress. Buddhism takes this one step further on – ultimate relief by dissolving the subject-object distinction altogether.

Ultimate upaya: cultivating 20/20 clarity

Around the time I was finishing the first draft of this book, I listened to a podcast interview with psychotherapist John Prendergast in which he asked a question that moved me deeply; one that invited a rewrite of this chapter to include a more personal take on what the teachings of *karma* mean to me: "If this experience was here forever, how would you relate to it?"

"If this anxiety was here forever, how I would I relate to it?" As I have shared, the experience of anxiety has persisted for many years, and I have had no choice but to allow it as a companion. Prendergast's question took me to another level of relating. It begged an intimacy; to know my anxiety like I would want to know a dear friend, a relative, a lover. As I say previously, the mirror of *karma* is an accurate one, and as such it has quality that is trustworthy. My anxiety is reliable. It communicates something to me. Not only does it give me the feedback I am alive, the seeing of it as it arises is an opportunity to connect to the awareness that knows it. In the way alchemists saw the vessel, and how therapists see the therapeutic frame, *karma* takes on the shape of a container.

The walls of a container allow process to show up against a boundary. When I was sharing these ideas with a friend, a fellow psychotherapist, she said my descriptions of *karma* as therapeutically relevant conjured up an image of something 'with solidity'; something that could be leant against, and from which something new could emerge, a new self. We might say from self to Self. Turning towards my anxiety – the speedy texture of mind, the fear in the pounding heart, the terror in the flipping belly – calls not for ridding or change, it calls for compassion. It is a call to transmute anxiety into courage. The *Vajrayana* Buddhist view that I am learning to integrate goes as far as to say that the apparent confusion of our patterns and habits are in fact THE gateway to waking up – a bit like how the peacock gains its beautiful feathers by eating poisonous leaves. When I see my anxiety, inherent compassion and wisdom are reflected back.

The law of *karma* can also be thought about across generations, not in the way traditional teachings spoke of reincarnation – we need not get into those esoteric and metaphysical debates here. I am referring to our ancestral lineage, and how family histories are passed from one generation to the next. I know that some of my anxiety is a trait inherited through the female line of my family; I even have a sense that an anxious mother (who was caretaker for her own anxious mother) offered me a quivering first home in the womb. Why would my nervous system gauge NOT be set to that end of the dial? There is a certain trajectory that we inherit, and at first this can be difficult to accept let alone allow. Hopefully this chapter has helped convey that while this '*karma* of results' cannot be changed, it offers a path quality; one along which we can move towards a whole, integrated, and individuated Self. Recognising the confused pattern, knowing it intimately as it is playing out, and sincere compassion for its appearance is the key to our liberation. As meditation master Yongey Mingyur Rinpoche says, "the problem IS the solution".

Before we leave the theme of suffering as the path, a brief note on reintegrating the bodymind. I'm writing this section of the book the day after facilitating a workshop with trainees. In these experiential workshops, students get to work in 'fishbowls' with another colleague on the course (with the rest of the group watching the dyad's work). Yesterday, both fishbowls brought up the power of working with the bodily experience. For first year trainees, the use of the body as the instrument for relational healing is a challenging prospect, sometimes leaving trainees with a mistaken view that the feeling function is more desirable than the thinking function. Emphasis on working with the bodily felt-sense must be seen as the attempt to rectify an imbalance set up by many of our *karmic* 'load-bearing' experiences; the tendency for lived experience to be quashed under layers of narrative and thought. Wholeness, the pursuit of our full health, means integration of body and mind (bodymind) not at the expense of one for the other. A client's thinking function is to be held with respect for its protective function or there is a risk of shaming the client or perpetuating but just another injunction of 'how to be'.

Notes

1 I feel it is important here to underline the two-way integration of mind and body. The best psychotherapy is one that understands the human being as a complex and interconnected system. The systemic and integrative practitioner stays open and curious regarding the aetiology of symptoms and presenting issues; to cast the net wide when exploring with the client what might be occurring and as to its meaning; referring to another health professional as needs be. The reader might find the work of Hill and Dahlitz (2022) of value.

2 As you read the description of the six realms, it might be interesting to keep in mind how Mark Epstein, Buddhist and psychoanalyst, has suggested that the psychodynamic view works with the lower realms and drives, whilst the humanistic paradigm emphases the capacities of 'peak experiencing' in the higher realms. Buddhism takes into account the whole; another way to think about the presentation of human nature, distress, and healing goals.

3 'Explainable' is not the same as a law of determinism.

References

Carel, H. (2016). *Phenomenology of Illness.* Oxford: Oxford University Press.

Chödrön, P. (2020). *Welcoming the Unwelcome: Wholehearted Living in a Brokenhearted World.* Boston, MA: Shambhala.

Cozolino, L. (2016). *Why Therapy Works: Using Our Minds to Change Our Brains.* New York, NY: W.W. Norton & Company.

Epstein, M. (2013). *Thoughts without a Thinker: Psychotherapy from a Buddhist Perspective.* New York, NY: Basic Books a Member of Perseus Books Group.

Hill, R., & Dahlitz, M. (2022). *The Practitioner's Guide to the Science of Psychotherapy.* New York, NY: W.W. Norton & Company.

Levine, P. (2012). *Healing Trauma: A Pioneering Program for Restoring the Wisdom of Your Body.* Boulder, CO: Sounds True.

Moffitt, P. (2012). *Dancing with Life: Buddhist Insights for Finding Meaning and Joy in the Face of Suffering.* New York, NY: Rodale.

Porges, S. (2011). *The Polyvagal Theory: Neurophysiological Foundations of Emotions, Attachment, Communication, and Self-regulation.* New York, NY: W.W. Norton & Company.

Sarno, J.E. (2011). *The Divided Mind. The Epidemic of Mindbody Disorders.* London: Duckworth Overlook.

Siegel, D.J. (2010). *The Mindful Therapist. A Clinician's Guide to Mindsight and Neural Integration.* New York, NY: W.W. Norton & Company.

Van der Kolk, B. (2015). *The Body Keeps the Score: Brain, Mind, and Body in the Healing of Trauma.* London: Penguin Books.

Chapter 5

Alleviation of distress
The Third and Fourth Noble Truths

Vignette

It is only when we turn on the light that we realise how much furniture is in the room. Similarly, in the first few weeks of my meditating, the light of awareness revealed how much thinking was going on . . . constantly, a background commentary throughout my life, during all my activities. I didn't only think, my thoughts had an opinion on how much (and how well) I was thinking. Clever thoughts, nonsense thoughts, random thoughts. Sitting in meditation and witnessing this felt quite painful. Thankfully, I was able to piggy-back on the wisdom and experiences of others: meditating wasn't causing me to think more – I was just becoming more aware of what was already there. The Tibetan word for meditation, *gom*, means to become familiar – and I was coming to know my mind and its activity.

Within a few months, awareness of 'the waterfall of thoughts' brought a change; remembering to come back to the breath started to slow the torrent. With more time, I noticed there were gaps between thoughts. Meditation became like a trip to the gym: the muscle of mindfulness (one pointed attention placed upon an object, often the breath), and the muscle of awareness (the quality that enables us to know we have left the breath) were getting stronger. At first, I noticed the change 'off the cushion' more than during the practice itself. People around me also noticed a change – I seemed more peaceful, less on edge, softer.

Evoking Gestalt's 'paradox of change', simply noticing the speed of the tumbling thoughts, gaps between thoughts came into view. In that gap, an opportunity arises – choice. The classical theories of conditioning speak of stimulus-response; the world provided a stimulus, and where I would normally react (from habit), the gap provided the time and space to choose another option. At first, slowing down allowed more consciousness of my thoughts and actions, but I was seeing them too late to avoid the consequences. I found this frustrating. With more time, the gap opened enough

DOI: 10.4324/9781003383710-5

to catch myself.[1] Reaction became response. With clients I often refer to this as response-ability.

Being in therapy at the same time as this unfolding allowed me to gain insight as to how habits of the mind were created, and to see how deeply those 'habit formations' were imprinted. I began to know a deep anxiety that led to controlling behaviour. I didn't like needing control; I didn't like who I became in moments I was triggered, even if I understood it was because I was scared of whence it came. Slowing down, I experienced my anxiety more clearly and began to catch the moments at which I was just about to contract around my world and solidify it in the attempt to make it predictable and safe.

One Sunday morning, I remember reading a quote from Buddhist teacher Pema Chödrön:

> In the next moment, in the next hour, we could choose to stop, to slow down, to be still for a few seconds. We could experiment with interrupting the usual chain reaction, and not spin off in the usual way. We don't need to blame someone else, and we don't need to blame ourselves. When we're in a tight spot, we can experiment with not strengthening the aggression habit and see what happens. Pausing.
>
> (2009, p. 7)

The mere suggestion of life being an experiment evoked a visceral "wow!" The freedom possible in not needing to get anything 'right', I simply had to open myself to the stimuli of life and see how I got pulled to react. Therapists reading this will also appreciate how helpful this is practically: the ability to notice the pull of the transference/counter-transference and bring curiosity to it rather than acting it out. I am offering this personal experience to set up how we can deal with the truth of suffering; how we can feel the tug in our experience to tighten and protect; and this is the very gateway to liberation.

Mind the gap

The teachings of the Four Noble Truths help us find the confidence to turn towards our suffering. The *Buddha* presented our 'dis-ease' in the familiar classical Indian medicine model of diagnosis, aetiology, prognosis, and prescription. We have already looked at the diagnosis, pain is inevitable; and an aetiology that explains suffering as the resistance to pain and the result of clinging onto a 'self' that is permanent, single, and independent. This is the 'bad news' message of the first two Noble Truths: we suffer, and very often we are the antagonists.

This chapter focuses on the good news! We can do something about our suffering if we start to take responsibility for our actions and their consequences, eliminating the false notion that we can always get what we want, and others (or the world!) are to blame that we don't. "There is cessation to suffering" (as posited by the Third Noble Truth) and a "path towards the end of suffering" (encapsulated in the Fourth Noble Truth). Before going into these in more depth, it might be helpful to detail how Buddhism describes the creation of the illusory 'inherently existing self' – the teaching of the five aggregates or *skandhas*:

- The first *skandha* is 'form', or the physical body, and is made up of our sense gates (eyes, ears, nose, tongue, body, and the mind).
- The second *skandha* is that of 'feeling' the sensations that arise through the sense gates as pleasant, unpleasant, or neither (neutral).
- The third *skandha* of 'perception' is simply a judging quality – when we experience something as pleasurable, it becomes a 'good thing'; or something unpleasant is 'bad'. We then react accordingly.
- Fourth, we have the *skandha* of 'mental formations' which describes the concepts and thoughts we carry.
- Finally, the fifth *skandha* is the 'consciousness' that has awareness of *skandhas* one through four.

As the word 'aggregate' suggests, each of these is a collection – not of parts but rather as five processes which with 'clear seeing' can be experienced as fleeting. Buddhist psychology explains how the ego function recruits these five processes to create a 'self' that is real and solid, and defended. Appreciating the *skandhas* as more than just another list we have a very sophisticated method of working with being activated. We can learn to interrupt the process and ease our suffering: the Third Noble Truth.

Working with the skandhas

Buddhist scholar and teacher Reggie Ray (2018), unpacks the process of the *skandhas* starting with resting in our innate *buddhanature* and coming to experience 'being' (material we considered in 'Comparing the Buddhist view with Western models', p. 40). However, when we encounter this boundless and brilliant basic goodness, Ray explains we can recoil in terror. It is through this abrupt pulling back that we objectify space and thus there is 'otherness'.[2] The first *skandha* of form is therefore the impression that something exists (self) separately from space. In the second *skandha*, we attach a feeling quality to this experience (whether that be pain, pleasure, or indifference) simply to create a relationship and orientation of whether this 'other' is friend, foe, or of no relevance. The evaluative felt-sense that arises brings subtle confirmation to a solid being-ness, and it is from here that we react. In the third *skandha*, we take up an attitude towards this 'other': we reject the unpleasurable, we want more of the pleasurable, and we close ourselves down to the neutral as "boring" or by numbing. You might recognise these three reactions as the *kleshas* (Chapter 3).

The fourth *skandha* of 'mental formations' is also referred to as *karmic* formations (*samskaras*). In this step, we move from the freshness of experience to concept; or as Ray describes it, a 'facsimile' of experience. There is an attempt to frame the experience within a framework of what we know; a coherent rationale as to why what is happening is happening, and why we are reacting to it in the way we are. A personal storyline is constructed from the identifications, labels, justifications, and judgements. You can perhaps see how this links to *karma*. The fifth *skandha* of consciousness is quite different to the quality of awareness associated with *buddhanature*. If we are resting in our inherent nature, we can receive sense perceptions and mental phenomena as a flux, arising and falling. In the fifth *skandha*, however, there is a limited and self-absorbed quality that decides what to include and what to exclude from awareness (arising from our *karmic* 'lens' in the stage beforehand). There is a fixation on aspects of experience that will fulfil the 'identity-project', that fits the facsimile into the concept of who we should/ need to be.

Catching the impulse

In psychotherapeutic work, therapists help clients to investigate how they are currently living their lives and how this is no longer serving them. This is the forward scope of working with *karma* (see 'The value-added of karma', p. 58). The *samskaras* are so subtle and ingrained that we don't notice how they continue to impact our living. *Samskara* imprints are like psychical springs of our thoughts and behaviours, and it is these that we bring under the spotlight (in therapy) and can loosen (using meditation). Ray (2018) explains for the meditation practitioner the most interesting and important moment is at the third *skandha*. No matter how much we understand our past *karma*, we cannot erase *skandhas* one and two; we must let it come to fruition, and in doing so, lay down new tracks. Ray calls the third *skandha* 'impulse', a label I appreciate as it reveals this stage as the moment for potential change and to "find ourselves really and truly free" (2018, p. 128). The home of impulse is the body, and Ray's invitation is simple, albeit not easy. If we can feel the impulse, not act, and come back to the body each time, eventually impulse is weakened. Essentially, we need to be able to sit with *skandha* two, our feeling evaluation, and avoid the invitation of the impulse to jump in and 'scratch the itch'. This is very much the work that "Claire" explored with her experience of chronic pain (as we saw in the previous chapter), and also the path that "Jake", a 32-year-old male client who was experiencing relational paranoia. A deep fear of abandonment would leave Jake constantly worried as to how those close to him perceived him. Any gap in communication – unreturned phone calls or messages – would leave him in a spin. Jake complained of being highly activated "nearly all the time", in the gap before a friend replied. On exploring the familial story and roots of this abandonment fear (the *karma* of results), the blue touch paper of Jake's curiosity was lit. How was he perpetuating this *karmic* tendency for seeming abandonment (the *karma* of causes)? Jake came to see how his 'checking' behaviour was sowing the seeds of the very results he feared – like a self-fulfilling prophecy, his "need to know" out of the fear of "being ghosted" got the certain return of rejection. Jake and I tried a few experiments in our work together. Bringing a relationship he was worried about to mind, I guided him to feel into the separation anxiety; to feel the impulse (for example, reaching out to his phone), and to learn how to bear the effect of "not knowing". Original experiences are overwhelming often because they happen alone. My presence helped Jake gain confidence he could bear the aloneness, that he could withstand the arising impulse. From here, I helped Jake try out how he could self-soothe in contrast to reaching out for someone else to calm his hot nervous system. This is the forward scope of *karma*, the influence we can bring to the *karma* of causes.

Working with impulse and the gap

Those of you familiar with CBT might notice some shared characteristics. Both Buddhism and CBT speak to the connection of thoughts, feelings, and behaviour. However, fundamental to the Buddhist view is a two-way street between thoughts and feelings. The body holds the story; a certain event or person triggers that story; and it floods back into our present. Emotion arising in any one moment is the thought and meaning in response to a feeling. In other words, our emotional reaction is not just the raw energy of a situation (*skandha* two) but rather the 'value-added' we attach because of our self-concept and the cultural influences (*skandha* three). The stronger the emotional reaction, the better the opportunity to work in the gap of non-response to the impulse. Can you see the importance of resting in the gap and feeling fully the emotion and the attitude to the emotion arising?

Opening up awareness and the resulting agency that comes from choice is paralleled in Western psychology; it is a fundamental tenet of Gestalt psychotherapy. However, Buddhism offers a more nuanced and practicable view given we can find our feet on the meditation cushion by consolidating awareness of bodily sensations, mindfulness of the resulting impulse, and the gentle encouragement to 'stay'. We can then move this same practice into the everyday: in relationship, at work, with family. Notice the sensations when activated, 'mind the gap', and then choose how to respond.

Ponlop Rinpoche (2017) describes a zooming out: to see not only the emotion but the emotional landscape within which it is contained – the setting, the pattern, the interconnection i.e., *karma*. Through this, suffering becomes optional.

Response-ability and choice

Cessation of suffering, the Third Noble Truth, is thus accomplished by resisting the impulse (and momentum of our *karma*) and resting in the gap. That is by no means easy. As I meditated this morning before my day of writing, I was witness to how often I am lured away by a stream of mental activity. Recognising this, I turned my attention to the thoughts as soon as they appeared to consciousness, and to see them for what they were before they could bloom into all sorts of stories and fantasies. Knowing I was to spend this morning writing about 'impulse' served as a reminder to come back to the somatic experience underneath. Research shows how meditation improves interoception (more on this in Chapter 7) allowing increasingly subtle felt experiences. Today my experience was of 'falling', and it was as if my thoughts, projecting to time points in the future, were acting like the webs Spiderman would shoot out for safety as he falls from a skyscraper. I didn't need to start thinking "why?" I just focused on relaxing and opening to the fall. As I say, this is not easy . . . but 'the only way out is through'.

What is out the other side? By resisting the impulse to think (in reaction to the falling and uncertainty) there is the opportunity to write a different *karmic* track. The more we open up the gap and stay with it 'as it is' we have the opportunity to loosen narratives about ourselves, others, and our world. The Buddhist framework offers us eight practices that can help ensure our *karma* is more to our pleasing. This Eightfold path (the "path to cease suffering" set out in the Fourth Noble Truth) is sub-divided into the threefold trainings of wisdom, ethical behaviour, and mental discipline and applied across all dimensions of experience, namely body, speech, and mind.

Developing the underlying philosophical foundation: Prajna or wisdom

There are two factors offered up by the Eightfold Path that cover the training in wisdom, the first being Wise View.[3] We have already discussed the error in expecting phenomena to be permanent. Another aspect of developing a more discriminating mind is being free of conceptualisation. By removing learned filters, we can take in more important information and stop distorting reality. An example is 'unconscious bias', the social stereotyping about groups of people that individuals form outside conscious awareness. In my work with clients, I often see how a person suffers from a rigid self-concept or inaccurate assumptions of others. Furthermore, I talk to trainees about the risks of losing sight of the person behind the label of a personality adaptation/diagnosis. Wise View offers us a way to take the opportunity for genuine encounters with others and our world. From Wise View springs forth Wise Intention. Seeing 'what is' without elaboration means we are not prone to the traps of wishful thinking or catastrophising. We realise there is no territory to defend nor gain and so there becomes an aspiration to not cause harm.

Creating a foundation of ethical behaviour: Sila or discipline

In this category, we have the practices of Wise Speech, Wise Action, and Wise Livelihood.[4] Wise Speech is communicating with truth. For example, I might work with clients as to how they can express their needs more explicitly rather than being passive-aggressive or potentially manipulative. I have found it helpful to use the *Buddha's* elaboration of what we need to consider before speaking (or indeed writing): Is what I am about to say true? Is it kind? Is this the right time? Am I the most appropriate person to say this? In the therapeutic setting we might also consider whether silence would serve this moment (and contact with Other) more powerfully? On retreat, some of the most profound experiences have come when I have sat the entire time without speaking a word to my partner in a dyad practice (an exercise of intentional speaking and listening). Connecting with Wise Speech we begin to communicate more authentically and congruently.

The second aspect is Wise Action, sometimes called Wise Discipline. Can we commit to a life of not causing harm to ourselves, others, and our world? For those who step more formally onto the Buddhist Path, this is committed to through taking of the 'precepts': the intention to abstain from killing, stealing, sexual misconduct, lying, and intoxication. By no means does this equate to a puritanical pursuit. I am mindful of this in my therapeutic work with Buddhists who, in following such precepts as doctrine, risk driving the 'bad me' into the shadow. We might see how some clients deny their own needs and never self-promote through the fear of being selfish. Wise Action encourages us to move towards what is important in life; towards seeing cause and effect rather than 'right or wrong'.

The third and final aspect of *sila* is Wise Livelihood. Whilst many on the path might desire a life in retreat, the real work is to be done integrating the spiritual into everyday life. Given the proportion of time we spend at work, this is an opportunity for spiritual and emotional practice. One client I work with refers to their workplace as a "playpen". In simplest terms, we might find a way to make a living that doesn't cause harm to others. Regardless of our trade, we can: bring more mindfulness of our behaviour and its impact on our colleagues; rouse compassion for self and Other in situations of difficulty; and consider how our way of earning a living funds an ethical purpose. I worked with one client who wanted to set up a non-for-profit venture to help the homeless. Another client uses their position as a solicitor to fund their volunteer work during summer vacations. Personally I feel very fortunate to have a vocation that fulfils my aspiration as a *bodhisattva* – helping others (client work); and helping others to help others (my work as an educator of therapists).

Training the mind: Samadhi or meditation

Cultivating a familiarity with the mind is central to the Buddhist path. In this category, three aspects of training the mind are to be applied, namely Wise Effort, Wise Mindfulness, and Wise Concentration. When we first sit to meditate, we can be overwhelmed with what we experience and the reaction can be to try too hard, or to get disheartened and give up. Wise Effort is like a string on a well-tuned musical instrument – not too tight, not too loose. Similarly in life, we can watch for becoming sombre and controlling, or flippant and careless. I often discuss with supervisees the interplay of effort and non-effort: when do we move into the therapeutic task, and when do we sit back and let the client demonstrate agency. Similarly, perhaps it is working with the polarity of serious work and serious play.

Wise Mindfulness is a quality that lets us step back from situations and gain a healthy distance from what we have noticed. 'Developing the watcher' (the differentiation of 'Knower and Known', p. 103) using meditation helps clients untangle from the storyline. In the therapy room I might invite them to lift-up in a helicopter and look down on what is happening, or climb onto the bank and watch the river. The quality of mindfulness allows a relationship TO the situation rather than being caught up and IN the knottiness.

Interestingly, Wise Concentration is the final aspect of the Eightfold path yet is the factor to which new meditators are often first introduced with a one-pointed focus on the breath. However, the aim of the practice is not to be champion breath watchers. By training attention, the mind and body become synchronised, breeding a relaxed and more pliable bodymind. The Buddhist teachings refer to the 'brilliance' and 'clarity' of knowing; one that illuminates the incessant, routine, repetitive, and self-serving thoughts. Wise Concentration helps us to be more present in our life because we come to see the thoughts as simply an undercurrent, NOT life itself.

Finding true refuge

An understanding of the Four Noble Truths, culminating with the practices of the Eightfold Path, clarifies our predicament as human beings and opens up choice. Perhaps most importantly it brings us more confidence in experience. With clearer seeing, less filtering, and less reactivity we begin to engage with 'what is' rather than what we want or don't want. We realise we can find peace in the midst of our life no matter the circumstance. Meditation with the underpinning of the Buddhist *Dharma* and View helps us find 'home' – not as a place, but rather as an experience in our bodymind. Wouldn't that be a wonderful outcome for our therapy clients?

This path doesn't depend on anyone granting salvation. With personal agency, we take responsibility for how we have lived and how we have reacted to the consequences of our living. Even in situations of extreme neglect or abuse, with courage there can still be a decision as to what to do with that experience. We might need the help of others, but we cannot rely on others to do the work for us. This is fundamental in any kind of therapeutic work – the therapist can provide a 'secure attachment', but then the client must be able to venture out into the world alone even with the huge uncertainty that presents.

Self is created in relationship; the young infant piggy-backing their caregivers until their neural function allows independent survival. Furthermore, given our childhood wounding took place in relationship, what better way to heal that wounding than IN relationship? (Welwood, 2005). Relationships are essential, we find out who we are in the contact made with others. We find friends that accept us for all we are, we share, and closeness grows allowing the basis of feeling 'good enough' about ourselves. Yet, we cannot take security from any one relationship, situation, or person. "Without forsaking our relationships with human beings or with the richness and goodness of life, we do not turn to them for refuge. Relationships with the world are one thing; taking refuge in them is something else altogether" (Kongtrul Rinpoche, 2006, p. 41). In my own life story, I am fully aware how long I sought refuge in external affirmation and validation, 'conditions of worth'. What Buddhism offered was the opportunity to take confidence in experience rather than in the opinions and expectations of others (whether real or simply perceived). As a *Vajrayana* student of Buddhism, each morning I take refuge in the path of practice or the 'three jewels' of the *Buddha*, the *Dharma*, and the *Sangha*.

- Refuge in the *Buddha* is refuge in the awakened heart and mind. We can look to others, like the *Buddha* for inspiration: to see and contemplate their wakefulness, openness, and stillness; and to practise remembering our own nature is also one of clarity.
- Refuge in the *Dharma* points to the truth of the present moment. The quality of awareness brings us into contact with the moment-by-moment experience: to notice when we are caught up in regrets of the past, or anticipatory fear of the future. Awareness helps us notice when we are caught up in habitual reactivity, to notice our thoughts, feelings, and emotions.

- Refuge in the *Sangha* comes from the quieting of thoughts and a subsequent softening and opening of the heart – this gives us a sense of safety and allows us to relax and entrust ourselves to reality, and to others in relationship.

Finding true refuge asks us to do things differently. False refuge is what many people are more familiar with – the strategies we employ when feeling hurt, angry, or confused. This can take several guises, and most of the time we are not aware that we are distracting ourselves from the painful feelings. Obvious examples would be eating when we need comfort or feel alone; drinking heavily when we've experienced rejection; or working long-hours to avoid going home to a volatile situation.

A less identifiable 'false refuge' many clients have learnt is the deflection into thinking as protection from feelings. Whilst we cannot help but think, at some level, believing the thinking above feeling IS a choice. Sometimes it is a very intelligent choice as a child, for instance, if exposed to abuse or a lack of love. Disconnecting from the physical pain of trauma or rationalising an inattentive parent allows the child to survive an otherwise intolerable situation. However, this strategy becomes ingrained. As I discussed with one client recently, the defence is obsolete. The obsessing mind is trying to work out a way to stay protected from something that has already happened.

Client case study "Carol": working with an anxious storyline

Existentialism points to anxiety as a common thread through our experience of being human. There is a sense of today's world ramping up 'normal' anxiety: growing uncertainty – politically and environmentally, to name just two aspects – combined with the rapidity and reach of the media and internet reporting of our predicament. One such anxious being-in-the-world, "Carol", came to meet me one morning explaining how much she had been struggling with anxiety and obsessive thoughts. She didn't need to say, as she spoke and moved with such speed it was like sitting in the room with the Tasmanian devil cartoon character. I noticed how hard it was for me to stay present and resist being swept up in her process. Bodily, I could feel myself being 'lifted up and out', the anti-gravity increasing as her speed increased. I sensed how important it was to not fuel the fire of that take-off, so rather than ask questions of what brought her to see me, I let the whirlwind blow itself out. I brought awareness to my feet so I could 'land down and in'. With time Carol slowed, and she landed with me. She looked at me as if for the first time she saw someone was in the room with her. From the look in her eyes in those opening moments I got a glimpse of the pain of this 71-year-old woman. She revealed to me "I can't help it. I get anxious about everything these days". Very few people could bear to be with Carol, her two adult children included; "pull yourself together Mum". My own experience of being in relationship with Carol was needing time to regroup after the session. My bodymind felt relief when she left the room, the bodily buzz taking some time to leave. When it did, an upswelling of sadness emerged connecting me to the loneliness Carol felt in this life. Anxiety receding, sadness emerging was to become a recurrent embodied theme in our relational field.

"Why now?" is a useful question to ask clients when they come to therapy. Carol explained her husband's Parkinson's disease had dramatically worsened. She and her two daughters had discussed moving him to a care home, but Carol couldn't bring herself to. It became clear why she was starting therapy. "I know I am losing Sam, but it is like I am losing me too. I don't know what my life will be; I don't know who I am". What struck me was the shock Carol was experiencing. "I've always been so sure of myself; I've always known who I was". With a confused expression and quivering tone, Carol told me, "I was so different to Mum. She lived on her nerves. But I've always been the opposite".

Over the first few weeks of meeting, Carol reported many memories from her "wonderful childhood" with three siblings evoking something of *The Sound of Music*, given the long summers playing in the mountain pastures of her native Switzerland, running wild and free. At first, this conjured nostalgia in me, yet it transformed into a deep sadness and longing as I pondered where her parents were. Then one day she told me of the day her older brother (himself only six years old) took kitchen knives from the house and started throwing them at their chickens in the backyard. Carol laughed. I was horrified. Yet Carol didn't break her stride or notice my bodily stiffening, so engrossed was she in the entertainment of retelling the story. Carol was used to horror being entertaining. She shared memories of sitting on the sofa with her brother and two sisters watching horror films – their combined age only just reaching the certification level of the film. Again, I wondered where the parents were; it was heart-breaking to envisage the four children left alone with such violence being normalised and even trivialised. No wonder Carol had developed her "little monkey" moniker. By being the family joker, she had found a way to run from her distress. Those of you who have studied aspects of family or systemic psychotherapy might utilise the ideas of vertical stressors (family stories, scripts, myths) intersecting with horizontal stressors (life events and developmental unfolding). Carol had developed a childhood script "I must make others laugh", but now in meeting her current life situation, something had shattered. In Carol's case, her "free spirit" identity was driven by "I must not be like Mother".

Carol's anxiety was extremely convincing and after a few months of working together, I noticed how I had been pulled into a pattern. Each week, Carol would bring another event or dilemma that had given her seemingly good cause to be anxious; and I was repeatedly extended the invitation to solve each anxiety provoking situation. I had become trapped in the content. Fortunately, in noticing the developing impasse, my focus corrected to process: the domain for effective therapy. I had to trust that holding my seat, while Carol's anxiety filled the room, was the genuine way to be of service. Carol's daughters couldn't deal with her anxious-being; providing a 'fix' for Carol each week would have been equally abandoning. I began to invite Carol's awareness to the process. Whilst I could help her look for a solution each week, didn't she at some point want to stop needing therapy?

After a few weeks of a kind but firm refusal to 'fix' Carol's distress, the intervention brought an interesting turn. A childhood friend from Switzerland had invited her on a holiday, and other school friends would be there. Carol was stuck, another dilemma. "If I go, I leave Sam behind – what will people think of me?" was countered with "If I don't go, I will be the only one of our school friendship group not going, what will people think of me?" By moving between two different chairs, I encouraged her to sit with the experience of oscillation – to choose one, to choose the other. In doing so, she noticed something quite different. "You know Helen, I don't want to make a decision; I don't want to actually decide". She was speaking to something we call 'secondary gain', motivations outside of awareness that fuel and perpetuate a given psychological experience. Who would Carol be if she wasn't anxious? And interestingly, who would Carol be if she wasn't there to be "little monkey" for her school friends? To not decide felt her only option; but that is also a choice – and either way Carol, was worried who she would be. The holiday was a cruise, and so with some irony the metaphor of Christopher Columbus' voyage helped us consider her sailing to the edge: an edge that felt like an abyss. For Carol, someone with a core of not existing except in the image of others' reflected light, this is akin to annihilation.

Interventions in the therapy

As I write this account of the work with Carol, I hold in mind the wish to convey what the Buddhist *Dharma* and practices bring to my psychotherapy work. So far, much of what I have written would be accessible from traditional Western psychotherapeutic theory and practices; and indeed, bringing the nature of the impasse and secondary gain to Carol's awareness might have been enough to secure a different way of being for her. Yet, it again feels important to stress that the awareness must be an embodied one. The Buddhist *Dharma* lends 'two wings' that help this lived experience get off the ground: wisdom and compassion.

In the Buddhist *Dharma*, wisdom is the quality of 'clear seeing' experience 'as it is' rather than fabrications and stories. In my work with Carol, I invited an examination of her thoughts. She wanted rid of them, but instead I suggested she simply get more curious. Together, we noticed how a thought became a story that then became a belief and then became "true". It was the "truth" of her stories that sent her in to a state of anxiety. One session her silenced phone buzzed. In not answering it, she shared the agony of proliferating thoughts. She was convinced her daughter, who had been feeling ill that morning, "has been taken in an ambulance to the hospital". I asked her "Is that true?" Examining what Tibetan Buddhist teacher Tsoknyi Rinpoche distinguishes as 'real but not true' (2012) demonstrates the 'cutting through' quality of the Buddhist teachings. Where do we add a layer over the present moment? 'Cutting through' requires a sharp blade of kindness. This is the reason Buddhist teachings emphasise the interdependence of wisdom and compassion. Compassion is our capacity to relate to experience with tenderness. The practice of 'RAIN' (the acronym we briefly visited with "Deena" in Chapter 3) outlines four steps that gives structure to processing present moment experience and lends the compassionate support that helps people in Carol's position to stay with the gap.

The first step of RAIN is to RECOGNISE what is arising in experience. The day I invited Carol to 'cut through' her holiday dilemma with the question "Is that true?" prompted her to pause and consciously acknowledge the stream of mental activity, feelings, and physical reactions. She reported back to me a sense of panic that was coursing through her body. The key here is observation not reaction. The 'recognise' step is to name simply what is present, thereby dropping the runaway train of a storyline.

The next step is to ALLOW the experience 'as it is', even if it's terribly unpleasant. The key is to stay with it – to acknowledge and allow experience, neither pushing it away, nor trying to change it. This was a very hard step for Carol – at first, she rebounded back into her thoughts, and this was a habit that required self-compassion rather than her usual self-critical voice. I invited her to close her eyes and to feel her feet grounded on the floor as a way of anchoring and supporting a 'letting it be'. Some people find whispering "yes" or "it's okay" help with the compassionate act of turning towards what is happening. I keep in mind an analogy John Welwood offered during my retreat time with him: holding an orange – not in the tight grip fashion we often do with our experience, but more akin to cradling fruit in a bowl, allowing experience to breathe.

Recognising and allowing enables a deepening in our curiosity through INVESTIGATION. Those of you familiar with Eugene Gendlin's Focusing will recognise the gentle questioning such as "How am I experiencing this in my body?", "What thought am I believing?" "What does this vulnerable part need from me?" Going inward, Carol was able to feel the tension in her facial muscles, increasing warmth in her arms, her "heart beating through a paper-thin chest". Going even deeper she noticed a knot in her stomach. For a few minutes Carol just rested in awareness of the knot. After a while, a felt-sense of shame and fear came forth. This step requires no intellectual inquiry or analysis, no 'why' or 'what', and instead touching into the 'how' this is being experienced here-and-now.

Through that step of investigation Carol fully sensed the extent of her wounding and what the deep-seated fear and shame needed. After taking a few moments, she said through tears "it is saying 'don't leave me'. The little monkey just wants my company, to know I am here". I asked if it would help to place her hand gently on her stomach and tell the little monkey "I'm here". At this point, some people find bringing in the presence of a loving being (friend, family, a pet, or a spiritual figure) can help support the message of NURTURING.

Repeated practice of RAIN in the therapy room gave Carol confidence in allowing the physical sensations to arise, sit with them, and witness them subside – which they will do in about 60 to 90 seconds, if we let them. Again, this takes practice – we have learnt to suppress emotions, so to allow expression of them goes against our survival logic. After a few weeks, Carol started practising RAIN between sessions. We talked about some potential scenarios which she knew to be activating and how normally she might start obsessing or using other coping strategies: Surfing the internet for solutions to her dilemma or opening the kitchen cupboard and eating biscuits were two "safe bets". The task was to pause, go to her designated 'safe place' (a cosy chair in her conservatory) and practice RAIN. She also started to use classical music for soothing after RAIN. Resting in experience more often, Carol was able to lessen the identification with her anxiety. With time, her language changed from "I'm anxious" to "I have anxiety", and finally to "there is anxiety in my belly".

Outcomes of the therapy

Therapy in combination with RAIN had helped Carol realise that she didn't have to take flight into her anxious thinking. Each time she was activated,[5] she sat and provided a bigger space for her distress; a bit like widening our physical stance to get a better sense of stability. In recognising her experience of dilemmas as a form of withdrawal, Carol became curious as to the message to be listened to each time a new dilemma arose. The existentialists understood 'anxiety strives to become fear' by locating an object it can hook itself on. Carol learned to stay with the subjective experiencing rather than locating it outside of herself and essentially leaving the vulnerable part of herself abandoned again just like in childhood. Carol stayed in therapy with me for a few months after we started using RAIN. It is good practice to co-create the timescale and work towards bringing therapy to an end, and for

Carol this included support during Sam's end-of-life and through another transition – moving back to Switzerland.

How this work shaped my human being

Working with Carol helped me to know the contagion effect of anxiety and the extent of its power. With clients experiencing anxiety, I can see how I am invited to fire fight – not just to help the client, but because I too am feeling the heat of the flames and the emergency to extinguish them. This case work in particular demonstrates how a Buddhism-informed psychotherapy can offer a working frame of wisdom and compassion. These "two wings free us from this swirling vortex of reaction. They help us find the balance and clarity that can guide us in choosing what we say or do" (Brach, 2012, p. 28). Rather than the reaction to rescue, wisdom brings the clear seeing of 'what is' during the moment-to-moment experience; compassion is the attitude with which we do this: with non-judgement, acceptance, and kindness. Carol's manifestation as 'Tasmanian devil' in a moment that in and of itself is safe[6] allowed me to really appreciate the descriptions that anxiety is a response to an event that has already happened; the alarm is stuck in 'on'.

Personally, it underlined the value of distinguishing bodymind anxiety feeling "real [but] not true". The work of Byron Katie (2008) suggests the prompt "is that true?", and when stuck in an anxious narrative, I give myself the chance to interrupt and disrupt; to look around in my environment while feeling down into my bodily experiencing. Each time, I realise the threat is not present and there is a gap to de-escalate. This is the task for each human being, to develop mind and heart. Clear seeing, compassionate presence. It is true for the therapist and client alike. The role of the therapist is to provide a compassionate presence and attitude through which the client can bring that kindness and understanding to oneself. The therapist's call to wisdom is to see with clarity what is going on; to maintain perspective and hold the hope whilst allowing the client to find agency and, using Paul Tillich's words, find the "courage to be".

Notes

1 With time I came to recognise the gap is always there. But we will come back to that later.
2 As neuroscience is revealing, this might be an evolutionary advantageous illusion in a universe that tends towards entropy (see the work on the free energy principle of Karl Friston).
3 The factors of the Eightfold Path can be pre-fixed with the label 'right', but translations using 'skilful' or 'wise' remove the moral imperative and instead invite agency and responsibility; and importantly the practitioner alone verifies through their own experience.

4 You might see different presentations of the Eightfold Path, often with these ethics of living placed at the beginning or at the end as they are considered both the seed and the fruit of the Buddhist path.

5 I prefer this to 'triggered'; but both words refer to moving into a survival state (in polyvagal theory terms, into sympathetic or dorsal).

6 I invite the reader to look at the neuroscience research on how 'predictive coding' helps us to understand how our nervous systems have developed this apparent paradoxical functioning.

References

Brach, T. (2012). *Radical Acceptance: Awakening the Love that Heals Fear and Shame*. London: Ebury Publishing.

Chödrön, P. (2009). *Taking the Leap: Freeing Ourselves from Old Habits and Fears*. Boston, MA: Shambhala Publications.

Katie, B. (2008). *Loving What Is. How Four Questions Can Change Your Life*. New York, NY: Random House.

Kongtrul Rinpoche, D. (2006). *It's Up to You. The Practice of Self-reflection on the Buddhist Path*. Boston, MA: Shambhala Publications.

Ponlop Rinpoche, D. (2017). *Emotional Rescue: How to Work with Your Emotions to Transform Hurt and Confusion Into Energy That Empowers You*. New York, NY: Penguin Publishing Group.

Ray, R. (2018). *The Practice of Pure Awareness: Somatic Meditation for Awakening the Sacred*. Boulder, CO: Shambhala.

Rinpoche, T. (2012). *Open Heart, Open Mind: Awaking the Power of Essence Love*. New York: Harmony Books.

Welwood, J. (2005). *Perfect Love, Imperfect Relationships. Healing the Wound of the Heart*. Boston, MA: Shambhala Publications.

Chapter 6

The role of the therapist-client relationship

Vignette

After finding meditation and first engaging with the teachings of Buddhism, I found myself describing it to curious friends as "a philosophy of life". I'm not sure I knew what that meant at the time. In all honesty, it was probably some kind of defence against being seen to practise a religion. Yet I did enjoy the intellectualism and the questioning of existence, reason, and values often seen as key to philosophy. I loved learning and building my knowledge of the lists (The Four Noble Truths, The Eightfold Path, The Three *Kleshas*, and The Four Reminders, to name but a few of the '84,000 *Dharmas*'). This is in part the intention of the early path or *Hinayana*: to ground oneself in the *Dharma* and, using the analogy of building a house, establish a firm foundation for the whole structure of the path. The *Mahayana* that follows is the main dwelling complete with windows and doors that allow communication with the world. Then finally, the *Vajrayana* is the roof that offers both protection and the completion of the whole.

The Four Noble Truths are often associated with the *Hinayana* because they are integral to the whole path. One aspect of Buddhism I have relished is the conceptual contact we can make with the teachings that then 'point like fingers' to the practical wisdom. 'Practical' because the teachings are tasks; and 'wisdom' because those tasks integrate knowledge with experience. Phillip Moffitt's *Dancing with Life* (2012), mentioned previously (in Chapter 4's case study of "Claire"), is a great guide on how to take the intellectual understanding towards the practical application. An invitation to dance with life; to see life as an experiment.

When I came to study the *Mahayana* – which builds on the foundation of non-harm by befriending oneself and others – I encountered the 'mind training' slogans of *lojong*. At first, out of habit, I set about trying to learn and understand them. It was only on my second exposure to them that it suddenly dawned on me how powerful they were as practices. It would appear Pema Chödrön had a similar experience, being "struck by their unusual message

DOI: 10.4324/9781003383710-6

that we can use our difficulties and problems to awaken our hearts. Rather than seeing the unwanted aspects of life as obstacles, [they are] the raw material necessary for awakening genuine uncontrived compassion" (2004, p. XI).

The 59 slogans direct our practice towards the taking on of suffering and the development of unconditional compassion. Traditionally, the focus of the *lojong* training would be towards others but, like many other modern-day practitioners of Buddhism, I have found incredible value in using these reminders to explore more directly how I suffer. Studying these slogans, a few have always stood out as incredibly powerful, helping me focus on where I perpetuate certain tracks of *karma* and therefore come to suffer. Slogan number 12, "Drive all blames into one", for example, is considered quite a radical slogan – instead of blaming others, we are invited to look at how our own suffering leads to tension and distress for others. Likewise, slogan number 13, "Be grateful to everyone", invites appreciation of whoever ignites our suffering. Everyone becomes a teacher exposing our blind spots. Generally, practice with these slogans has helped me come to know intimately how I suffer, to accept my imperfections, and with the light of compassion, to understand that these imperfections do not make me unlovable. It is not always easy to admit where I have come up short in my treatment of others or my need to hide less comfortable aspects of my being. Vulnerability is exposing; and yet also connecting. The *Mahayana* teachings in general have highlighted my soft spot, a place from where I can connect to others' suffering because I know my own more deeply. "Vulnerability is the birthplace of love, belonging, joy, courage, empathy, accountability, and authenticity. If we want greater clarity in our purpose or deeper and more meaningful spiritual lives, vulnerability is the path" (Brown, 2013, p. 34).

I share my experience of working with the mind training slogans not as a direct suggestion for their use within a Buddhism-informed psychotherapy. Rather, I wanted to convey how "mixing our minds with the *Dharma*", or a true integration with the dance in the phenomenal world, allows us to truly *know* our experience, including an intimate knowing of how we suffer. Every person we meet, every situation we find ourselves in becomes a teaching and a learning environment. The more light thrown on my experience, the more I understand what activates me, how I live that out, and importantly, how I perpetuate patterns that often don't serve me or others. Through meeting Buddhism, I feel I have truly come to know myself and the markers of my distress. To know the aching in my chest, the knot in my belly, the holding in my shoulders; and to know what situations bring these about.

To know our suffering

Prior to my master's research, my psychotherapy training had already highlighted the integral place of the relationship between therapist and client in the healing task. Many of us will be familiar with the 'common factors' research (Wampold, 2001), a detailed meta-analysis revealing the therapeutic relationship and alliance to be far more important to therapeutic outcomes than the theoretical approach or interventions. I was therefore curious how my psychotherapy colleagues and research co-participants would view what Buddhism could offer to support the relational conditions.

Like me, my co-participants had come to Buddhism to get relief from suffering. Like me, they didn't anticipate going deeper into the suffering. My co-participants shared their personal experiences of how the path called them to pause, turn inward, and recognise what was present in their being the moment they noticed their distress. I have come to consider this like a 'vertical dialogue': where we pause and allow our awareness to know what is to be known. To 'know the known' is a relationship, and dialogue can occur.

As Buddhists, rather than contracting around our pain we are encouraged to open to it and bring gentle, kind attention (as we saw in the previous chapter and the practice of RAIN). This attitude has become pivotal in my practice as a therapist. I remember my curiosity when I first realised sessions with clients felt 'easier' when I was experiencing a struggle in my life. The times when I felt at my rawest or my most tired, I seemed more present. When a friend introduced me to the work of psychotherapist Sheldon Kopp and his practice orientation, it gave me the courage to bring more vulnerability into the therapy room.

> Patients are often disappointed to learn that I too wander unredeemed, that I am no better off than they are. Eventually, they may realise comfort through my turning out to be just another struggling human being. At least then I can bring a fellow-pilgrim sort of understanding to his journey.
>
> (Kopp, 1976, p. 134)

My co-participants and I agreed: knowing our own suffering, and not seeing it as a failing, brought an equalisation to the room. We are companions, travelling in the same boat. It is easy as a therapist in training to yield to the client's wish to make us idealised, perfect and experts or, "the guru" (Kopp, 1976, p. 11). Yet, if we take the role of companion we don't have to lead, we can sit alongside. This is incredibly valuable to help the client find the power and responsibility for their own journey.

Relational wounding, relational healing

As relational psychotherapists we understand the power of coming together with Other to share our distress. I won't apologise in repeating John

Welwood's notion that we are wounded in relationship; it makes sense we are therefore healed in relationship (2005). When we take our inner experiencing (the vertical dialogue) to the horizontal dialogue of therapy, we not only get to hear our words out loud but also to know those words are being witnessed by Other. To be heard, to be seen. The presence of Other offers an opportunity of validating that we exist in ways that we have not experienced in our childhoods. The power of mere presence in 'dyad' practice reminds me of the storytelling tradition the ancients practised for community healing and protection.

My research co-participants pointed to three ways in which Buddhism has helped to enhance the quality of the therapeutic relationship, all building upon the knowing of their own suffering: presence, compassion, and interdependence.

Presence

Carl Rogers is perhaps the name we associate the most with the relational conditions of counselling and therapy: psychological contact, the therapist being more congruent than the client, the empathic attitude, and unconditional positive regard. When I first read Rogers' text "On becoming a person" (1967), I was so deeply touched and inspired by the simplicity of his view – to sit alongside and attend fully as enough to bring relief from distress. Although I now take a more process-directive style, I have not neglected the relational conditions Rogers implored as necessary. Later in his life, Rogers added another factor,

> that when I am closest to my inner intuitive self, when I am somehow in touch with the unknown in me, when perhaps I am in a slightly altered state of consciousness, then whatever I do seems to be full of healing. Then simply my presence is releasing and helpful.
>
> (Rogers, 1995, p. 129)

Knowing my own experience allows me to be more present to the experience of the Other. I can 'know' yet not be 'caught up in' my experience. Freud used the expression 'evenly suspended attention' in reference to how we can regard our clients. We can hold all the information coming from our client (content, along with how it is being delivered including tone, bodily posture, gaze, etc.) and allow it all to be taken in. We are like an open vessel, opening to our own experience and receptive to that of the client's impact on us. The meditation practices of the Buddhist tradition have certainly helped me develop this inner congruence, thus offering the client an experience of my sincerity.

Compassion

As an open vessel, I can receive a client's being and let it mingle with my own, including the experience of what it is to suffer. We can consider this within the context of how sympathy, empathy, and compassion relate to one another, as set out by Germer and Siegel (2014). When someone we know suffers a loss, we often extend our sympathy, yet this is not a sentiment we would necessarily convey in the therapy room. Sympathy includes a reactive element: we hear of the loss, and we respond from loss. This differs from empathy, a mirroring of another's state. We hear the loss of the other and we know what it is to have that experience. In other words, empathy includes more mindful awareness – the knowing of, rather than from the place of, experience. Compassion goes beyond empathy. We know our suffering, there is empathy with the suffering experienced by the other, and importantly, there is an allied wish to alleviate it. Compassion includes the feeling of love; not personal in nature but one combined with equanimity. Thus, a skilful response to the suffering witnessed is enabled. When we are open to our own experience, we can hear and see the suffering of the Other in the same open-hearted awareness. We are not attached to either the suffering or the need to rid the other of their suffering. We are simply connecting deeply to feeling that state yet not reacting.

Germer and Siegel also offer this three-part breakdown of compassion: "I feel for you" (affective), "I understand you" (cognitive), and "I want to help you" (motivational). Kopp's attitude of 'fellow-pilgrim' speaks to this 'fellow-feeling' quality of compassion. We don't feel pity for Other – this is distancing. Instead, we know all humans suffer YET they also have *buddhanature*; everything is workable. Whenever we see a client's suffering, we can bring attention to the part of them that is always present, a witness to their experience that is not suffering. The *Vajrayana* tradition of Buddhism realises this through the understanding that where there is confusion there is also wisdom.

Interdependence

As we learnt in Chapter 3's section on 'Non-self' (p. 36) we are not independent, single, and separate beings, although it can feel that way. In 'selfing', we form ourselves in relation to Other and our world – we are interdependent. Knowing this inter-being can become a basis for an ethical and compassionate life. Doing 'good' doesn't become a 'should' but rather a motivation when we recognise that in hurting others, we hurt ourselves ultimately. I remember an interview with Buddhist and yoga teacher Michael Stone in which he joked the motivation to help others to their awakening soon arises when we realise *nirvana* would be a lonely place otherwise! I think psychotherapists get a sense of this when training;

the contrast between the developing relationships with likeminded peers and those pre-existing relationships that can start to feel inauthentic and unfulfilling.

During my psychotherapy training, I became incredibly interested in the challenge to feel autonomy yet also need of Other: how do we exist in the to-and-fro between being-as-self and being-with-other? My needs and the needs of others. I offer an extract from a blogpost I wrote after returning from a month-long retreat:

> On retreat, life is lived in community – being in contact is the default, and energy is used to withdraw, to find solitude. I found a good balance between what Paul Tillich explains as being-self and being-a-part-of. In this post retreat transition, I am back to experiencing a familiar struggle – to not end up lonely when alone: back home, life is lived in isolation – and energy is taken in making contact. I find this harder. How tempting to live the life of a hermit, to be on my own, to withdraw into my working life (to use client work as a link to humanity) or into my books. I notice my black and white thinking, the search for certainty and ground. To withdraw avoids the risk of reaching out and not being met. Trying to live in the middle ground, neither black nor white, neither alone nor together, brings uncertainty, brings a loss of control. On retreat, living in community meant I was in control of when I needed aloneness – I could simply put on my walking shoes and head for the forest. At odds with Winnicott's 'the capacity to be alone', I completely withdraw to feel safe alone. I often note that when I want to be alone, I fear being intruded upon. On retreat I would wake early and go to the kitchen for breakfast and reading time. I would often feel a contraction when another retreatant would come in, no matter who that person was. Thank goodness for the practice periods of 'golden silence', I was saved from having to connect when I had a desire to be alone. Does all this sound contradictory? It is, and maybe that's a truth.

Fellow therapists might recognise this 'dance of intimacy'. The awareness of the bodymind generated through meditation (or from other somatic practices) greatly enhances the capacity of this dance to be felt. Through this we can begin to get curious about *karmic* patterns and dynamics. Once I come to know the aching in my chest, the knot in my belly, the holding in my shoulders, I can bring awareness to this in everyday life; and I can notice such 'character armour' invites situations to unfold in a certain way. 'Julia' was a client who came to see me to talk through a recurring work situation where she felt bullied by a colleague, yet in the next moment this same colleague was being incredibly kind. We worked on ways to help her notice how this 'push and pull' played out in her body. With greater attunement,

Julia began to notice the contraction in her body started before she even came face-to-face with her colleague. She realised "ahh, it's like when predators get a smell of blood, they attack. He is smelling my fear, and it's his signal to pounce". We worked on a bodily sense of 'safe and whole', and she soon found the 'push and pull' in their relationship to lessen.

A great opportunity arises when such relational dynamics come up between therapist and client. This can be painful and difficult to work with, particularly for the trainee and/or novice therapist; yet working directly in the here-and-now allows the *karma* generated in previous relationships to be pinpointed and worked through as it comes to fruition in the room. How do therapist and client meet? What is the quality of contact? Is one person reaching out, the other retreating? Is one searching, is one hiding? Gestalt therapist Ruella Frank has built a whole system of body psychotherapy around such 'fundamental movements' (2013) laid down in childhood and perpetuated in adulthood. As we have explored earlier, *karma* can be considered in terms of human development, exploring where a client becomes 'arrested' at a certain emotional age. Furthermore, it can be applied to reveal patterns as an intergenerational phenomenon. Many clients I have worked with came to reflect upon how their anxiety was 'inherited' as a mode of being.

Knowing our suffering and knowing how this plays out in our relational experience is paramount for healing. Critically, the more a therapist understands their own patterns, the more they can be there for the client in theirs. It is accepted wisdom in therapy that we cannot work with clients in areas we have not explored ourselves. Moreover, knowing our own tendencies helps us to understand what is being co-created in the therapy room. Buddhism allows us to understand our interdependence, our inseparability; not expert/client, nor guru/student. As 'fellow-pilgrims', we can go beyond empathy to compassion.

Presence, attunement, resonance, trust

Daniel Siegel (2010) uses the acronym 'PART' to explain how the therapeutic relationship becomes a vehicle for healing. Presence is the way in which we are open to and receptive of our experience, and to find a grounding from this place. Siegel describes it as an 'inside-out' view; or in my words, a vertical dialogue from which a horizontal dialogue can spring. Presence is a gateway to the very deepest forms of listening, one in which our whole being is involved. Therapeutic presence is the ground of congruence. From presence springs attunement. When we can touch on our experience in relationship, a 'subterranean' communication exists between selves. This capacity is dependent on holding an attitude of unknowing, or 'beginner's mind' (Suzuki, 2006). A vessel filled with assumptions won't have capacity for vital information. Next is resonance, described by Siegel as "the physiological result of presence and attunement, the alignment of two autonomous beings into an interdependent and functional whole" (2010, p. XX). Resonance describes how we feel felt by others. Imagine a tuning fork vibrating causing another to resonate in tune. This brings qualities of being seen, being heard, and opens us to intimate connection. Finally, trust comes when we experience validation by Other that lays down safety and security. Neural networks that are not in alert mode allow us a freer and more adaptable response to our environment and those in it. Consider how young children require parents at the playground to feel safe playing; or how in education settings it is crucial to understand the anxious brain is not available for learning.

Siegel argues that PART leads to integration; a trajectory from either chaotic or rigid presentations to one where our clients gain more flexibility and harmonious functioning. PART uses the instrument of the therapist's self. As Kopp offers "The therapist can interpret, advise, provide the emotional acceptance and support that nurtures personal growth and above all, he can listen . . . with the personal vulnerability of his own trembling self" (1976, p. 5).

Client case study "Penelope": working with the internal critic

I clearly remember the first time I spoke with "Penelope"; our conversation being punctuated by the sound of seagulls. Penelope had phoned from the seafront to prevent her ageing father overhearing she was speaking to a therapist. Adopted at the age of nine months when her biological parents died in a car crash, 52-year-old Penelope was petrified of her 79-year-old father. When Penelope and I met face-to-face for her first session, she broke down in tears almost immediately. She had been wanting to come to therapy two years earlier. Having found me on the internet, her husband Derek "thought I would find you approachable, I needed someone to talk to about Dad". I asked, "What stopped you coming two years ago?" "Dad would have been livid if I was talking to a stranger". What finally brought her to therapy? In a tragic symmetry to her parents' death, Derek had died in a car crash the summer before, and Penelope was bereft. In the five years I worked with Penelope there was a sense we were working on a few different levels: her experience of everyday life as being threatening without Derek, her "shield and chaperone"; the frequency with which she felt let down by others and singled out by life; and the excavation of her early life experiences of abandonment, abuse, and neglect.

Since Derek died, Penelope experienced terrible anxiety – her main complaint was how her head hurt with all her thinking. Head in hands she would say "it just won't stop, thought after thought". She often had migraines and found it hard to get more than two or three hours of sleep each night. "I have so much to do", dealing with Derek's paperwork, the upkeep of her house, looking after her father and his demands – the list went on. Each week she would detail this list and the panic if one ball got dropped. Penelope believed if she controlled her world (and the people in it) she kept the threat at bay. She once came to her session terribly upset that the supermarket didn't deliver the right tea bags. "I had to drive to the corner shop at 11 o'clock, after Dad had gone to bed, just to go get the right ones". Penelope felt she was living under a tyranny: both her father and the version of him she had internalised. When Derek was alive, he would have intervened, but "now it is all down to me". Often these stories were followed with a deep sigh and plea "why did he die, why did he leave me?"

Derek wasn't the only person who had let Penelope down. For the first few months of working together, it was common for Penelope to focus on experiences of how friends were not asking her questions as to how she was, or not calling her at the weekends when "they know I am alone". Some complaints were specific, but others were a more generalised sense of "the world is out to get me". One week she described how a trip to see her daughter was ruined because a suicide on the tracks had left her stranded on the train. Even as she described the carnage at the accident site, her focus remained on the consequences for her. I remember it crossing my mind what would happen if I left her stranded; and I felt an inner jolt as if reminding me to never let her down. The oft 'victim' position was an indicator of fragile Narcissism, and it became important for me to avoid invites to persecute or rescue, as with Karpman's 'drama triangle' (2014), and instead look to the deeply held pain.

The self-centred orientation was a much-needed protection Penelope had developed in childhood. Her highly critical father "was always moving the bar, so all I could do was make sure I never made mistakes". Penelope's mother was equally scared. At first, Penelope found it hard to see her mother's part in failing to keep her safe and not standing firm against her husband. It took a number of sessions before Penelope began to see her mother's love was conditional: it was Penelope's responsibility to keep her mother 'intact'. Penelope's mother would keep her close, recruiting Penelope as an object and extension of herself, and consequently Penelope was not ready to be an adult. As Masterson describes in his writing on Narcissism (2004), where a mother's own neurotic presentation requires the child to resonate with her, mirroring of the child's experience will be unempathic and defective. We might follow this through to explain Penelope's tendency to 'split' the world and others into 'right' and 'wrong' (compounded by her father's critical and opinionated worldview). Like a baby bird kept under her mother's wing but never encouraged nor prepared to leave the nest.

Undoubtedly, another layer of complication came from a mother-child unit shaped in adoption. When she met Derek, she found her new 'wing'. Now he was gone, and her fragile self was yet again exposed to the dangers of the world.

Interventions in the therapy

In supervision, the notion of my role as 'Mummy bird' arose, and the need for me to foster a sense of dependability for Penelope. Only then could Penelope develop the full set of feathers needed to fly the nest. Yet it wasn't easy to experience Penelope's growing need, at times quite severe and 'limpet-like'. The task for me was to expand and open despite the strong sense to withdraw and get away from the pull; essentially, a task to reject the invite to persecute thus becoming another critical voice in Penelope's experience. Providing an unconditional presence to both my own embodied response and Penelope, attuning to her lived experience, and allowing an empathic resonance were fundamental to gaining Penelope's trust. Both psychodynamic and humanistic theorists underline this. As Stolorow (1976) states, in this empathic stance "The client [thus] comes to experience himself as 'prized' . . . much as does the Narcissistically disturbed patient immersed in a mirror transference" (p. 29). Rogers (1951) might see the immersive presence I offered Penelope as "almost [becoming] an alter ego of the client. . . . The whole relationship is composed of the self of the client, the counsellor being depersonalized for the purposes of therapy into being 'the client's other self'" (p. 42). The reader might hear the echo of Siegel's PART.

Only with trust could Penelope begin to loosen the protections that held at bay primitive feelings of rage, and to experience the painful depths of her fragile self. This was the main thrust of the therapeutic work – to support Penelope first in noticing when her internalised critic entered our relational field and questioning its 'truth'; secondly to come to value her anxiety and thinking as protection yet go below to feel into her experience; and finally, to gently facilitate awareness of the rage she contained and how she projected this on to the world and others. In essence, to come to know 'the full catastrophe' of her suffering.

Interventions with clients like Penelope require a lot of care, such is the fragility and the likelihood of inflaming the Narcissistic injury. To say I often found myself treading on eggshells doesn't get across the extent to how constricted and bound I felt. This is where I have found Masterson's three-step 'mirroring interpretation' incredibly powerful (2004).[1] Firstly, identify and acknowledge the patient's painful affect with empathy and understanding; secondly, emphasize the impact on the patient's self to indicate understanding of his or her experience; and thirdly, identify and explain the defence or resistance, which can be tied to step one, by observing how it protects, calms, and soothes the patient from experiencing the painful effect. In our sessions together, I came to see Penelope's pointing the finger of blame under an empathic light; it brought protection, yet it had the potential to isolate her further at a time a core need was really connection and the security of closeness to others, including me! When I felt the inner jolt of Penelope's judging and partitioning the world into black and white, I would respond

> I imagine it is difficult for you to hear your friend's differing view of the situation because as a child you learned your father's 'right and wrong' as the truth (pain). You feel exposed and threatened by this difference in opinion (self). I wonder if in protecting yourself you turn to me to take your side? (defence).

I would gently invite Penelope to close her eyes and just notice how her body responded to my ideas. This took many months of work for Penelope. At first, she would say "I don't feel anything", and I would assure her this was okay and perfectly normal, inviting her to notice the absence of feeling and just stay with how that was. As Penelope turned inward, I would do the same, like a tuning fork reacting to Penelope's story and experience. I would offer my bodily reactions to her story "When you tell me about this situation with your friend, I notice my heart is beating quite hard", and that allowed her to get curious in her own body. I might then offer how I read the message of the hard beating heart as "telling me I need to act, like to be 'on alert'". Linking affect with meaning in this way, Penelope was able to make sense of her own experience. We might go back to the metaphor of the young bird – learning to trust their own experience rather than relying on that of the mother during the process towards separation.

One week, Penelope was recounting her visit to the GP for a check-up. "He suggested medication [for her anxiety], but I wondered if meditation might be better. Can you teach me please?" To notice a need and ask someone for help with it was itself a breakthrough for Penelope. Moreover, it signalled she was recognising the stickiness of her thoughts and a need to change her relationship to them. Most impressively she added "I've already downloaded an app and listened to a podcast. I know it's not about stopping my thinking but making the thoughts less believable. . . . I could do with some of that!" Bringing meditation as a practice into therapy room is a recurring theme of a Buddhism-informed psychotherapy. In Penelope's case, it was a pivotal point in our work together, sealing the working alliance. She had joined me in taking of responsibility for the healing task; and from here on in, committing to a process of 'turning toward' rather than defending against and running away (from her pain). We began to routinely start our sessions with a short meditation to help her arrive and to see what persistent thoughts were playing out. Penelope might then bring an event from her week that gave the context for her present preoccupations. Sometimes we used RAIN to bring awareness to where the pain lived under the story. Through this, Penelope began to grow confident that her somatic experience was tolerable and wouldn't overwhelm her. At first, Penelope practiced with mindfulness of breath meditations at home and reserved the more 'somatic' meditations for when with me. Eventually, with growing confidence she started to do both RAIN and Focusing in-between sessions.

Outcomes of the therapy

About half-way into our work, Penelope's father died. Penelope saw the deep need to separate from the internalised critical father voice that continued after his death. It was only now Penelope was able to allow herself to feel the full extent of her rage towards him; and indeed, a rage rooted in losing her biological parents so young. "Perhaps I have only been able to let this all out now because it is safe – he can't terrorise me anymore". Rage, which is considered to have a different developmental root than 'anger' (Parker Hall, 2009), needs gentle holding and firm containment of therapist presence. Penelope came to see that the long-held belief of a 'personal deficit' was actually a 'relational deficit'; and no wonder Little Penelope was terrified. In sessions, Penelope would use my presence like scaffolding whilst feeling into her terror and rage. For many like Penelope, rage is 'feeling angry for being scared'. Our caregivers might fail in the responsibility to protect us from threat when we are too young to do it ourselves. Penelope's internalised critical father was simply the result of an imaginative young girl who needed protection – the voice simply got too loud and outlived its welcome. 'The tyranny of the shoulds' (Horney, 1950) needs retiring or transmuting to a more compassionate internalised parental presence. Penelope played with turning the 'should' to 'could', finding she had choice; less black and white, more shades of grey. One week, she announced "I would like to talk about ending Helen; it is time to start living in the present, not the past or the future". She saw this as a choice, one that only she was responsible for. I let Penelope lead our discussion on the timescale for ending and how she would like to work towards it. It was quite incredible to see a client attain such an empowered position given she had started out so crushed nearly five years before.

How this work shaped my human being

A colleague asks the applicants to our counselling and psychotherapy courses the question "who would your nightmare client be?" There are certain ways-of-being in the world that we all find difficult. Ask many therapists and they would say that clients with Borderline process are often the most energy-demanding and the presentation type to keep at a low ratio in a caseload. However, as I share later, working with BPA (see Chapter 9's case study of "Charlotte") can also be the most rewarding. Narcissistic presentation, especially the sticky-feel in the transference with the fragile variety, is my nemesis. I found it hard to like Penelope, and it made the systemic principle of 'joining the system to disrupt the system' hard-going: to do so felt like I would be stuck forever! But intuitively, I knew I had to find something to bring us together. When I felt her attempts to merge with me, and her invitations for me to merge with her (in taking her side) it flagged up my need to turn inward and know my own experience of suffering. Our stories are different: Penelope's focus has been on partitioning the world into right and wrong for protection, my version has been to focus on threat and find allies; but we (like many fellow human beings) have experienced a relational deficit that felt like a personal one. The call to feel the embodied sense of deficit as not the same (confluence) yet no different (common humanity) helped me connect to that in Penelope.

Note

1 By no means am I laying claim on Buddhism's behalf to Masterson's 'pain, self, defence' approach, but for me it does evoke the empathic 'cutting through' when dealing with persistent narrative.

References

Brown, B. (2013). *Daring Greatly: How the Courage to Be Vulnerable Transforms the Way We Live, Love, Parent, and Lead*. London: Penguin Books Limited.

Chödrön, P. (2004). *Start Where You Are: A Guide to Compassionate Living*. Boston, MA: Shambhala.

Frank, R. (2013). *Body of Awareness: A Somatic and Developmental Approach to Psychotherapy*. New York, NY: Taylor & Francis.

Germer, C., & Siegel, R.D. (2014). *Wisdom and Compassion in Psychotherapy: Deepening Mindfulness in Clinical Practice*. New York, NY: Guilford Publications.

Horney, K. (1950). *Neurosis and Human Growth: The Struggle Toward Self Realization*. New York, NY: W.W. Norton & Company.

Karpman, S. (2014). *A Game Free Life. The Definitive Book on the Drama Triangle and the Compassion Triangle by the Originator and Author*. San Francisco, CA: Drama Triangle Productions.

Kopp, S. (1976). *If You Meet the Buddha on the Road, Kill Him! The Pilgrimage of Psychotherapy Patients*. Toronto: Bantam Books.

Masterson, J.F. (2004). *A Therapist's Guide to the Personality Disorders. The Masterson Approach a Handbook and Workbook*. Phoenix, AZ: Zeig, Tucker, & Theisen, Inv.

Moffitt, P. (2012). *Dancing with Life: Buddhist Insights for Finding Meaning and Joy in the Face of Suffering*. New York, NY: Rodale.

Parker Hall, S. (2009). *Anger, Rage and Relationship. An Empathic Approach to Anger Management.* London: Taylor & Francis.

Rogers, C.R. (1951). *Client-centered Therapy. Its Current Practice, Implications and Theory.* London: Constable.

Rogers, C.R. (1967). *On Becoming a Person.* London: Constable.

Rogers, C.R. (1995). *A Way of Being.* Boston: Houghton Mifflin.

Siegel, D.J. (2010). *The Mindful Therapist. A Clinician's Guide to Mindsight and Neural Integration.* New York, NY: W.W. Norton & Company.

Stolorow, R. (1976). Psychoanalytic Reflections on Client-Centered Therapy in the Light of Modern Conceptions of Narcissism. *Psychotherapy: Theory, Research and Practice, 13,* 26–29.

Suzuki, S. (2006). *Zen Mind, Beginner's Mind.* Boston, MA: Shambhala.

Wampold, B.E. (2001). *The Great Psychotherapy Debate: Models, Methods, and Findings.* Mahwah, NJ: Lawrence Erlbaum Associates Publishers.

Welwood, J. (2005). *Perfect Love, Imperfect Relationships. Healing the Wound of the Heart.* Boston, MA: Shambhala Publications.

Chapter 7

The role of meditation practices

Vignette

Having spent 2012 training as a meditation teacher, I was keen to share the practice with others. What started with running a small local group soon grew to regular classes and weekend workshops. By the end of 2014, there was enough demand for MBSR and MBCT to run eight-week courses, three or four times per year. Not bad for a small town with little culture of meditation or Buddhism. I also began to run weekend workshops for education institutions, small businesses, and therapists.

I was one practitioner riding on the wave of the 'mindfulness revolution'. Across the world, people were turning down medication in favour of meditation to deal with a whole array of physical, mental, emotional, and social challenges. Presented as a secular practice backed by science, mindfulness was no longer marginalised. I was happy to help people find the benefits of the practice. The eight-week formula of MBSR and MBCT has helped thousands of people find mindfulness and make meditation mainstream. However, the deeper my own meditation experience, the more I began to see 'stress reduction' as a misnomer. Those who sustain the practice for any period of time will come to see the actual benefit of the practice comes from changing the relationship to the stress rather than its reduction. In my case, it was coming to befriend the anxiety originally regarded as foe. And so teaching these courses I felt part of a system setting people up for a fall.

When I started meditating, I was amidst a time of great change. As with many people approaching mid-life, things weren't turning out as I had thought, and my identity was shifting as if on quicksand. My head was a waterfall of thoughts, and my heart pounded to keep up. Meeting meditation didn't take these 'symptoms' away – I came to know them more intimately. Slowly, a process unfolded whereby the daily act of 'just sitting' for 20 minutes allowed me to see and appreciate how desperately hard my anxiety was trying to keep me safe. I came to realise that no matter how hard I tried, I couldn't stop thinking but I could learn to stop believing the contents.

DOI: 10.4324/9781003383710-7

As I shared earlier, with practice my thinking had slowed from the waterfall torrent to more like a flowing stream. 'Hot boredom' (the quality of restlessness) started to melt towards 'cool boredom' (a kind of surrender). With gaps between thinking, I started connecting with the feeling tone underneath and discovering what my body wanted to say about the situation of my life. This was not a comfortable time. If anything, I experienced more discomfort on meeting the physicality of the anxiety. I empathise with those who drop out of a meditation practice. My meditation teacher guided me through this time of utter groundlessness, or as Chögyam Trungpa explains in his inimitable style, "The bad news is you are falling, a million miles an hour, no parachute. The good news, there is no ground". Years of unmet emotional material was visiting me each day on the cushion and all I could do was to 'hold my seat' and open to my experience. At times it was barely tolerable. Ramping up the practices to cultivate compassion alongside my normal practice offered an internal benevolent parent to soothe the anxious "Little Helen". With time (and this was many months) the story loosened, and I came to trust the sensations and energies.

As a teacher on MBSR and MBCT courses, my main aspiration was to help students realise a similar journey – meditation isn't a practice of 'getting rid' of thoughts, but rather allowing them to arise, to flow through, and to fall away. However, what I describe of my experience is not a quick process nor a linear one. This will disappoint many people who are looking for an instant answer. Further disappointment is in store once it's realised that only continued practice sustains benefits. Typically, only around 60% of participants complete the eight-week courses; and of those, 80% do not sustain a practice after a year from finishing a course.

With some regret I chose to stop teaching the eight-week course model, partly because of the 'quick fix' mentality and becoming fatigued with managing expectations of participants. However, one of the most significant factors was a growing conviction that meditation presented in this way endangered a technologising of Buddhism and a loss of its 'spirit', what has been called McMindfulness (Neale, 2018). As presented in Chapter 5 ('Response-ability and choice', p. 69) meditation is but one aspect of the threefold training, and I am more likely to teach meditation in circumstances where there is a desire on the part of the student/client to explore and integrate – rather than eradicate – experience.

De-bunking some meditation myths

When you hear the word meditation, what comes to mind? I imagine you may hold some preconceptions; you may even have your own experiences of what 'meditation' practice is – whether it be from another religion or wisdom tradition; or perhaps a secular presentation from participating in a mindfulness course.

We have already met *gom* or Tibetan for 'familiarisation' as one translation for meditation. Another is *Bhavana*, Sanskrit for 'cultivate'. Meditation encourages wholesome qualities that remain dormant within us unless we apply effort to draw them out. Chögyam Trungpa Rinpoche described the meditation journey as "making friends with yourself" (2015) to capture the gentle curiosity towards our own experience and the attitude we would take when getting to know someone. Before going deeper into what meditation is, I would like to take some time in explaining what it isn't. Again, it bears reinforcing that much good has come from the mindfulness revolution. However, if the practice is removed from its roots, meditating without the context or the View may lead people down rabbit holes, or even to end the practice prematurely. For the therapist thinking of using these practices, it feels pertinent to bust a few meditation myths.

Myth #1: Meditation is a tool for self-improvement

Many people find meditation because of issues with physical and mental health, and the practice can be helpful; but this is a side effect rather than the intended aim. When the *Buddha* sat in meditation, he came to see the nature of mind 'as it is' rather than attempt to better it. The practice works because it challenges our conventional position relative to the world. Most significantly, as meditation teacher Susan Piver (2015) explains, the heart softens and from that we access our inherent quality of compassion. Meditation is a spiritual, not a self-betterment, practice.

Myth #2: Meditation takes us to a more peaceful place

Our gateway to meditation can come from a wish to not hurt anymore. We see posters advertising retreats or a spa with people in full-lotus sitting on an idyllic beach with a soft smile and closed eyes. It infers we meditate to leave where we are and find bliss. When we come to try the practice, we are surprised to be greeted not by bliss but internal chaos. The good news: there is NO place of bliss that we need to escape to, nor does the practice have to convert our life to all good and peaceful. What actually happens is we soften to ourselves with no need to change experience. Peace is the attitude we hold TO our internal warfare; we allow it. Ethan Nichtern, with whom I trained to become a meditation teacher, uses the phrase "the road home" to describe the path of meditation (2011). We learn to dismantle the wall designed to shield our vulnerability that disconnects us from our more genuine and authentic self.

Myth #3: Meditation will help me to stop thinking

Good luck with this one! Our mind is designed to think just like our eyes see, and our ears hear. Even if you could, why would *not* thinking be a good thing? We need thoughts to access our wisdom, compassion, and confidence. When we sit in meditation we do work with our thoughts, but the actual instruction handed down over 2.5 millennia is to change the *relationship* to thoughts. We become more aware of where we pay attention, and realise our thoughts are there but not necessarily true. Believing our thoughts is what leads to distress, so we learn to let them be – and they dissolve back to where they came. In Chapter 10, we will look at the Buddhist model of mind ('*Karma* and the Eight consciousnesses', p. 166) that can help us take our thoughts less personally.

Myth #4: I don't have time

Who doesn't have ten minutes to find? The more truthful statement is probably "I don't make (or take) the time" to meditate; and often underlying this is the sentiment "I don't have time to sit around, I need to do things". A fear-based thought, a fear of being passive, a fear of what might be felt; a need to be doing to reinforce an idea of self and identity. Interestingly, the traditional teachings point to the need to be busy as a form of laziness.

Myth #5: I don't need to meditate, running* is my meditation

(*or some other activity). Whilst the Buddhist teachings talk about the cultivation of mindfulness in all activity (whether walking, standing, sitting, and lying down), it is interesting to explore more deeply what people mean when they say they already have their 'meditative' space and don't need to sit in a more 'formal' way. People have explained to me that running gives them space to let their mind wander. This does have benefits – we need time to be mindless; daydreaming helps our creativity! Yet, it is different to working with mind, to notice where our attention is and to transfer it back to 'an object'. There are movement practices, including walking meditation. But these offer an object – the foot contacting the floor being the anchor to come back to.

Myth #6: Meditation will bring you more control

Well, yes . . . and no. A meditation practice WILL help you notice where your mind has gone (thoughts of past or future) and develop the 'muscles' to bring you back (to the present). This is not controlling our thinking but rather training where we place our attention. We learn to notice the thoughts and direct our attention to experience rather than the stories. Nor can we control what life offers: we can merely choose our response to it – and the good news is that is the SAME muscle developed in meditation practice.

Myth #7: I'm no good at it

This myth makes me mad and sad. 'Mad' because in my experience this is a direct consequence of mindfulness being taught unskilfully and hooks into low self-esteem prevalent in the Western mind. 'Sad' because this is the very practice that offers a badly needed befriending and 'road back home'. With too much emphasis on 'being with the breath' people get the message that 'losing the breath' is a failure; and we will ALWAYS lose the breath. If we realise there is no 'Champion Mediator' title up for grabs, there is possibility for a kinder, gentler form of practice. Tibetan meditation masters explain how the essence of meditation is awareness. Losing the breath and knowing you are lost in thought is the epitome of good practice. Another way people lose faith and motivation is thinking they must sit (perfectly) still with the posture of a full-time yogi. Undoubtedly, there are benefits to a good posture: including how it allows us to recognise the faintest of impulses to move – but we still CAN move. I remember one teacher I trained with simply invited the slowing down and pausing before moving (for example, to scratch an itch) so that the underlying desire could be felt and gently explored. Following this invitation, in one long sitting my foot started to go numb. I stayed still and investigated the sensations as I lost feeling. When the bell rang to indicate a period of walking meditation, I rose from my meditation cushion and promptly fell over – a warning that all instructions can be taken to the extreme. Practice the Middle Way!

Myth #8: Meditation is a panacea

At the height of the mindfulness revolution, it was as if the solution to every human predicament was meditation. "Don't medicate, meditate", "become a more effective leader", "improve your parenting", "lower your golf score", "why waste your money on therapy?" Hopefully the previous list of myths busted have helped a little more understanding of what meditation is not. However, there is one more aspect to consider, especially for those of us in the therapeutic setting. People come to therapy to acquire help with their distress – whether that be surfacing in relationships, at work, during transitions, health concerns and so on. What we know as therapists is that the presenting issue (that is conscious) might morph into something else as therapy unfolds. It feels important to make mention at this point therefore that meditation is NOT suitable for everyone, and at first this may not be apparent. Clients can be unaware of deeply held trauma, and it is possible this may suddenly hit the surface once they are delving into embodiment practices. I would also add that not all clients presenting with anxiety will benefit from mindfulness meditation that (commonly) uses the breath as the anchor – given anxiety is often experienced in the chest, overt attention placed here can ignite an 'anxiety of anxiety' and take people on to panic.

It is pertinent to introduce the more disturbing and adverse effects of adopting mindfulness meditation, as researched and presented by Dr Willoughby Britton. Most contemplative traditions offer maps of spiritual development that indicate a period of difficulty on the path. You might have heard of "the dark night of the soul", the metaphor used by St. John-of-the-Cross in the 16th century when chronicling his journey through loss, abandonment, and transformation. On the Buddhist path, experiencing 'non-self' (which can be thought of as a type of depersonalization) can evoke a 'dark night', leaving the meditator groundless and fragile. Arguably, this is compounded if practice is not within a frame of reference. According to Britton's research team (Lindahl et al., 2017), there are many possible acute and chronic effects of this spiritual wilderness that don't fit the 'meditation as panacea' narrative: sensory overload, disturbances to the sense-of-self and time, increases in amplitude in emotions such as fear and anxiety, manic manifestations from euphoria and grandiosity to severe depression and nihilism, perception changes including hallucinations and lights, and physiological responses such as inexplicable musculoskeletal pain and headaches. When attending my first week-long retreat there was a month-long *dathun* being held onsite at the same time. On the third day of my stay, I walked from the meditation hall to see a young man being lifted into an ambulance. I later heard the *dathun* was his first experience of meditating and he now found himself being taken to hospital with a suspected psychotic break. I was to start my counselling training just four weeks later and this was incredibly impacting. One cannot say if meditation caused the break; we can only wonder if the practice, the intensity of ritual, and the basic environment contributed to something already dormant. For now, at least, it is a flag to be cautious. Therapists need to know the territory of meditation themselves rather than adopting it as part of a 'toolbox' (more on this in the next chapter).

Types of meditation practice

In attempting to provide an overview and explanation therein of the most common meditation practices, I must make mention of how the various traditions, schools, and lineages of Buddhism offer different systems and categories. Being a practitioner in the Tibetan system, what I offer here is mainly influenced by the three vehicles or *yanas* presentation.

The 'condensed method' (Rosenberg, 2004) presents the Buddhist path in two, simple steps:

- Practice with the breathing until a certain level of concentration and calm is achieved.
- Open the awareness to whatever arises in the bodymind process and see that it is all impermanent, unsatisfactory, and lacking in an essential self.

These two steps are known as *shamatha* and *vipashyana* respectively.[1] You might see them referred to as discrete or sometimes rolled together into the practice of '*shamatha-vipashyana*'. Let's explore what they mean and how they relate.

Shamatha

Mindfulness is the foundation of our work as meditators. It is a training in noticing what you are doing WHEN you are doing it; we might say it is when our bodymind is synchronised. In the Tibetan system, the main 'workout' for the muscle of mindfulness is called *shamatha* (Sanskrit for 'calm abiding'). Meditation practices of this type allow the mind to settle into the present using an object to attend to – the breath is a common object. In bringing attention to the breath, we can learn to recognise thoughts and patterns of thinking without getting caught up in them. We use the breath like a stabilising anchor to the present moment.

The object of meditation need not be the breath. A practitioner can use external objects (such as candles) or other sense perceptions (such as sound, bodily sensations). The Four Foundations of mindfulness is another way we can explore what is arising in the present moment, and I have found this to be of particular use in the therapeutic setting. We will return to this shortly when we meet "Sebastian".

The corollary of mindfulness is awareness. If mindfulness is the muscle that helps us place where our attention is, awareness is the muscle that keeps us cognisant of the whole. When teaching meditation, I like to use the analogy of chopping carrots while cooking a meal: we must cut the carrots mindfully, paying close attention to the knife so we don't cut ourselves. Equally, there is a broader quality of knowing what is going on in the kitchen – does the heat of the stove where the potatoes are boiling need adjusting? Mindfulness is a focusing of mind down to something specific, and when awareness notices we have lost the object, a panoramic knowing is the invitation back.

Vipashyana

As our mindfulness stabilises and our awareness sharpens a quality of 'insight' may arise, *Vipashyana*. As in the second step, awareness leads to the realization that there is no enduring or permanent self. Thinking no longer leads to conceptual confusion but rather clarity of 'what is'. It is this 'wisdom' aspect of Buddhist meditation that differentiates it from other meditative traditions.

As simple as 1, 2 . . . and 3

Having tamed and calmed our mind (*shamatha*) and awakened wisdom to see the true nature of phenomena (*vipashyana*), we go beyond the constricted sense of self and towards connection with Other. There are a whole range of practices that cultivate open-heartedness and compassion. *Bodhicitta* (awakened heart-mind) is the inherent quality of our *buddhanature* that can be reconnected with through practising the Four Immeasurables – lovingkindness,[2] compassion, joy, and equanimity. These compassion practices still draw upon the concentration (of mindfulness) and awareness (of our embodied response), but it is useful to consider them as a third type of meditation practice. Practices such as lovingkindness, *tonglen*, and RAIN might be placed here.

Other practices

As one progresses on the path of meditation many variations on practices are introduced but essentially the View stays the same – the essence of meditation being the recognition of awareness (or the quality of 'knowing'). In the *Vajrayana* vehicle of the Tibetan system, for example, visualisation or mantra might be used to cultivate qualities of awakened-mind. Before I started out on the *Vajrayana* path, I found the brightly coloured *tangkas* with deities all rather disturbing and more reminiscent of a theistic religion than a mind science. However, I have come to understand the advanced psychology: Visualisation of *buddhas* and deities is akin to role modelling – visualising an archetype whose 'heroic and holistic' qualities of mind need waking-up in ourselves. Similarly, we might use a mantra to calm a mind filled with compulsive negative thoughts. As you may come to realise, visualisation and mantra may also take on some roles within (or as) *shamatha*, *vipashyana*, and compassion practices.

As we move towards consideration of the practices within the therapeutic context, we might also classify the practices according to their main aim:

1. **Concentrative:** These are the practices that aim to slow and still the mind. Providing the mind with an object to attend to allows a gathering process, a reigning-in of the dispersed and scattered mind. Mindfulness of breathing is one example practice.
2. **Generative:** These are the body of practices that help us grow and develop certain qualities – kindness, generosity, or patience, for example. The development of lovingkindness is a key practice of this type.

3. **Receptive**: This is a key capacity for the therapeutic journey – to be completely open and able to turn towards our actual experience, beyond and below our layers of conditioning and assumptions of 'how things are'. The practice of 'open awareness' is very simple, but not easy. Mindfulness of emotions and the various embodiment practices are examples; we might also recognise this quality in the practice of Focusing.

4. **Reflective**: The practices contained in this category are typically grounded in the three aforementioned capacities. With relaxed and present-moment focused attention, deeper and more intuitive insight may arise in our awareness. Contemplation practices are housed here.

How meditation may help the therapeutic journey

When I conducted my MSc research, the Buddhism-informed therapists I interviewed saw the benefits of meditating alongside the therapeutic journey. Some participants in the study considered meditation as a way clients could continue to process material between therapy sessions; others preferred to emphasise the power of the practice in helping clients tune into their experience in the room. In my experience the practices are technically compatible and mutually reinforcing.

If I think back over my own personal journey these last ten years, "being more aware" would encapsulate much of the change. But what does that mean exactly? I know more of my experience in any one moment; there is more 'data' available to me. Whether humanistic or psychodynamic in therapeutic bent, we can think of it as more of the iceberg being above than below the waterline. Certainly, awareness is one consistent thread across Eastern and Western thought, being both the essence of meditation and in-and-of-itself the key to wholeness.

Stabilising the mind

When we bring a 'typical' client case to mind, we might remember how they appeared to us in the first session. We might have seen how bound up in their story or their scripts they were. We might have experienced them as slightly cut off, preoccupied, or disconnected from us. It might have been apparent that their depression or anxiety was being placed as central to their being. In any of these instances, we are (to lesser or greater extents) able to see the person 'underneath' despite how they presented to us, because we ourselves are not attached to the story, script, or belief. I would propose that this is the first place that meditation can assist a client – in the opening of a gap between self and their story.

The concentrative practices of mindfulness allow the mind to be placed on an object one-pointedly. With time of course, the meditator might lose the object and find themselves lost in thoughts. In noticing the attention has drifted from the object to thinking, the 'stickiness' of mental activity is loosened. Take clients with anxiety: in meditation they are encouraged to drop the perpetual future-thinking and come back to the reality of the here-and-now. With time, they might distinguish what is present versus what is a catastrophic prediction. Likewise, the client presenting with depression might find relief from their preoccupation with past events by anchoring to an object in the here-and-now.

Research[3] supports two main hypotheses as to why mindfulness meditation can be therapeutically assisting. Firstly, providing the mind with an object for one-pointed attention enhances cognitive restructuring. Repeatedly returning to the object, the breath for example, cuts through false cognition and de-automatises consciousness. In other words, the questionable story is undermined. Secondly, the practice retunes physiological arousal: desensitizing anxiety through 'reciprocal inhibition', or conversely bringing more vitality for states of depression. Stabilising the mind can be thought of as a reducing of the flames, or more traditionally, a slowing of the flow of water from rapids to a still pond.

Knower and known

Mark Epstein, Buddhist teacher and psychoanalyst, has proposed that mindfulness practices set up a 'therapeutic split' (1990) in which the ego becomes subject and object, the observer and observed; to be the Knower and simultaneously to see what is Known (see 'Non-self', p. 36). The ability to 'stand back' and witness experience whilst experiencing it, loosens identification with what is unfolding. This brings two benefits to the meditator in therapy: firstly, the practice brings familiarity to mental processes and preoccupations; and secondly, a state of 'active passivity' allows material previously out of awareness to come forward. It is perhaps understandable why parallels have been made between meditation and psychoanalytic techniques of free association and dream work in their capacity to loosen defences.

Some teachers and writers talk of 'developing the watcher', and this is indeed a useful way to think of this split into knower and known. However, we need to keep in mind that non-identification with what we are experiencing is not the same as disowning our experience. Being in the river but not of the river allows us to become acutely aware of the rapidly changing nature of experience and start appreciating a disruption to the self-concept. Similarly, no longer immersed in the storyline, clients get to see their contribution to perpetuating dynamics that they struggle with. This ability is referred to as 'meta-awareness': the ability to observe thoughts, feelings, sensations, and impulses as they are happening and how they contribute to a situation. As we saw in Chapter 5, the more we can open up this gap, the more we notice our choices and how we might respond.

Experiencing and digesting emotions

In getting underneath the storylines, we move from the waves at the surface and come to know the subtle currents in the depths of the ocean. We come to appreciate the very stories that have been in service of deflecting us away from the seat of pain (and potentially, past traumas). Stripped of the escape lane of thinking, we get an opportunity to sit with the sensations within the bodymind as a whole and work with any arising 'impulse'.

I would add there is something of an enhanced bodymind dexterity that comes with meditation: awareness may allow sets of psychological and embodied contents previously separate and unrelated to be connected. I've certainly witnessed in my own process, and that of clients, simply sitting with a situation as felt in the body allows a deeper-held wisdom to come up; we learn to trust what the body wants to communicate. And, in knowing our needs, we can begin to understand what was lacking (from our childhood) and seeks resolution in the present.

Research suggests that meta-awareness is linked to affect-tolerance. Present-centred attention, along with clarity and acceptance of one's experience, allows emotional regulation and a return to within the so-called 'window of tolerance'. The scientists tell us this is down to neuroplastic changes in the key areas for emotional reactivity (amygdala, insula), and body awareness or interoception/exteroception (insula, somatosensory cortex). Experientially, it is as if opening to and accepting what is present provides a bigger container in which we can give space and oxygen to the processes within. The container offered each time we sit in meditation can be thought of as a temporary and controlled regression, one that becomes trusted to hold a re-experiencing of previously undigested emotional and psychological material.

I have witnessed this happening in the here-and-now of the therapy room. With my encouragement and support, clients can turn towards the emotional texture of the current situation as felt in the body. Opening to the sensations within, given enough space, the story breaks down into sensation plus an awareness of the interpretation/label applied to it. By dropping the latter, the sensation begins to be appreciated as energy; and once here, it has an opportunity to be transmuted or 'composted'. For example, anxiety may rise in the body with sensations of pulsing, gripping; and with our direct witnessing, this can be transmuted to courage. Likewise, sensations of anger if given space may convert to skilful action.

Clients that meditate outside of the therapy session are allowing more dedicated time for these processes. I have experienced the interplay between clients' understanding arising in the therapy room, and that new awareness getting processed and digested on the cushion. This may lead to new insight which can be brought back to therapy for deeper exploration and more understanding . . . and so on.

Bringing compassion and gentleness

Psychotherapy brings about healing change when we can find the courage to feel what has previously not felt safe to experience. Understanding and insight around the conditions of our wounding is helpful, but ultimately, we need to feel the pain of the past to move through it. Experiencing and digesting emotions takes a lot of courage. I use this word in preference to 'bravery' because it evokes the quality of heart opening where we have habitually closed down.

My own experience of healing turned a corner when I was able to view and hold my story with compassion. I would talk about the terror and anxiety of my felt experience using words like "I can't bear it". Only in coming to realise the "it" was the little girl still residing inside were my eyes opened to the need for a gentler and kinder attitude. I am not alone in this reaction. Even when we have found the strength to turn towards our vulnerability, subtle undertones of doing so simply to 'get rid' can remain. Bringing an unconditional presence is to provide our own parenting, one we missed out on during childhood.

Client case study "Sebastian": working with unfolding experience

When looking back over my case work to illustrate the ideas from this chapter, two priorities came to mind: firstly, how to illustrate the power of awareness of a moment-to-moment unfolding of experience in dissolving the stories that limit living to the full; and secondly, to bring a client case that demonstrates how the neuroscience of 'interoception' can be a useful concept in psychotherapeutic practice. With these priorities in mind, let me introduce you to "Sebastian", a 35-year-old man working in the world of marketing.

Sebastian's father wanted him to become a lawyer, just like he had been and his father before that. There was a strong sense in Sebastian's story that he had disappointed his father and betrayed the male lineage of his family, exaggerated by his being an only child. Quite simply, Sebastian didn't enjoy the academic side of school, much preferring to play sport. Sebastian met his partner through a rugby club he joined on finishing college and starting his career. Now married, Sebastian and Vanessa enjoyed "a good life", but he felt the pressure to maintain their standard of living. Working long hours, keeping at the top of his game, "or else". When I asked what the apparent consequences were, Sebastian told me failing would be giving his father the opportunity to say "I told you so". Furthermore, there was fear that Vanessa would leave him if he were not wealthy and successful. There was also tension in the relationship because although they had met through the rugby club, Sebastian was increasingly aware of Vanessa's disapproval of his time out of the house at the weekends given she wanted them to start a family and renovate the house. Sebastian was annoyed at her apparent turnaround, but also because she became a reminder of his father's disapproval of what he loved most.

Sebastian contacted me given my background in mindfulness meditation. A work colleague worried for Sebastian given his stress and "panicky moments" before meetings had recommended a meditation app. Sebastian was finding it useful and was eager to learn more. He had also used some sport psychology techniques for his rugby performance, so he was open to "working with the mind". Sebastian had recently been making the connection between his life issues and the relationship to his father. He shared with me in our first session "As I feel the escalating panic, it feels like there are eight of Dad sitting around the meeting table".

When we started breaking down what was happening in the build-up to his work meetings, Sebastian told me that it was as if he constantly lives in the next moment. "When I am eating breakfast, I am thinking about what to wear; and when I am getting dressed, I am thinking about what to take for lunch . . . and it goes on. When I am driving to work, I am thinking about the emails I need to send; and when I am writing those, I have one eye on the clock and what the morning meeting will bring". Internally, I felt a knowing of a perpetual "what's next"; a world I too once inhabited and momentarily got distracted into again. Realising this and feeling how it distanced me from Sebastian, I returned and asked how this was for him. Wearing a pained expression, he described how distant he felt from Vanessa each evening, even if they sat side-by-side. As Buddhist teacher Gaylon Ferguson points out,

> all too often, direct experience of the real-time present is replaced, forgotten, hastily bypassed. In our rush to get to the next moment, we substitute a fantasy life, an imagined double in the future, for the actual life we are living. . . . Mindfulness lets us reclaim the lives we are actually living.
>
> (2010, p. 31)

Interventions in the therapy

Sebastian's story indicated to me we were working in the haunting shadow of his male ancestral lineage. I got a sense that he was looking for an anchor in his (own) life beyond his beloved rugby. In finding new solace in meditating on the breath, I asked Sebastian what he thought of using more of his experience to 'ground'. His curiosity ignited, I went on to introduce the 'Four foundations of mindfulness', a practice from the very earliest teachings of the *Buddha*. By moving through a series of different objects (body, feelings, mind, and objects of mind or 'phenomena'), we get an opportunity to directly recognise, in real-time, the totality of experience.

Mindfulness of body: By the time Sebastian and I embarked on the project to deconstruct his stories and clear the way to direct experience, he had been meditating for four months and had been in therapy for two of those. He already understood the benefits of good meditation posture, the benefits of practising daily, and adopting an attitude of 'curious explorer'. I introduced the first foundation as an extension to what he had already been doing – so just like the breath is an anchor to what is present and happening, we can also use other aspects of the physical to access the 'here-and-now'. We started with the practice that people often meet on MBSR courses – the body scan. In this practice, often performed lying down, the object of attention becomes bodily regions. Over a period of time, typically 20 minutes to 30 minutes, the meditator is invited to notice any sensations arising in the feet; moving up to the ankles; the shins and calves; the area around the knee, through the rest of the body to the top of the head. The practice can culminate with a noticing of the whole body, and how it feels relative to the start of the body scan. Sebastian would practise the body scan at home between sessions. After initial difficulty establishing a rhythm, after a couple of weeks he was settling into practising as soon as he woke up, and then again in the evening before bedtime. Vanessa was supportive, having seen Sebastian become a little calmer. After this encouraging start, Sebastian and I talked about developing a more 'natural' mindfulness of his body. We transitioned into a practice whereby he would simply rest with the breath and notice what other regions of his body called for his attention: What were the sensations? Was there a speed or intensity? Could he locate sensations of pressure? Or temperature? At first, Sebastian continued with the body scan twice a day and added in short practice sessions of this 'tuning in' during his working day: at his desk, on the park bench where he ate his lunch, on the train home. He then moved on to making this his main evening practice. As pointed to in the original teachings of the *Buddha*, rather than recognising the body as one solid, unified 'thing', Sebastian practised recognising the collection of parts in process – with feelings arising, staying, and then falling away. Going back to the experiment of 'Non-self', (p. 36) if we close our eyes, how do we *know* we have a body?

Mindfulness of feeling: In the practice of mindfulness of feeling we get an opportunity to remember that just like the body, feelings can be identified, seen as interconnected, and experienced as impermanent. In the Buddhist teachings, the practice focuses on 'feeling tone', or *vedana*. Transitioning from the mindfulness of body practice, I would invite Sebastian to notice the physical sensations he was experiencing, and to then label the quality of that sensation as either pleasant, unpleasant, or neutral. We then moved to the sphere of the other senses – sounds, sights – and to notice what was the reaction to his experience. This rudimentary feeling tone is an important experience to detect and work with the 'impulse' before it becomes a full-blown emotion. Sebastian noticed how much of his experience was either pleasant or unpleasant, and how little 'neutral' there was. When a police car with siren blaring passed the room one time, we talked about his reaction to it and how easy it is to move away from the unpleasant and want more of the pleasant (silence). He was noticing this moment of labelling and reaction as a moment when stories ignite. Based upon that realisation, I invited Sebastian to investigate the moment feeling became emotion, and to explore how emotional experiences feel in the body. It also became a bridge to the therapeutic exploration of his life. As he settled down to practise, starting with mindfulness of breath, then mindfulness of the breathing body, I invited him to recall a 'pleasant' experience from the previous week. He recounted sitting in the park one lunchtime and a moment when the clouds parted and he felt bathed in sunlight. He was able to capture where that experience 'landed' in his body. I encouraged him to rest in those feelings and explore what was it about the sensations that led to 'pleasant' and 'happy'. Within the exploration of adjectives, he described how 'open' he felt in his chest, and I invited him to really know that feeling for a while. After coming back to the breath for a short time, I invited Sebastian to visit an experience of stress from his week. After recalling the experience of the team meeting the day before, I invited him to drop the story and see where 'unpleasant' resided in his bodily experience. How did he know it was 'bad'? Where was the anxiety and distrust located in him? Again, he came to the chest – and rather than the 'openness' he described a moment ago, he could feel a "constriction, heavy pulling in". The reader can probably recognise the importance of 'presence' and 'holding' the therapist offers here. In the earlier detail I have deliberately left out my own experiencing and response to Sebastian's in the service of clarity, but this fails to convey the true embodied sense of the encounter. In each experiential move, I was participating alongside present to my own experience and using that to pace and guide Sebastian. To instruct from a place of conceptual mind risks due care, and endangering experiences that might flood or activate – in Sebastian's case, his panic. Furthermore, a client wishing to use these practices at home needs to be able to manage how intensely to 'lean in', or as Chögyam Trungpa Rinpoche describes 'touch and go'.

> The idea of 'touch' is that you feel a quality of existence; you feel that you are who you are. The 'go' part is that you are there, and then you don't hang on to it. You don't sustain your sense of being, but you let go of it.
>
> (2010, p. 86)

'Touch' is not just to acknowledge but to greet and experience; only then do you come back to your breath and let the emotion dissolve on the exhale. Learning and trusting the 'touch and go' attitude was critical for Sebastian – to bring experience fully to his awareness, yet to 'titrate' its impact so it was tolerable. Sebastian and I used the metaphor of good clutch control, feathering the accelerator and brake pedal to ride the experience.

Mindfulness of mind: Sebastian spent a good deal of time on mindfulness of body as he felt it gave him a resource to use 'on the spot'. It was some weeks later that we moved on to mindfulness of mind, and Sebastian shared his fascination with the "two-way traffic" of his bodymind; how his thoughts caused reactions in his body, and how his body provoked stories in his mind. I suggested we try a practice that my own meditation mentor recommended: After settling into the body using a period of mindfulness of breath, I invited Sebastian to imagine he was sitting on a railway station platform. Each thought that came into his mind could be imagined as a train. I invited him to observe the trains coming and going, but not 'board' any one train; essentially to become a dispassionate observer rather than an actor in his mental flow. I asked him to watch where the thoughts came from, how long they stayed at the station, and where did they go after leaving? After a week of practising with this instruction, Sebastian came back to the therapy room the following week visibly excited. "I get it! I might have a thought, but I don't have to follow it. I've always considered my thoughts to be MY thoughts, that I created them . . . but they pop out of nowhere and go back there . . . if I leave them alone". Of course, on a relative level they ARE our thoughts – they aren't exactly random (to be explored in 'Karma and the Eight consciousnesses', p. 166). Like the comet clusters that exist on the edge of our solar system, our 'thought clusters' reside in a storehouse because of our karma. When they get pulled into our 'orbit', they don't have to become our personal possession, we can let them exit our orbit and return to where they come from. Sebastian made some links to his upbringing, and how his storehouse was full of beliefs and 'script decisions' he made in response to observing his father's behaviours as a child. As Jung so accurately pointed to, the greatest tragedy for any child is carrying the unlived life of the parent (2014). Sebastian's father didn't assert his own wishes to his father, and by not addressing his shadow, this became

Sebastian's inheritance. Other ways to explore mindfulness of mind include becoming familiar with the 'texture of mind'. Is mental activity heavy or dull? Fast or slow? Doing this, Sebastian developed a witnessing consciousness, or a meta-awareness of mental states and contents, without indulging or empowering them or needing to suppress or avoid them.

Mindfulness of phenomena: The first three 'foundations' had broken the grip of Sebastian's family story. The fourth foundation of mindfulness brings a complete breakdown of all experience into 'bite size chunks'. If the systematic investigation across the first three domains lends a set of stabilisers; the fourth foundation is transitioning to ride the bike without. 'Just sitting' in open awareness, the fourth foundation is to notice what arises in awareness. In psychotherapy speak, we move from content to process level; in Buddhist terminology we "mix the mind with the *Dharma*" (Trungpa Rinpoche, 2013, p. 68): to work with the *skandhas* (how we take raw data from our senses and tend to label them); how to work with the Four Noble Truths (how our suffering is rooted in making things permanent rather than in flux); and the rising of 'mind' out of consciousness when an object is perceived. Sebastian found this practice of all-inclusive awareness incredibly challenging, and I agreed! Many hours of practise (indeed a lifetime) might be required to find sufficient stability to set up the 'auditorium' and experience it without jumping in.

Outcomes of the therapy

I mentioned in the opening to this case study my wish to offer an account of client work that brought forth the concept of 'interoception'. Referred to as an eighth sense (after the five senses; the vestibular system for balance; and proprioception for location in external space), interoception is the sense of our internal world. Not only biological (awareness of heartbeat, breathing, hunger, thirst, bowel control, etc.), interoception interacts with emotion and mood. Interoception was the quality that allowed Sebastian to recall events in his week that had sparked happiness or stress. For some, interoception entails a super-sensitivity to the environment, so isn't always desirable. It is associated with anxiety-specific arousal symptoms; and might also be the channel through which 'empaths' are exposed to vicarious trauma. However, the more of our experience we can bring into our awareness, the more information we have available to us to help us consciously decide how we respond to our life. Researchers are currently developing programmes that might help the development of healthy interoceptive processing. Unsurprisingly, the basis of such programmes are activities such as mindfulness meditation and reflection on interoceptive processes: body scanning, visualization, bringing awareness and attention to the sensations of breath, heartbeat, gurgling, stomach, the weight of limbs, and so on. The aim of these programmes is an improved capacity for self-regulation. Within the context of therapy, language and communication of affect strengthens the command of interoceptive capacity.

Interoception theory explains what centuries of practitioners of meditation have come to appreciate through practices such as the Four Foundations. As Sebastian came to recognise, underneath the habitual stories and solidification of thoughts, experience is made up of many moments and sensations always in flux. Attending the flow helped Sebastian break down the long-held beliefs about himself and the expectations he thought others held over him. Towards the end of our work together, Sebastian was beginning to see the actual people in the meeting room, not as projections of his father. 'Touch and go' helped him to stay in contact with the feelings of anxiety, and honour the needs of "Little Seb", and then to come back to his adult self, attend to others in the room and the agenda of the meeting.

Sebastian also reported he felt less 'top heavy', and being more in his body, he became better able to notice when he was activated and at the risk of spiralling off. As hoped, this bodily anchor gave him more support – to the extent he happily reported his weekend "sanity anchor" of rugby became negotiable. His relationship with Vanessa improved as the interpersonal resentment decreased. Something similar was also shifting in the relationship with his father. He found himself less defensive when they spent time together, in part because he had seen how his father's unfinished business was not his responsibility and he was now able to refuse the baton.

How this fit in the therapeutic frame

Whenever a therapist is moved to work outside of a set therapeutic frame, they are called-upon to be curious as to 'why'. This is a conversation I have with supervisees, especially those who have undergone additional training to their core, humanistic modality (for example EMDR, CBT, sand tray work). Interventions are key to bringing about second-order change. However, a therapist who has worked with a client in the way I have described with Sebastian will need to visit any 'out of awareness' transaction potentially playing out. Did I reach for meditation to avoid a difficulty in the room? Did I unwittingly fall for the 'praise' of my expertise in meditation, or was I excited from my side to share the practice? Given that more and more people contact me to work in this way, it is a self-enquiry that is now a constant thread through my work: what might be avoided or not seen by bringing meditation into the relationship?

What I have not detailed in the previous account is the exact nature of how the meditation and therapeutic dialogue interweaved – and by no means was there a set format followed week-by-week. The principle of 'co-construction' was paramount in Sebastian and I setting out and co-piloting a path. This negated the risk of therapy becoming a one-on-one version of an eight-week mindfulness course. Sebastian would travel to his session with me by train, giving him a chance to practise in his transition from work. So, by the time he came to the therapy room he was quite centred and aware of what he wanted to bring. We could therefore get started in the dialogue shortly after a period of settling together. Typically, the progression of practices would occur in the middle-third of the session; but some weeks we didn't do any meditation work at all, and some weeks it was more akin to the practice of Focusing (Gendlin, 2010).

It was also in our contracting around the meditation teacher/psychotherapist roles that I discussed with Sebastian how we would both be responsible for monitoring the 'dual relationship' and its ability to meet/ frustrate needs. An example of this was his request to record the practice we did together in the room so he could subsequently use the audio for a guided meditation at home in between sessions. We talked about the audio as a 'transitional object', what it meant to him to have a female companion and might there be a maternal role for me to help him step out from his father's shadow. This was all very much part of the work and was always weaved back and forth. Similarly, Sebastian and I also discussed how it was for him when I overtly used Buddhist terminology to underpin the practices. Growing up in a Catholic family, Sebastian was opinionated about religion. From my own personal experience of finding meditation in the secular context, I was able to understand Sebastian's openness to the practice in the same vein. We were open about our 'difference': he could honour my Buddhist view and path without having to subscribe to it nor dismiss it. Having such a conversation was again therapeutic, as part of the judging eye he had projected on to his father was rooted in the family's belief system.

How this work shaped my human being

Sebastian's story invited me to contemplate my own story and relationship to ancestral lineage. Before I started my therapy training, I held my suffering as a personal deficit; the training helped me appreciate it was borne of a relational deficit. But what if it doesn't stop there? My inheritance wasn't the burden of expectation that Sebastian inherited from his father and grandfather; more likely mine was the baton of anxious-being along the female line. At first when we come to therapy and begin exploring our 'presenting past', our fingers can point to our caregivers; mothers particularly get a raw deal! Blame doesn't help. If anything, it locks us in the story . . . I know. Coming to appreciate that my parents had parents too, and my grandparents had parents too (ad infinitum) has been a lot more beneficial. When I was starting *Ngondro*, the first practice is to take refuge in front of a lineage tree. Insightfully, my meditation mentor invited me to consider who else is in my lineage, and not just family ancestors; it could include people that inspire me. I share all of this to communicate how much our world imprints on us; not just the world we live in now, nor the world we can ordinarily experience (if we acknowledge a collective or archetypal realm). This has helped me take up the baton, to choose to do this work of healing not just for myself, but for my female lineage.

Notes

1 This is the Sanskrit. You might also come across *samatha* and *vipassana*, the Pali.
2 From the Sanskrit *maitri*, this is a mind stance of friendliness: kindhearted, benevolent, with goodwill.
3 I would encourage readers to also follow the latest in neuroscience around 'predictive coding', as this offers a very convincing explanation as to how our brain interacts with the external world and how meditation practice might modulate experiencing.

References

Epstein, M. (1990). Beyond the Oceanic Feeling: Psychoanalytic Study of Buddhist Meditation. *International Review of Psychoanalysis, 17*, 159–165.

Ferguson, G. (2010). *Natural Wakefulness. Discovering the Wisdom We Were Born With*. Boston, MA: Shambhala.

Gendlin, E. (2010). *Focusing*. London: Ebury Publishing.

Jung, C. (2014). *Collected Works of C.G. Jung, Volume 17: Development of Personality*. Princetown, NJ: Princeton University Press.

Lindahl, J.R., Fisher, N.E., Cooper, D.J., Rosen, R.K., & Britton, W.B. (2017). The Varieties of Contemplative Experience: A Mixed-Methods Study of Meditation-Related Challenges in Western Buddhists. *PLoS One, 12*(5), e0176239.

Neale, M. (2018). *Gradual Awakening: The Tibetan Buddhist Path of Becoming Fully Human*. Boulder, CO: Sounds True.

Nichtern, E. (2011). *One City: A Declaration of Interdependence*. Somerville, MA: Wisdom Publications.

Piver, S. (2015). *Start Here Now. An Open-Hearted Guide to the Path and Practice of Meditation*. Boston, MA: Shambhala.

Rosenberg, L. (2004). *Breath by Breath: The Liberating Practice of Insight Meditation*. Boston, MA: Shambhala.

Trungpa Rinpoche, C. (2010). *The Collected Works of Chogyam Trungpa: Volume Four*. London: Shambhala.

Trungpa Rinpoche, C. (2013). *The Bodhisattva Path of Wisdom and Compassion. The Profound Treasury of the Ocean of Dharma, Volume Two*. London: Shambhala.

Trungpa Rinpoche, C. (2015). *Mindfulness in Action: Making Friends with Yourself Through Meditation and Everyday Awareness*. Boston, MA: Shambhala.

Chapter 8

Practical implications and applications

Essential ground for the therapist

The intention of this chapter is to highlight some of the practical aspects of bringing the Buddhist teachings and practices to the therapeutic act. We start with a few ideas as to how the *Dharma* can provide the therapist with a sense of 'ground'; or as one of the therapists I interviewed for my research spoke of it, how Buddhism is a "mothership" to return to.

In the second year of my initial counselling training, a new tutor arrived on the course. Jamie was a big man – in stature but also presence, and that impacted me immediately one afternoon in the experiential workshop. He sat quietly as we all arrived, and I was struck by his arms covered in tattoos of the *Buddha* and Sanskrit writing. With excitement, I asked him if he was a Buddhist. He replied, confusingly, "nah". With time, however, I have come to realise Jamie wasn't interested in the label nor the identity of being an "ist". There was no separation between Jamie, therapist, Buddhist, nor educator. There was simply his being. A being that I came to experience as a healing presence. This encounter communicates a key aspect of working within a Buddhism-informed therapeutic frame. The teaching is merely a vehicle to describe the truth, not to be mistaken for the truth itself. To inform *how* we are, not *who* we are. As the *Dharma* explains, a finger pointing at the moon is needed to know where to look, but the finger is not to be confused for the moon itself.

Following the path of Buddhism provides practitioners with a View; a wisdom that guides authenticity and clarity within practice; and expresses itself in kindness and compassion. Buddhism has become the ground or container that holds the ideas and interventions of my practice as a humanistic psychotherapist. One way to explicate this container principle is to consider the teachings from the *Mahayana* on relative and absolute truths (first introduced in Chapter 2, when considering 'Why bring together Western psychotherapy and Eastern wisdom traditions?', p. 14). When a client enters my therapy room for the first time, it is through a Buddhist lens that

DOI: 10.4324/9781003383710-8

I first connect with the client. In choosing to come to therapy, the client has already found enough connection with their inherent wisdom or 'basic sanity'. This 'absolute' is simultaneous with the 'relative' experiencing of pain and suffering. Wisdom and confusion. This is the view from which I work. The theory I have learnt as a practitioner of Western psychotherapy can then be considered as the *upaya*; our relationship being the vehicle that takes the client on the 'road back home'.

We have previously considered how important being truly present is for our client work (see 'Presence, Attunement, Resonance, Trust', p. 86); and undoubtedly, practising meditation is a great training for slowing down and arriving in the here-and-now of the therapy room. However, our ability to stay present will be tested as soon as we encounter everyday life and relationships with Other – including our clients. Like a tree, the deeper our roots go, the more we can withstand emotional weather. It is one thing to access meditation as a technique and stay present with an object (such as the breath); it is another to stay present without such an anchor. The further I have travelled along the Buddhist path, the more I have encountered the object-less or 'formless' meditation practices that train resting and relaxing with 'what is'. The Buddhist View therefore can be thought of as the fertile ground in which our roots get stronger; a deepening in trust (of *buddhanature*) and faith (that this is the path to uncover it).

From personal experience, I have realised how much courage it takes to intentionally be present to our lives. Beside my desk, I have a postcard carrying the quote from Franklin Roosevelt "Courage is not the absence of fear but the ability to continue in spite of fear". In the Tibetan Buddhist tradition, fearlessness is not the reducing of fear but using the fear to move through. Truly resting in experience 'as it is' acknowledges the deep sense of emptiness – no-thingness – at the very core of our being. We may try to distract ourselves away from this existential abyss with the activity of 'project identity' but, developing the courage to feel the groundlessness that is the absolute reality of our existence is the only way through. The Buddhist path provides both the stability of mind (through *shamatha*) and the experiential insight on absolute reality (through *vipashyana*).

To have such a container, or a mothership to which we can return, fosters a sense of surrender. This is not an optimistic "everything is going to be okay", but rather everything is already okay 'as it is'. Holding this as the backdrop of our experience is one way we can learn to let go and truly relax. Having a trusted way of returning to source, or re-sourcing, is vital as a therapist. All *bodhisattvas* need to apply their own oxygen mask before helping others with theirs; our being is the tool or instrument of our trade. One place to explore this is at the end of each client session. Many therapists have rituals they will use in the ten minutes between ending with one client and starting with the next. A few moments of mindfulness of breath can bring us back to ground. My own ritual will depend on client encounters: it might be about restoring my own being, but equally it might contain a reflection on a client's suffering, bringing compassion, and a rousing of *bodhicitta* ahead of my next session.

The place of ethics

The universal rules[1] addressing malevolence and benevolence lie at the cornerstone of ethical practice in Buddhism and psychotherapy and so it felt essential to speak to this area in a book integrating the two. Moreover, I wanted to share my experience of bringing together professional *ethics* and personal *values*.

For therapy to be effective, the therapist is called upon to cultivate an environment of trust whereby clients feel safe in revealing sensitive personal information and their deepest vulnerabilities. Although not a regulated profession in the UK, it would seem consistent with the values of preventing malevolence and cultivating benevolence that any practitioner would seek thorough training to qualify, and then work to a code of conduct. There are two main professional bodies in the UK responsible for guarding professional standards of care for the therapy client. As a registered psychotherapist, I work to the code of professional practice set out by the UK Council for Psychotherapy (UKCP). The UKCP outline numerous key areas which they expect practitioners to commit to holding in their practice, namely: the best interests of clients; professionalism; communication and consent; records and confidentiality; professional knowledge, skills, and experiences; social responsibility; trust and confidence. Counsellors in the UK have a similar code under another membership body, the British Association of Counselling and Psychotherapy (BACP).

In my role training counsellors and psychotherapists, I teach on a module covering the professional, legal, and ethical aspects of the profession. The main points of the ethical frameworks of the BACP and UKCP are introduced and discussed, and we encourage students to develop reasoning and critical thinking as applied to practice. Delivering this module has been a valuable opportunity to reflect on my own approach to ethical working. Firstly, teaching is an effective way to remain up to date with safeguarding standards that I can then apply to my practice. Furthermore, in helping trainees move towards a personalised value-based system, teaching is an opportunity to 'walk my talk' and work with integrity. I would go as far as to say that it is through teaching my therapeutic ethics have taken on greater profundity than simply a set of rules.

It feels useful to take a moment to consider how we might distinguish ethics (perhaps most relevant to the professional) from values (as held and lived through the personal). Essentially, ethics are a set of rules established by a group or culture that govern the behaviour of a person. Ethics determine what is right (and what is wrong) and can be considered a system of moral principles that typically constrain. Values on the other hand refer to the beliefs for which a person has an enduring preference. In contrast to 'right and wrong' thinking, values stimulate action from a place of personal motivation. Working with trainees and supervisees early on in their practice, I often witness the risks inherent when social imperatives rather than personal values drive a path of service. 'Good' therapeutic behaviour tends to be driven by 'fear'. Over the evolution of a career, a shift comes when the inner compass is set by trust and intention; i.e., practice becomes more 'value'-based. Whether it be the teachings of the Eightfold Path met in the *Hinayana* or those of the *paramita* fundamental to the *Mahayana*, the *Dharma* emphasises engaged practice rather than rules. The goal is not simply to behave properly but rather to understand why one behaves the way one does. If we align actions of body, speech, and mind with our own well-being, we will naturally make choices that lead us to the well-being of others. It might be useful to return to the *Hinayana* and *Mahayana* aspects of the Buddhist path.

The Hinayana practice of non-harm

The universal rule of 'do no harm' is emphasised in Buddhism through the Eightfold Path. If practised deeply, the practitioner sees the connection between motivation, action, and consequences. Internally experiencing the consequences in meditation is a great motivator to be more mindful of behaviour and to drive self-responsibility. The Eightfold Path (as presented in Chapter 5) might be seen as relevant to therapists in the following ways:

- Wise View. One tends to take ownership of one's conduct when one understands there is no external authority to evade. When I teach trainees, shifting from a fear-based to a value-based practice helps develop reflection and reflexivity; i.e., developing the ability to ground practice in reasoning, decision-making, and examination of consequences from actions. Taking ownership, or *karma*, means practice based on firm yet kind acts.
- Wise Intention. When the practitioner engages in an honest attempt to understand motivation, this is bound to inform the relationships held with clients and colleagues. Ethical practice cannot be shied away from. One might recall how we react to a client's request to move a session or break the frame in some other way – is our reaction punitive, or do we stay curious as to what is going on for the client with their well-being in mind?

- Wise Speech. Any therapist grounded in humanistic theory understands the importance of congruence and empathy: to speak honestly in a warm and gentle way. In reading this book, you might also come to reflect upon the healing quality of talking only when necessary (presence and deep listening). A therapist can practice skilful speech in everyday life; and with this, decisions such as when and where to break confidentiality and reveal client information flow more naturally.
- Wise Action. The Buddhist *abhidharma* explains how unwholesome actions lead to unsound states of mind, while wholesome actions lead to sound states of mind. I've mentioned previously how hard it is to meditate if we feel we might have caused harm. Practising non-harm in daily life leads to less questioning of what proper conduct might be in the therapeutic environment.
- Wise Livelihood. Choosing the career of therapist might seem automatically in harmony with this aspect of the Eightfold Path. However, we can keep looking at our motivation and the trap of serving others to feel good about oneself. Times such as when a client describes financial challenges just as we mention raising our fee might also ask of us "what is skilful here?"
- Wise Effort. The more confident an individual can be in trusting the core of being, the more in tune with the appropriate effort to be applied they will be. Supervision sessions are a good place to reflect on when we are trying too hard and not trusting that the client will (or needs to) go at their own pace and find their own solutions.
- Wise Mindfulness. Clear perception is important if we are not to get carried away by conceptualisation and assumptions; i.e., sticking to the phenomenological method by employing deep listening and understanding of the client's world/experience.
- Wise Concentration. With deepening concentration and stability of mind, one has access to any experience of discomfort. From experience, noticing this comes with an in-built, self-correction factor – we will be motivated to act with more mindfulness and compassion in the future.

If we take the eight factors here as practices, not rules, we have an opportunity to notice where we come up against dilemmas. This encourages deep reflection ahead of informed decisions. The Eightfold path is a bit like the rumble strips on the edge of motorways – if we notice a jarring quality in our work, what line may have been crossed leaving us feeling uneasy? A carrot rather than stick approach, the invitation is to examine the consequences of our action with kindness and to develop healthy remorse in order to not feel the discomfort again (with the benefit of not harming others along the way). Fundamental is the joining of the ethics with the meditation practices. As mental activity quietens, the increased mindfulness helps us know we are experiencing the rumble strips at the level of body, speech, and mind; and we gain insight as to the origins of behaviour and choices being made in response to our world. Arguably, the capacity for critical thinking and skilful intention are sharpened if meditation is retained with the more over-arching *abhidharma*. We keep in remembrance our intention and how we are not just a suffering self but a self that exists within a dynamic, social web and has impact on others.

The Mahayana recognition of interdependence and compassion

When we have glimpsed the interconnected nature of our being, we come to recognise a 'soft spot' or *bodhicitta*. With this 'awakened heart-mind' there is a more organic intention to not only avoid harm to (self and) others, but an aspiration to go out of our way to serve. Buddhism's alignment to this second universal rule asks that we investigate our own heart, discover what gives us pain, and then refuse under any circumstances to inflict that pain on anybody else. If we do, an opportunity arises for us to get to know the lost part of ourselves that is driving the harmful or unkind behaviour. At first, *bodhicitta* is an aspiration that needs help realising and so *bodhisattvas* take on the practices of the *paramita* (transcendent actions), another list! It might be helpful to expand upon these in the way we did previously with the Eightfold Path:

- Generosity. We tend to think of generosity as the giving of an object (even if the object is something like the gift of our time). Transcendent generosity also includes "just simply doing what is required at any moment in any situation, not being afraid to receive anything" (Trungpa Rinpoche, 2010, p. 201). Early in my practice days I would refuse gifts from clients, yet now I see the healing in my accepting what a client needs to offer. Vulnerability begets vulnerability, and offering an open heart elicits this in others.
- Discipline. Again, there is a traditional view of discipline that can be a hindrance on a path towards wholeness and integration. With the view of the *Mahayana*, discipline is less about restraint and more about resting. Whilst there is undoubtedly a conventional discipline in practising therapy, the transcendent aspect is the commitment to attending to 'what is'; to keep coming back to our experience now. Therapists can integrate this into their practice through the discipline of staying present (and thus making themselves available for attunement, resonance, trust).
- Patience. This *paramita* is perhaps more in line with our everyday understanding of patience and builds on the *paramita* of discipline. When we commit to attending experience, we can open, learn to relax, and rest there. The *paramita* of patience gives us time we need to develop the

unconditional trust that the situation is workable. I think of the times in my life when I have served the internal critical voice, or lived too speedily, including the rush to get rid of my suffering (that leads to further suffering!). If we are not careful, this can play out with our clients, rushing them through the therapeutic work with our 'clever' interpretations rather than letting them come to their own realisations.

- Exertion. This *paramita* resembles 'wise effort' in the sixth aspect of the Eightfold Path; yet here there is emphasis on the rousing of energy as an antidote to three types of 'laziness'. As well as an 'ordinary' laziness, there is also the experience of disheartenment, and the tendency to avoid our true priorities through 'getting busy'. We might consider how we use 'techniques' similarly to avoid the uncomfortable feelings of impasse in the relationship with clients.

- Meditation. Whereas the *Hinayana* path emphasises the calming and taming of mind, in the *Mahayana*, the quality of meditation is one of cultivating co-ordination and suppleness of mind, both on and off the cushion. The act becomes one of befriending ourselves and our experience; a critical attitude if we are to protect ourselves from the narrative that we are not doing a good job with a client. It is with meditation we can open to and ride our experience without taking it too personally.

- Wisdom. This *paramita* is a sharpening of intelligence that moves beyond theory to integrating knowledge with personal experience in the service of others. A good example of this is remembering what it is like to sit in the client chair and relate to the difficulty and struggle of the fellow human being in the room.

The *paramita* are thus qualities to cultivate in the service of reducing the suffering of all beings, including the 'being' performing them. Being a 'baby *bodhisattva*' myself, consideration of the *paramita* in my personal and professional life has been transformational. Within the context of my therapeutic work, the opening that comes with aspirational *bodhicitta* has softened the edges around my practice. For example, while mindful of 'self-disclosure' principles, I am more likely to bring aspects of myself and my journey with suffering into the therapy room.

The ethics of applying Buddhist ethics

Whether we explicitly tease out professional ethics from personal values, values are an inevitable and pervasive part of psychotherapy. In the humanistic tradition, importance is placed on 'bracketing'. An integration of spiritual values into psychotherapy requires an even more open and honest acknowledgement as to the implementation of the therapist's own value system (Bergin, 1980), and a great deal of critical thinking. From my experience of integrating the spiritual-psychological, I offer a few ideas that need consideration, especially in the realm of potential paradigm conflicts.

The humanistic tradition already goes a long way in distancing itself from the predominant medicalised model: for example, the process being acceptance not curing, and the self-as-fluid rather than fixed. However, the practitioner who straddles the humanistic and the spiritual does need to consider where divergent conceptualisation remains. For example, from a Buddhist paradigm, one's ethical behaviour – through the law of *karma* – is integral to mental well-being, a view therefore potentially at odds with Western psychotherapeutic view where ethics are viewed as primarily separate from examination of one's mind. Buddhism dispels the separateness of self, whereas the humanistic concern is towards individualism (Batchelor, 2007). Another divergent aspect to keep in mind is how spiritual aspirations might not conform to accepted views of mental well-being. We will visit this in the case study of "Jacob".

Other areas where care is needed include the use of Buddhist language and terminology, the holding of distinct views and avoiding the leading of clients (although this is not peculiar to a Buddhism-informed therapy). Social responsibility, such as activism, is another dimension therapists are invited to reflect upon. It was not an intention of this book to go too deep into the debate around therapy and positioning within the political agenda, but to not make mention of it here would be remiss; especially as I am writing this five months into the Covid-19 pandemic. Questions around social responsibility (the obligation to act for the benefit of society at large) is high on the agenda at micro, meso, and macro levels, and this necessitates looking at where I stand across the social, political, economic, and environmental. Buddhism as traditionally studied and practised came with a focus on the cause of suffering being personal and individual; but contemporary situations like Covid-19 point to how the three *kleshas* can operate on a vast scale in our political, social, and economic systems. As a Buddhist I have taken a vow to reduce suffering; how can I ignore injustice? Through meditation, and coming to see we are not separate selves, a deep sense of compassion arises and with it, the call to action. Whether this can or indeed should be actioned in the therapy room is an interesting question and requires contemplation within 'wise livelihood'.

My MSc research uncovered ideas as to how ethics might be integrated into clinical practice, my co-researchers suggesting a multi-stage process: Firstly, having reflected on one's own personal values, help to orient a client towards awareness of theirs. Secondly, help clients explore current obstacles through the lens of that value-set and develop mindfulness of behaviour that deviated from intentions and the arising consequences. Finally, support behaviour in alignment with the stated values and reflect on the effect of behaviour change in the relief of suffering.

Working with Buddhists and non-Buddhists

I imagine we all have had experiences when working with certain people feels more easeful; perhaps those who hold a similar worldview and values. There have been numerous times this has come up for me in my therapeutic work and where I have had cause to discuss it in supervision – reflecting upon why some clients feel easier to work with, while with others I feel on a different wavelength. With complete transparency, it can make the therapeutic task more straightforward when we think, feel, and communicate through the same worldview. And so, many of my early ventures into a Buddhism-informed practice felt less awkward and clumsy, and more harmonious with clients who identified with following the Buddhist path too. Of course, this is something to watch. Commonality in worldview and difference aren't mutually exclusive. Holding difference is integral in the work of a therapist; complacency and assumptions must be avoided. Equally, I have come to experience the power of the Buddhist teachings in contributing to a psychotherapeutic approach regardless of the client's worldview, presentation, or relationship to spirituality.

I consider my own journey towards a Buddhism-informed psychotherapy as having had four phases. At first, my practice as a Buddhist was one that offered personal support. My meditation practice generally fostered a greater sense of well-being and capacity to be there for others. And, on days of seeing clients, short moments of sitting helped me ground and prepare. In a second stage, my study of *Dharma* was like a backbone of intention – to help with the world's suffering as much as I can. Time, study, and practice brought a deeper sense of coming to know not only my-self, but the nature of 'self' generally. The teachings started to shape my view of human nature: how we come to be, how we come to suffer, and the potential to heal that suffering. To not only become a 'fully functional person' and reduce distress, but to transcend suffering completely. Even though the Buddhist teachings were greatly informing my practice, they remained as a backdrop with no appearance in the room other than my shrine in the corner. A third phase brought a more overt integration of my two paths of practice. As I wrote earlier in this book, there came a time when I could no longer distinguish Helen the Buddhist, Helen the therapist. My being was imbued with the teachings and practices; to leave the *Dharma* outside of the room would have been an artificial separating out, taking effort better placed in bringing presence to clients. The assistance I offered to clients in making meaning of their situations was rooted in the *Dharma*; and the interventions to invite them deeper into the experiencing of their situation was grounded in meditation and awareness of body, speech, and mind. My practice is now in a fourth phase: one in which clients are coming to work with me *because* of my psychological and spiritual integration offering, whether Buddhist or not. With this approach I can offer clients an 'arc' that encompasses the humanistic (becoming fully human) and the transpersonal (exploring the nature of experience beyond the self). This continues to evolve, with therapy clients commencing work with me as spiritual mentor – a shift to be made 'in-awareness', and consideration of aspects such as the renegotiation of boundaries and contract.

I see a Buddhism-informed psychotherapy having much to offer clients from all backgrounds, secular or spiritual, and across faith traditions. What I have found helpful in ensuring its applicability and accessibility is recalling some of the conversations I had with my co-researchers who I interviewed in my MSc research. Those dialogues revealed several aspects that I would like to delve into now.

Holding not imposing a view

In the training of counsellors and psychotherapists, our lecturing team encourages the students to 'hold theories lightly', as none are 'truth'. Like all therapeutic frameworks, the Buddhist *Dharma* offers a lens through which we can view the human condition – the trap is to confuse the lens for reality. There is a danger that having all these wonderful theories leads us to impose what is only a map directly onto our clients; to mistake the theory for the truth leaves no-room for the client's experiencing. The *Dharma* may inform my interventions, but first and foremost, it reminds me to stay 'experience-near'; to stay with the immediacy of a client's experience. Rarely do I find the need to mention Buddhism directly, unless a client is a Buddhist and brings a teaching to the situation or asks specifically how their experience can be understood through the *Dharma*. If the *Dharma* does enter the room, it might be likened to the attitude of 'psychoeducation' – a didactic knowledge transfer between therapist and client. A therapist using Transactional Analysis might offer a description of the three-part ego structure of Parent, Adult, Child to help a client recognise these 'parts of self' co-existing and to help the process of separation (in service of) integration. Likewise, in Cognitive Behavioural Therapy, much can be gained by bringing worksheets and tools to help clients look at how thinking, feeling, physical sensations, and behaviour link. Similarly, explaining how meditation works using both the *Dharma* and neuroscience can bring much benefit to clients in helping them be compassionate-with and understanding-of their experience.

Skilful means

Upaya is a key principle within the *Mahayana* teachings of Buddhism. It describes ways in which wisdom can be tailored to deliver what might be helpful at the right time and in the most effective manner. As therapists, we know the power of being able to meet clients where they are; to find a way to share our sense of a situation in a way that they can be heard. Buddhism has a history of transferability and translatability crossing time, countries, and even continents to convey its message in the local language, and through the imagery and metaphors familiar to the indigenous population; the methods and means of Japanese Zen compared to those found in Tibet, for instance. Speaking with my co-researchers, several therapy-relevant examples came up:

- Cutting-through: Bringing the 'empathic challenge' to clients is often considered a learning edge for trainee and experienced therapists alike. 'Cutting through' is symbolised by the *bodhisattva* Manjushri and his *vajra* sword of discriminating wisdom or insight. The sword cuts through ignorance and the entanglements of conceptual views. It cuts away ego and self-created obstacles. It takes confidence and courage to speak directly to a client's responsibility and contribution to their own distress – how do we use this more directive approach and still wield the sword with compassion, to cut cleanly? To "be clear to be kind" (Lesser, 2021). For the Gestalt-trained practitioner, cutting through helps to support compassionate 'experimentation'. Skilful means is a balancing of wisdom and compassion.
- Languaging: language shapes our perception and therefore our reality (Wittgenstein, 1955). A sensitivity to language is critical when bringing the Buddhist teachings to therapeutic practice, especially when working with non-Buddhist clients who have heard and may misconstrue Buddhist terminology. We have already considered some of this when we looked at *karma* and the case study of "Claire". Clarity of meaning is essential if on hearing a client make a complaint about a friend letting them down, we use the teachings of *karma* to explore choices made and actions taken that contributed to that scenario.
- Middle Way: on meeting the clients who come to our consulting room, we might begin to see how black and white they view the world, splitting situations and others into camps of good and bad, right or wrong. The Western psychological theories such as Gestalt's 'polarities' and Jung's 'shadow' help clients to see the 'both/and' rather than the 'either/or' in any situation. The Buddhist teachings go further.

The Middle Way describes the middle ground between attachment and aversion, between being and non-being, between form and emptiness, between free will and determinism. The more we delve into the middle way the more deeply we come to rest between the play of opposites.

(Kornfield, 2008, p. 376)

Being with this inherent paradox of the universe, clients will come to feel their basic okayness independent of external circumstance. It has proven a useful teaching to help clients find a way of living that is neither 'too tight' nor 'too loose' – and it's astonishing how often this type of energy shows up in working with 'parts of self'.

- Holding relative and absolute truths: Chapter 2 introduced the teachings on absolute and relative truth; the ability to hold both these views on reality simultaneously can be beneficial when sitting with a client and holding their distress. You might remember that the relative truth is conventional reality, and on this level we suffer (because things are never totally satisfying). However, ultimately everything is 'empty' of an inherent, everlasting existence – including the 'self' who suffers! This is the teaching of absolute truth. I see a client's humanity in their suffering; and at the same time, I can appreciate their empty, *buddhanature*. We might also see Buddhism as an absolute lens (the possibility of complete transcendence), and Western psychotherapeutic models as relative means to alleviate suffering.

Discerning between roles of teacher and therapist

One area working in counselling and psychotherapy that has proven interesting ground for me has been one of working with role and power differentials. This has surfaced in my twin role as a teacher and supervisor. Furthermore, before I qualified as a counsellor, I had completed my meditation teacher training and was hosting regular meditation classes. When I qualified, it was a natural step to integrate meditation as one of the offerings in my private practice. Indeed, it felt like the classes could become a useful 'shop window' to my therapeutic services and getting myself known in local networks. I was soon being asked to teach mindfulness to other counsellors looking to integrate the practice into their own self-care programmes; and inevitably I was asked how to integrate meditation into client work. Meditation students began asking me to help them with more therapeutic issues, and at times the nature of our working relationship risked getting blurry. Those early days taught me a lot about holding boundaries and the potential traps of the 'dual relationship'.

It remains somewhat of a dilemma. I am passionate about the power of meditation and how helpful it can be as a practice – I hope this comes across in this book. I also know the benefit that clients gain from meditation (the vertical) alongside relational psychotherapy (the horizontal). However, I think there is an ethics of 'teaching' in the therapeutic space that needs to be brought fully into awareness and deeply reflected upon. From my experience:

- I am not supportive of therapists teaching meditation to clients if they do not have their own regular meditation practice. Furthermore, I believe it is imperative therapists seek good training to become a meditation teacher.

- Similarly, I am not comfortable when I see therapists calling meditation a 'tool', inferring it can be applied for certain 'mental health' conditions, or used 'off the shelf' in times of need. Benefits from practice come from the View, and from a sustained relationship with the practice. I hold the view that meditation is a long game – a discipline one engages with for life, and best not associated as a thing one did in therapy as a 'fix' or part of self-development.

- I am very aware that clients whose character is organised around compliance might ask for meditation instruction to be a 'good client'. As a therapist, I hold great importance of clients being able to explore all the feelings that come up in our relationship, including negative feelings. A compliant client might not be able to disentangle internalised resentment to having to please me from the benefits of meditation. For any client presentation, there is a risk the practice will become associated with the therapist teaching it – negatively or unhelpfully positive.

- On a practical level, how do we manage the dual role of being a meditation teacher and a therapist? Do we charge the same fee for our time? And if a therapy client asks for instruction, how can we take on the role and expertise of a teacher and then, even in the same 50-minute 'hour', avoid the invitation to give advice?

Given I would not want to deny someone's chance to learn the practice, especially if I am not able to refer a client to a teacher that I feel holds the relevant training and view, I have taught meditation to clients. However, I have found a few things helpful to navigate the territory I set out earlier. There is a convention in Buddhism, following the lead of the *Buddha* himself, to only teach if the prospective student asks three times. I don't keep count, but I do try to stay true to the underpinning principle here – that teaching meditation to a client must come from their motivation and not from mine. Furthermore, I may offer the practice if it becomes a natural extension to our work, like bringing Focusing into the work. Whether to teach meditation in the therapy room remains something I take on a case-by-case basis.

Spiritual friendship

The more deeply I go into an offering of psychological and spiritual integration, the more I have considered the role of spiritual friendship, or *kalyanamitra* as it is formulated in Tibetan Buddhism. The spiritual friend is a practitioner who helps a lesser experienced practitioner on the path; someone "who reflects you like a mirror does" (Trungpa Rinpoche, 2001,

p. 171). In my experience with spiritual mentors, there may be some elements of instruction and advice from the more experienced practitioner, but importantly this is an eye-to-eye level, highly meaningful, and personal relationship.

There is much commonality across spiritual mentoring and the therapeutic attitude; and undoubtedly all I have learnt as a therapist underpins my mentoring. Not only do the relational conditions form the bedrock of the *kalyanamitra* role, the humanistic and Buddhistic views share an understanding that the individual has all they need to come through the other side of obstacles and challenges. A mentor is part of the fertile environment that holds and honours the process in a person's natural tendency for growth. Sometimes that environment needs more challenge – 'cutting through' allows a clearing of ground to help sturdier growth. Each therapeutic modality brings nuances, yet we can suggest that both therapeutic and mentoring roles are empowering.

When clients have ended therapy and transitioned into a spiritual mentor relationship, that process has allowed me to highlight key differences between the therapist and *kalyanamitra* roles. One considerable shift is the degree of disclosure. As both a mentor and a mentee, I have come to appreciate the deep sharing of personal processes and experiences between two people. While humanistic therapists don't subscribe to the 'blank screen' of early psychoanalytic practice, disclosures rarely include sharing of personal experiences of the client's presenting issue. In a spiritual friendship though, much of the role is in the knowing that the mentor has been through something of the mentee's path. As a *Vajrayana* practitioner, knowing that both my therapist and my meditation mentor have been through the practices of *Ngondro* (and understand the types of challenges and intensity I may go through) has opened up something quite profound within; being a part of something bigger, taking courage from being in that lineage. Coming to know that being shaken and stirred IS the path, having a role model who embodies the spiritual values on the path is deeply inspiring and containing.

Another aspect that differentiates across roles is an almost indescribable shift in presence. Listening is intrinsic to both therapist and spiritual mentor, yet there is a quality of 'deep listening', a whole-body listening afforded by the presence of both practitioners in the room, that allows the mentor to 'listen someone into their own wisdom'. Relatedly, I sense that this is perhaps how spiritual mentorship shifts beyond therapy; from empathy to compassion; from unconditional positive regard to lovingkindness. Chögyam Trungpa Rinpoche talks about the mentor as speaking the "same neurotic language" (2016, p. 27), who knows and shares the experiences of suffering, and at the same time is accepting of the student's "neurosis as well as their sanity" (2016, p. 22). Part of the containment fulfilled by the spiritual mentor is holding the confidence that the student is already awake and conveying gentle reassurance that everything is workable. Working with my own mentors, I have a sense of their gentle nudge towards my account-ability and authority; that the path is my own and requires 'wise effort' to form the experiential bridge between habitual confusion and underlying wisdom, albeit with a co-pilot at hand. In some ways, we can see the remit of the therapist to help get a client 'back on track' towards wholeness; a spiritual mentor, however, sees the student as already on track, nowhere to go other than be with 'what is'.

Summarising, we might make two distinctions: firstly, we are talking about the nature of boundaries – both therapist and *kalyanamitra* make possible a container for process, but the therapist role feels more like a guardian, holding a boundary firm so that process can 'bump up' against it. Spiritual mentors might place more emphasis on the creative chaos within and less on holding the order around – and as fellow practitioners, they take part in the dance of the mandala. Secondly, a therapist could be considered as helping the client 'to grow up' (in developmental terms), whilst the *kaly-anamitra* helps the student 'to wake up'. This is part of what differentiates the humanistic and transpersonal views of therapy, and in fact would be part of therapeutic work integrating the psychological and spiritual. Perhaps we might even go further in spiritual mentorship – maybe the two practition-ers in the mentoring partnership are 'waking up' together? As I write and reflect on this, author Sheldon Kopp comes to mind: I credit him with a turn that my psychotherapy took back in 2018 when his work invited me to be a fellow-pilgrim to clients. Looking to take on more spiritual mentoring work involves taking that invitation more deeply.

Client case study "Jacob": working with a spiritual emergence

In the case study that follows, the client came to work with me because of my Buddhist background. My hope is to provide a sense of the issues we might encounter specific to clients on a spiritual path; and where arguably our Western training might begin to hit its limits. A Buddhism-informed psychotherapy could find itself in the category of the so-called 'transper-sonal' psychotherapies. I am particularly influenced in this regard by the writings of Carl Jung, John Rowan, and Michael Washburn. A thorough explanation of what makes a therapy transpersonal is beyond the scope of this book, but I will briefly overview the model of Washburn (1995) to give some context behind my work with "Jacob".

Washburn, originally a student of Ken Wilber, founder of the 'integral approach' (Wilber, 2007) offers a complete model of human development from pre-ego, ego, to trans-ego (or we could say pre-personal, personal, to transpersonal). Wilber and Washburn alike suggest a path of development where the human being first separates from the ground, develops an ego-structure, and later in life returns to the ground. For Wilber the ground to which is returned resides at a higher point. For Washburn, travel through the three phases is neither hierarchical nor linear, following instead a spiral where the return is to the original ground, or source. Providing this basic description of an 'arc' of development might help us understand why a spiritual experience can appear and indeed be confused with a fragmentation consistent with psychosis. Washburn's model allows for a process whereby the mental ego laid down and solidified in adulthood must go through a period of undoing the repression of earlier years. In Washburn's words, there is a "regression in the service of transcendence" (1995, p. 171): the ego becomes open to pre-ego consciousness, and this is often crisis territory. To fully integrate and reconnect with the ground of being, repressed material needs to be engaged with.

Washburn's spiral path resonates with my own experience. I have needed to become courageous enough to return to childhood material and embrace the lessons it offers. "Jacob", a practising Buddhist in his late 30s, also needed to go back to reclaim the past in order to move forward. Encouraged to find a therapist by his partner Neil, Jacob had chosen me to work with because the shared connection with the Shambhala teachings. Jacob wanted to address "health anxiety". He often experienced discomfort in meditation particularly in his stomach and was convinced something was wrong with him despite medical examinations revealing nothing. Offered medication for his anxiety by his GP, Jacob preferred to find another way. Our early work explored the nature of the physical sensations and pain. We were able to locate the origins in his childhood – a very critical father and a complicit mother who rather than protect Jacob and his brother Sid could only advise "be careful, your father's having one of his moods". Jacob said he and Sid spent most of their childhood "tiptoeing in the shadows" around the house so as not to upset the peace. Jacob took on the role of "Mum's little helper" holding up the shield protecting both his mother and his brother. This responsibility called for skilful vigilance and scanning; to step up and "take care of everything".

Jacob was a joy to work with, always eager to explore his lived experience and understand what might be going on in accordance with the Shambhala Buddhist teachings that he studied with enthusiasm. I was trained to be cautious of such joy, and in my own scanning and vigilance caught the incidences of arriving slightly late for sessions or cancelling with full payment. Jacob was inspired by the Shambhala teachings on 'basic goodness'; and holding the benign boundary lapses in mind I became curious about a polarity of 'badness'. Bringing these incidences into awareness through this lens, Jacob came to recognise that his boundary pushes were a resentment towards having to pay for my care; a parallel with his mother who demanded protection in return for her love. This released a powerful phase in his therapy. We explored the relationship to his anger; how it resided suppressed in his body, and fundamentally, how he repressed badness as "Rebel Jacob".

'Rebel Jacob' surfaced in the world as a teenager. At first, Jacob channelled this energy into sport, but it soon became alcohol and drugs that he turned to. Living under the same roof as his oppressive father became too much to face directly. One session, Jacob explained how a dope-smoking session got out of control and he nearly died when playing on a canal bridge and falling into the river below. Shaken up, Jacob gave up substance-use and has been 15 years sober. The 12-step programme he attended was run by a Buddhist organisation, and that is how he came to the path. We reflected upon the 'Good Buddhist' Jacob had become and discussed together how 'Rebel Jacob' was still present only quieted. Following this revelation Jacob found our sessions difficult. He felt ashamed of his past life, doubting that 'Rebel Jacob' could co-exist with 'basic goodness' and impatient that this darker side could still be in control. We worked on self-compassion, helping Jacob to open not only to the young "little helper" but also the "teenage rebel". At the time, Jacob was finding it hard to meditate and was losing faith in his path. Having talked to his meditation instructor, Jacob booked on a seven-day retreat hoping to reflect on where he had found himself.

I met Jacob for his weekly session the day after he returned from retreat. As soon as I opened the door to greet him, I felt him to be different, as if he were emitting electricity. I plugged in, eager and curious. We sat down, made eye contact and immediately tears came into Jacob's eyes. I simply sat while he explained his experience in the past fortnight since we had last seen one another. The theme of the retreat had been "who am I?" Whilst there was an emphasis on meditation, Jacob also participated in the deep sharing practice of dyad. One day, Jacob worked with a member of the community he had often struggled with. As the woman shared her experience of the retreat's theme Jacob felt a deep annoyance at this "Good girl". By the end of her 15-minute sharing, Jacob was experiencing many of the symptoms in his stomach and lower back that he had come to know recently in our therapy work as deeply held anger. 'Good girl' was triggering his 'Bad boy', and this threw Jacob out of the calm he had craved. With a broad and soft smile on his face, Jacob went on to explain that it was in that afternoon's sitting that he realised that "who I am" also included the rebel, and that "Rebel Jacob was no different to Good Jacob"; nor was he different to (not-separate from) 'Good Girl' he had just worked with. He had deeply recognised the truth of his nature by going more deeply into his emotional suffering of anger and his aversion to it.

As I write this description of that post-retreat session with Jacob, it is difficult to convey the felt-sense of being in the room with him. His pace was slow, he was incredibly coherent, and something felt 'other worldly' about him, almost ecstatic. I found it very easy to follow him and it was as if every cell in my body understood what he was trying to explain to me. Very little words were needed, nor would words be enough. His presence was emitting the very bliss and joy he was describing. As a therapist, I have had moments of relational depth with clients and yet this was beyond that, 'a no-different to' like communion. It was necessary to apply a conscious effort, from my own awareness, to keep shuttling back and forth – staying with the closeness to Jacob and his experiencing and yet acknowledging my separate self. I felt an interplay of knowing his realisation yet a necessary cautiousness concerning his 'loss of self'. I was holding in mind the recent challenges to his ego-strength when encountering his 'bad', rebellious self and how disturbing this had been to him. Yet, I didn't want to deny his spiritual realisation.

The following week, Jacob was still in touch with his awakening experience and sense of non-separation. However, he had been having trouble integrating back into life. He spoke about how in our session he felt met and understood. "It was important you didn't find me weird", but others in his life found it hard to understand what he had been through and the depth of his realisation. His brother, who had a history of his own mental health challenges, even expressed his concern for Jacob. We spent the session exploring what it means "to be in the world and yet not of it"; to have touched the absolute but live in the relative.

A week later when we met, Jacob described a sense of declining into estrangement: a growing distress involving both a losing touch with what he had glimpsed and losing connection to the world he lived in ordinarily. This included struggling at home with Neil. Having built the frame of relative and absolute, now our dialogue focused on separation and non-separation. Jacob's experience of aloneness brought up previous experiences of loneliness and isolation as a child and young adult. Just like the period of our work before his retreat, Jacob was again experiencing difficult territory but this time his glimpse of awakening was a support. As was a feature of his sensory experience – since returning from the retreat, he had been experiencing tinnitus. Knowing such auditory perceptions can be a sign of emotional distress, I was careful to bracket such an interpretation and allow Jacob to make his own meaning of this 'presence'. Far from distressing, it served as a reminder to "be with" experience 'as it is'.

The coming weeks involved a slow integration of Jacob's experiences. We talked through the "dark night of the soul" (Moore, 2011) that had preceded the awakening experience on retreat; how the retreat gave him a confidence to 'fall back to ground', even if that meant a turbulent re-entry through material that was previously repressed. We worked through his childhood anxiety and loneliness, and the anger held not just towards his father but also towards his mother for not fulfilling her protective role. Key at this time was a trust in Jacob's 'fall' back to source; and I'd like to detail what helped me hold my seat and thus hold Jacob.

Therapeutic interventions

I understand a few key co-created aspects of our work assisted Jacob transmute 'breakdown as breakthrough' (Bollas, 2012). In the five years we had been working together, Jacob had moved through the phases of deconstruction typical of long-term psychotherapy. Being able to review our work in the context of the transpersonal arc gave a place to seat his experience, an explanation, and a meaning. Furthermore, my training in predominantly Western psychological theory had prepared me for meeting psychosis in practice; my personal interests had me study and research concepts such as 'dark night of the soul'. I thus had alternative hypotheses as to what Jacob was going through and trust this was a spiritual emergency that heralded a spiritual emergence (Grof, 1989). Secondly, we found creativity to give Jacob a sense of holding between sessions. Jacob had studied English literature at university and was very open to journaling by way of supporting his process. He ended up writing short poems or drawing when prose couldn't articulate his experiences. Thirdly, having not long returned from a retreat myself – one where I had a deep realisation in practice experience – I was more receptive to Jacob's glimpse into non-duality and could normalise what he was going through. As Cortright (1997) explains, "when the person shifts into seeing what is occurring as positive and helpful rather than bad and sick . . . they know that this is healing and growth . . . to turn toward rather than run" (p. 173). Finally, we discussed ways he could adjust his spiritual practice to integrate what was unfolding. Jacob found the introduction of countryside walks reminded him of the connection to his true nature. Spending more time walking and less time sitting tempered a re-creation of his retreat experience and eased the transition to everyday life. Body work and awareness in movement is considered a less intensive yet integrative way to work with the subtle body and consciousness. Jacob and I discussed this as our 'both/and approach' – his realisation on the absolute level, yet the need to integrate into ongoing life on the relative level.

Challenges and learning in the work

Working with Jacob in this time was both fascinating and testing. Looking back at my work with Jacob, I realise how much of the work was recognising the cusp between the humanistic and the transpersonal, and how I naturally oscillated between the two views. I recognise the fear of dropping Jacob in what many might have viewed as a state of fragmentation. In that first session post-retreat, a hesitation and swaying "is this a psychotic break, or is this a spiritual event?" was touching upon my own 'good girl': fear of getting the differential diagnosis correct was hard to work with in the here-and-now. I remember after the session wondering if I should call my supervisor, yet at the same time worried I might be 'swayed' into quashing the potential in Jacob's experiencing. Gestalt therapy calls for a 'shuttling' back and forth between what is figural and what is ground; and this was also helping me join but not merge with Jacob's reality to evaluate risk. Therapists will know the importance of the 'internal supervisor' that develops with experience: to be both present with the client but also take the meta position observing the relational encounter.

Lukoff (1998) developed a 'spiritual competence' frame for healthcare professionals, and on studying these while working with Jacob I gained confidence. Firstly, Jacob had a spiritual path in place. An event out of the blue and without context might have suggest a great risk. Furthermore, he recognised the experience rather than being IN it. A non-psychotic person clearly acknowledges the extraordinary and unbelievable nature of their experience. Jacob was also able to develop meaning and a shared intersubjectivity where psychotic individuals would have difficulty establishing this. As Laing (1982) noted "both what you say and how I listen contribute to how close or far apart we are" (p. 38). Finally, whilst a challenge, Jacob did retain an everyday sense of functioning.

Working with clients such as Jacob has given me the opportunity to ponder the complete, and transpersonal 'arc' of being a human. I believe it is fair to say the humanistic frame helps a person to become 'fully functional' and 'actualise'; but maybe its emphasis on autonomy and 'self' limits the move to experiences of interconnectedness and non-duality. A complete arc allows therapists and their clients to go to a realm beyond the personal and interpersonal. Subsequent to working with Jacob, I pondered a distinction between curiosity and wonder. Gestalt psychotherapy, in contrast to the interpretive attitude of psychoanalytic and psychodynamic approaches, adopts an attitude of curiosity towards what is unfolding in the here-and-now. The therapist 'notices' a phenomenon in the relational field and facilitates an opportunity for the client to make meaning of the phenomenon. Frank (2020), however, talks of developing 'wonder' – "different from curiosity, which can be intellectual, as in thinking 'about' something". Felt bodily, wonder is arguably more in line with Heidegger's concept of lived experience. We have lost the capacity for wonder; probably since the Greek philosophers proffered curiosity as a more active (and higher) engagement with the world and one that distanced themselves from the mystery intrinsically linked to the religious tradition (Ball, 2013). Essentially, curiosity and wonder might be seen as a philosophy/spiritual polarity. Certainly, as I sat with Jacob that first session post-retreat, it was a "primordial and fundamental moving-feeling link [to Jacob's] subjective world" (Frank, 2020) that motivated my therapeutic enquiry.

A second reflection after this case has been concerning the work of Martin Buber and the 'I-Thou' (1958). For therapists early on in their career, experiencing I-Thou moments with clients indicates progress in their working – to experience this is to have experienced an 'authentic moment of meeting' the client. As I mention earlier, the meeting with Jacob felt beyond experiences of relational depth. Charmé (1977) writing on the I-Thou has helped me consider a second dimension to Buber's work: namely, as well as [wo]man's relationship to fellow-beings, Buber was trying to speak to the relationship held with God or the divine. In both, I-Thou exits the temporal dimension – as if time stopped. In the ordinary understanding of I-Thou, that exit is an ethical move to not treating others like an object. In the extra-ordinary, there is an exit from the spatial dimension that takes us towards an epistemological level – a mystical 'knowing' or a momentous union with the divine or absolute. I wonder how much of my therapy with Jacob was calling me to straddle the humanistic – transpersonal in the shuttling between closeness (and the relationship felt in the between) and non-dual ("Thou" and "I", not different yet not the same).

I hope this chapter has conveyed the therapist's ability to embrace the entire lived experience of what it is to be human will influence the work and its outcomes. The concluding words go to the brilliantly unconventional R.D. Laing. "Attempts to wake before our time are often punished, especially by those who love us most. Because they, bless them, are asleep. They think anyone who wakes up, or who, still asleep realizes that what is taken to be real is a 'dream' is going crazy" (1998, p. 82).

Note

1 Said to originate with Confucius but seen in all the major world wisdom traditions.

References

Ball, P. (2013). *Curiosity: How Science Became Interested in Everything*. Chicago, IL: University of Chicago Press.

Batchelor, S. (2007). *Alone with Others: An Existential Approach to Buddhism*. New York, NY: Grove Atlantic.

Bergin, A.E. (1980). Journal of Consulting and Clinical Psychology. *Psychotherapy and Religious Values*, 48(1), 95–105.

Bollas, C. (2012). *Catch Them Before They Fall: The Psychoanalysis of Breakdown*. London: Taylor & Francis.

Buber, M. (1958). *I and Thou*. Edinburgh: T. & T. Clark.

Charmé, S. (1977). The Two I-Thou Relations in Martin Buber's Philosophy. *The Harvard Theological Review*, 70(1/2), 161–173.

Cortright, B. (1997). *Psychotherapy and Spirit. Theory and Practice in Transpersonal Psychotherapy*. Albany, NY: State University of New York Press.

Frank, R. (2020). Developing Presence Online. *The Humanistic Psychologist*, 48(4), 369.

Grof, S. (1989). *Spiritual Emergency: When Personal Transformation Becomes a Crisis*. London: Tarcher.

Kornfield, J. (2008). *The Wise Heart: Buddhist Psychology for the West*. London: Random House.

Laing, R. (1982). *The Voice of Experience*. London: Allen Lane.

Laing, R. (1998). *The Politics of the Family and Other Essays*. London: Taylor & Francis.

Lesser, E. (2021). *When Women Are The Storytellers, The Human Story Changes*. Retrieved from www.youtube.com/watch?v=sX724z5xtF4.

Lukoff, D. (1998). From Spiritual Emergency to Spiritual Problem. The Transpersonal Roots of the New DSM-IV Category. *Journal of Humanistic Psychology*, 38(2), 21–50.

Moore, T. (2011). *Dark Nights Of The Soul: A Guide to Finding Your Way Through Life's Ordeals*. Boston, MA: Little, Brown Book Group.

Trungpa Rinpoche, C. (2001). *The Lion's Roar: An Introduction to Tantra*. Boston, MA: Shambhala.

Trungpa Rinpoche, C. (2010). *Cutting Through Spiritual Materialism*. Boston, MA: Shambhala.

Trungpa Rinpoche, C. (2016). *Glimpses of the Profound: Four Short Works*. Boulder, CO: Shambhala.

Washburn, M. (1995). *The Ego and the Dynamic Ground. A Transpersonal Theory of Human Development*. Albany, NY: State University of New York Press.

Wittgenstein, L. (1955). *Tractatus Logico Philosophicus* (Vol. 23). London: Routledge & Kegan Paul.

Wilber, K. (2007). *The Integral Vision*. Boston, MA: Shambhala.

Chapter 9

Working with complex presentations

Up until this point in the book, focus of the theoretical ideas and their practical application has been on client presentations that the psychodynamic modality might frame as 'neurotic': the presence of mild symptoms of stress yet a maintained contact with reality. At times, therapists might get an opportunity to work with more extreme suffering and the complex presentations of trauma and personality disturbance. Classical psychoanalytic explanation would offer that the neurotic maintains the ability to see the two levels of relationship with the therapist, the real and the transferential. This can be brought to the attention of the client, and the therapeutic task is to work through the difference between the real and projected. In psychosis, however, this distinction cannot be made – the personality organisation is considerably disturbed, and the individual loses accurate perception, logic, and orientation to time, place, and people.

With evolving psychotherapeutic theory and method, a structural dichotomy doesn't always seem to hold. Take for example the clients who come into therapy who maintain contact with 'reality'. They remain able to live within society yet contend with extreme emotional pain and frequent issues within relationships, work, and with identity. This points to a continuum in between the poles of neurosis and psychosis, with people presenting symptoms somewhere along it. This fluidity is perhaps more palatable for the humanistic therapist, acknowledging that we all have the potential for sanity and madness, and where we might lie on the continuum is an interaction in the factors of personality development – nature, nurture, and fate[1] (Greenberg, 2004). A humanistic therapist will also be keeping in mind any diagnosis is of the pattern NOT the person. These 'personality adaptations' are set down in childhood as protective functions in response to persistent environmental conditions. We saw this in the case of "Penelope" (Chapter 6), where a deficit felt as personal is in fact a deficit in the early holding relationship.

How might Buddhist teachings expand our view of personality adaptations further? In my experience, there are three useful aspects provided by the *Dharma*. Firstly, the Buddhist view of 'non-self' brings even more

DOI: 10.4324/9781003383710-9

fluidity and temporality to the process; secondly, the teachings on *karma* open us to a sobering and compassionate view – that if we, the therapist, had lived through the same causes and conditions, we too could be experiencing the life of our client; and thirdly, having the view of human nature as inherently awake takes us beyond the honouring of protective strategies and seeing them as expressions of 'basic sanity'. I will elaborate on these three notions as we travel further into the territory of complex presentations.

Disturbance to the organisation of self: trauma

Yontef (1993) explains that psychological function in personality adaptations is more disturbed than the neurotic position and yet not as disturbed as the psychotic. Broadly speaking there are three personality adaptations we might encounter in the private practice scenario: Borderline (originally named because of its proximity to the psychotic tipping point), Narcissism, and Schizoid.[2] Using a Gestalt lens, Yontef explains how all three adaptations exhibit a dichotomy of personality functions, and to some degree, a deficit in the ability to integrate polarities into the whole. For the Borderline pattern, there is a splitting into good and bad; in the Narcissistic pattern we see inflation and deflation; and finally in the Schizoid adaptation, there is difficulty in reconciling connection and separation. Adaptations arise from deprivations or distortions in the satisfaction of needs. Sometimes we might see that deficit as neglect, or sometimes it might come as abuse. As we live in an era when people coming to therapy are more societally and culturally savvy, it is not uncommon for clients to offer a description of their 'trauma' – a personal narrative on the particulars of neglect or abuse they experienced and what trace it left behind in the bodymind.

Vignette: emptying the vessel

I wanted to share a personal narrative that has only recently come to light through a powerful combination of insight gained in therapy and the experience in my practice as a student of *Vajrayana* Buddhism. Many aspects of the *Vajrayana* path are esoteric and furthermore protected from being revealed from anyone who has not taken the Refuge, *Bodhisattva* and *Samaya* Vows along the Buddhist path, simply to prevent misinterpretation and confusion as to what the methods are aiming at. I am therefore heedful of conveying my personal experience of entering the *Vajrayana*, especially with the 'preliminary practices' or *Ngondro*. As explained by Buddhist-Jungian Rob Preece, the *Vajrayana* practices resemble much of the path of the alchemists, as drawn upon in the Jungian approach to psychotherapy (Preece, 2011). The practices contained within *Ngondro* prepare the student for the main *Vajrayana* practices to come. There is a quality of 'emptying the vessel' of impurities before engaging in the practices that cultivate our true (or *buddha*) nature. In psychological language this can be understood as the healing *en route* to wholeness.

Ngondro has four components, the first including the physical movement of prostrations. This physicality (with an accompanying visualisation to support the practitioner's remembrance of *buddhanature*) supports emergence of emotional and psychological material which up until that point were out of awareness (or deep in the unconscious if that terminology is preferred). We might think of a motorboat stirring up the seabed, bringing the sand to the surface so it is now seen. I started *Ngondro* in the autumn of 2019, and my first experiences of the practices whilst in solitary retreat brought up quite severe reactions: cycles of shame, depression, despair, anger, and anxiety like I had not experienced before. Some of these emotions felt impersonal, almost as if I was being asked to heal an ancestral lineage trauma as well as my own personal, deeply held psychological wounding. At first this was considerably destabilising. Nonetheless, talking to other *Vajrayana* Buddhists about the intensity of the experiences who normalised this reaction convinced me something powerful was happening in my process towards healing. Over time I became accustomed to cycles of oft times intense, other times rather mundane practice experiences.

One Sunday morning I settled down for *Ngondro*, a session that lasts just over two hours. As I sat in meditation ahead of the main practice, I recognised a growing sense of lethargy. Once into the rhythm of prostrations, I felt a stiffening in my back and neck. I have come to know these as precursors to migraine and a physical expression of grief and loss, and so I slowed my pace a little, a gesture of gentleness towards what was arising. Sure enough, that opening invited to a deep sadness; and after about 30 minutes of prostrating and taking refuge in the example of the *Buddha*, I lay prone, sobbing.

What I have not yet described is an undercurrent to that pre-prostration lethargy; one not unfamiliar to me in meditation; one I first got to taste a year before I started *Ngondro* through the somatic practices of pure awareness (Ray, 2018). These practices put me in contact with what the Tibetan Buddhists refer to as energy winds, the channels in which they travel, and where these channels get blocked and thus stop the flow of the energy winds.[3] During these somatic practices, bringing close attention to the back of my body – what the Tibetan system refers to as the central channel – would bring forth an awareness of nausea. It was at a time I was experiencing a lot of sinus pain and headaches as symptoms of my chronic fatigue. There was something connecting all these somatic sensations that invoked a sense that I was falling from a great height. You can only imagine how disconcerting that was, to be falling at speed yet I was sitting still! I began to contact a life-long, yet until now held back from my awareness, feeling of terror.

Forward in time again to that morning in *Ngondro*, the lethargy and the sense of falling underneath didn't trigger terror. Going deeper into the experiences of intense somatic practice and unpicking this in therapy has given sufficient understanding for me to know my everyday anxiety prevents me from feeling the pain of loss, and the deficit of holding and verification of my existence as a child. What *Ngondro* is enabling, with its very sophisticated view of the nature of mind, is a strengthening of awareness that illuminates the experience (of falling) without an identification or merging with the experience (the terror).

I mention that Buddhism offers a very sophisticated window to the nature of mind: in describing the mind's essence as empty (that is, if we look for it, we cannot find some 'thing'), and its nature as luminous (or cognisant) allows awareness and appearances that arise in awareness to be distinguished. Rupert Spira provides a model of mind and consciousness (2019) which I have drawn in Figure 9.1. Consciousness is like a piece of white paper, a field of aware being with no form. First bring your attention to Circle A, representing the finite, individual mind: the dotted line symbolises its porous form, simply a localising of consciousness. Inside this circle, we draw a second. Again, not solid, this is our waking state mind, and is smaller than the contents of the finite mind (Circle A). When we sleep at night, the inner circle expands, taking in more material of the total finite mind. Similarly, relaxing in meditation the small mind expands so that more content outside of the waking state comes into the light of awareness. The outer circle (in bold) fills almost the entire page – this largest circle represents the total content of mind: this isn't just the individual mind but that also containing 'platonic forms'[4] and archetypal ideas. This circle is a medium of mind that all finite minds share, a store for all those dreams that seem more impersonal and not explainable by events of ordinary life. A final circle, just inside this, would carry culture and other collective content.

How does this description offered by Spira (2019) help us understand not only my experiences described previously but also those with more 'definitive' trauma? Spira explains that trauma exists in the area outside the innermost (waking state mind) and inside the circle outside of that (the total finite mind). Traumatic experience is not evident to us in the waking state, yet it informs the waking state: we may not understand why we act a certain way. This is an area we don't have access to in the waking state; buried in the body, outside of sight. Both dreaming and meditation might lead us to become aware of any scars and residues in the 'back' of our minds. For Spira, trauma is the trace of something that has happened left in the bodymind. The trauma may have happened personally, but as the circular model presented previously conceives, it can also be inherited from family

Consciousness

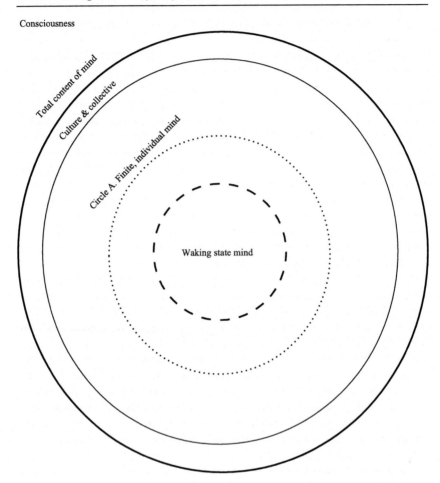

Figure 9.1 A model of consciousness and its localisation into aspects of mind

or culture. We are minds coming from minds. Like water channel imprints on a sandy beach slowly washed away with the tide, "meditation is like the bathing of these etched traumas in the bodymind with the warm water of awareness" (2019).

I would not describe myself as someone who is 'traumatised', but like many fellow human beings who relate to 'neurotic' positioning on the continuum, I have life experiences early on in childhood that have left a trace in the bodymind. The physical movement of the prostrations stirred up bodily held memory, allowing awareness to illuminate the appearance in the mind. The more experienced we are at resting in the awareness and not merging with the appearance, the more able we are to simply bear witness (and heal) rather than react (and perpetuate) the narrative.

Client case studies in complex presentations

There is a dearth of literature exploring complex presentations through a Buddhist lens, the exception being 'Narcissism', as we will come to see. For an aspiring Buddhism-informed practitioner, it is important to consider how such adaptations can come about given the central Buddhist teachings on 'non-self' and *Buddhanature*. Who is the self that is 'adapted'? And if there is no fixed self but instead inherent purity, how can this nature be disturbed?

In this section we will come to see lesser or greater degrees of misattunement (whether deficient environment/relationship; abuse or neglect) are at the root of all psychological/emotional disturbances. Three case studies are provided. In each case we start with a description from the Western psychotherapeutic (which, because of historical development of theory, is psychoanalytic/dynamic). I will then present how humanistic literature has moved that to a more relational understanding before exploring how a Buddhistic view might help inform thinking. After this theoretical base, the client case illustration will cover aspects such as the presenting issue, client history, the aims and interventions, and how the therapeutic work played out in the room. I also include some reflections on the work and its outcome.

Client case study "Simon": working with Narcissistic Personality Adaptation

We start this exploration of more complex presentations in the therapy room with the adaptation of Narcissism; a pervasive pattern of grandiosity, comprising a constant need for admiration, and a lack of empathy (American Psychiatric Association, 2013). The person with Narcissistic Personality Adaptation (NPA) expects others to recognise their superiority. In relationship with them, we might witness theirs as a fantasy world, one where we feel their attempts to exploit and the expectation of our compliance with their view and wishes. Their arrogance blocks any kind of empathy. They are the centre of the world, and those around are simply 'players' in their life. This latter point is important when we consider the flipside of the grandiose presentation, the more fragile type of Narcissism: rather than being 'the best', the people still orientate the world with self at the centre, but this time 'the worst'.

Many writers have pointed to the prevalence of Narcissism in Western society, perhaps understood through shifts in value systems towards individualism. Kohut (2013) explains there is a normal and healthy developmental dependency of the infant on caregivers. A cohesive sense of self-hood is needed ahead of separation; yet if this is not appropriately supported, the infant's development (towards a mature interdependency) is arrested. We might also keep in mind that a healthy narcissism (with a lowercase 'n') is vital for a positive sense of self-regard.

Imagine the recently mobile toddler, delighted at their new-found power. As they encounter the world, appropriate mirroring by the caregiver provides both the fuel for their explorations and the holding when the infant encounters frustration and disappointment. There is a back and forth between adventure and disappointment that slowly allows the toddler to separate intrapsychically. In arrested development, where NPA arises, the caregiver's own needs overshadow those of the infant – mirroring will not be empathic and thus defective. Badness is internalised by the infant and pushed into the shadow, leaving an outward facing grandiosity protecting an empty and fragmented core of being. Those readers familiar with object relations will understand this as a split in their internal representations of themselves and others into two parts; each part contains one extreme view of the self (part-self), and one extreme view of the other (or part-object). In NPA, the maladaptive relations between infant and caregiver have become internalised as two fused, object relations: the grandiose part-self/omnipotent part-object unit; and the empty part-self/aggressive part-object unit.

As humanistic practitioners, we might continue to feel the discomfort of labelling such adaptations, reflected by a less complete literature base. Where there is literature, the empathic understanding towards the initial wounding and the difficult experience for the person with the NPA (as well as anyone that encounters them, including the therapist) is emphasised. Yontef (1993) explains how field dependent NPA is; the self always needing the affirmation and admiration of others (the ongoing fuelling of part-object that is omnipotent). Furthermore, he points to the "twice alienation" (1993, p. 43) experienced in NPA: alienated from others because they are self-centred; alienated from themselves because they are centred on their image rather than their actual experience. Indeed, my experience of working with such clients has been to make contact with the sadness and loneliness of their stories. Greenberg (2016) explains that the primary goal for the NPA individual is to receive praise; and for the therapist, feeling the demand for that in the therapy room can be both irritating and heart-breaking.

As mentioned, there is a general lack of literature on how Buddhist ideas might help the therapist working with complex presentations and the personality adaptations detailed in the DSM-V (American Psychiatric Association, 2013). However, the teachings on 'non-self' (p. 36) have been used to discuss the trappings in ego-inflation. In working with the NPA, we consider the sensitive use of pointing out the fixation on self and opening the client to an experience that is less fixed and more in flow with the field (rather than dependent upon). I will attempt to illustrate the use of this teaching, and that of the Eight Worldly winds, through the description of my work with "Simon".

When Simon walked into my consulting room, I was immediately struck by his presence. His tall and broad-shouldered physique, and his posturing at first left me paralysed: like there was no room for me and I must stay small. As he sat down, Simon explained it was his wife's "see a therapist or I'll leave" ultimatum that brought him to see me. Two things in that first session got me thinking about a narcissistic injury. Firstly, I was being recruited as a "trophy therapist" as a bitter pill to adhere to therapy; and secondly, his insistence that it was his wife's envy of his career that was the real root of their recent relational issues. She had stopped working so that they could start a family. I found Simon charismatic, yet aspects also revealed why his wife and colleagues shunned and criticised him. As I left work after that first session, I reflected upon a bodily inflation-deflation cycle, as if I was changing size with the energetic shifts in our relating, depending upon Simon's need of me as Other.

Simon explained to me his sense of "falling apart". A successful tennis career converted into a high-up position in an internationally known leisure group that relied on his confidence and magnetising persona. Lately, however, the cracks in his relationship with Clara were starting to impact his ability to perform at work. Always "her fault", the increasing frequency of rows meant he was "dropping the ball" at work and "flipping out". He had always considered himself "cool as a cucumber" but knew his anger bursts were inappropriate and untimely. What Simon hadn't realised before our work was how superficial his work relations had always been, his self-centredness clouding any kind of experiencing of others. In fact, I wondered if he ever experienced me. With less reinforcement from Clara and his boss, he was starting to contact the fragility at the very core of his being – his response was to get angry, even rageful that he would be exposed. Again, I wondered if this was coming my way too.

Simon was keen to emphasise he had a "great childhood" with parents who were always supportive of his sporting endeavours. He was always very happy to share with me the stories of his success, the tournaments he won, the opponents he defeated who were now "top professionals you know". I found myself with an invitation to simply "hang out" and become adopted in his adulating audience. An only child, Simon was recruiting me as a sibling – and this 'twinship' transference is not uncommon in NPA (Kohut, 2013). He knew sport was a common bond, and he needed me to be as great a therapist as he was client. He would find any way he could to compliment me, yet I held a deep knowing that once he experienced any kind of misattunement, in the disappointment he would become highly critical. Repeatedly, I felt myself inflate and deflate.

Sure enough, some six weeks into our work, Simon experienced my inability to move a session time inexcusable. He clearly took deep umbrage that I was not only failing to prioritise him over my other clients "who could surely accommodate this one off", but that I had not understood how important this was to him. In his reaction, I could empathise with Clara who would call-out his "toddler temper tantrums". Earlier on in my therapy career during such situations I naively defended my decision, or had given in (sensing it was easier to back down and avoid the wrath). I owe part of my progress to hold this kind of situation (and be better able to tune into the bodily sense of inflation and deflation) to the Buddhist teaching on the 'Eight Worldly winds'. Set out in four couplets – Pleasure and Pain, Gain and Loss, Praise and Blame, and Fame and Disrepute – the teaching offers the invitation to stay grounded when the wind might blow us from one extreme to another. In my relationship with Simon, it was critical I didn't believe his praise of me (and inflate); and in that way I could later see his blame with the same distance and non-attachment (and not deflate).

With deeper roots, I could stay more grounded in response to Simon's anger and retain a faith that this was in fact an opportunity. For our relationship to heal the wounding from a childhood that had prioritised his worldly success yet neglected his emotional needs, I knew I needed a way to affirm his experience and avoid the prodding of his shame-filled fragile core. Yet, I also needed to provide some modulation of his grandiosity through appropriate limit-setting. As with "Penelope" (Chapter 6), I used Masterson's mirroring interpretation: "I can see that my inability to move your session time is deeply disappointing, Simon" (PAIN); "I know it is important for you to feel I understand you and your needs, and the fact I can't might leave you feeling unseen and vulnerable" (SELF); "To protect yourself from being vulnerable, you see fault in my decision and you get angry with me" (DEFENCE). What I have come to appreciate in this three-step approach offered by Masterson is the honouring of the client's 'basic sanity' and the wisdom of the defence. This skilful means prevents wronging the client and brings compassion to the part that creatively adjusted to the wounding situation.

Feeling the "no" in response to his demand risked exposing Simon to the "Four D's": deflation, depletion, depression, and despair (Yontef, 1993). The individual with NPA struggles with any situation of conflict or confrontation that might burst the illusion and fantasy that everything in the field is there to serve their needs. Feeling the "no" allowed a contact with me, and with that, my needs. This interrupted a confluence with the field; i.e., others are no different to me and therefore serve me. Whilst most clients find their way with the learning situation offered by therapy, the shame-oriented NPA with the protective block against self-reflection moves from inflation to deflation quite dramatically. I shared my own inflation-deflation experience of the relationship alongside repeated efforts of Masterson's mirroring to help Simon notice the dynamic of disappointment in his life and to make links between these present life experiences and (until-now denied) disappointments of his upbringing. Slowly, he learnt to dismantle the pedestal on which his parents stood.

Simon's awareness of the repeated dynamic of disappointment brought into the room the Buddhist teachings of the Eight Worldly winds. Simon was able to identify problematic arenas in his life: the experiences where he sought pleasure but ended up 'bored' or unfulfilled; times when he had worked hours on a project in the hope of getting the 'praise' but in its failing, blaming others. We were able to predict scenarios, and in using mindfulness practices, he learned to 'lean in' and contact how that felt in his body. A key lack in NPA is not having learnt to deal with emotional affect. Mindfulness of the body and breath-based meditation is an excellent way to encourage self-soothing. We also practised relational mindfulness, exploring the awareness of his experience within our relationship, flagging up when he was feeling the deflated (small) self. Within the relational support, Simon began to allow his vulnerability without going on attack. As Simon became confident in the practices of mindfulness, he recognised how experience is always shifting. I once asked him if he could notice anything in his experience that is permanent. He went quiet and then exclaimed "no, in fact the more I stay with the flow, the less real I feel". When we talked about this, it seemed to help knowing there was no self to defend.

The realisation that there was no-fixed Simon he could find in his experience was key to Simon's ability to leave therapy after two years. For me, Simon's case is an example of how the insight offered by therapy can be supported and augmented by the awareness developed in meditation. The two offered Simon more flexibility in his self-representation or identity. Simon's journey might be described as a kind of relational differentiation or interpersonal reconciliation. In developing a more realistic positive sense of self, he had less need to treat others as objects (the I-It) and moved toward meeting others in subject-subject relation (the I-Thou). "All real life is meeting" (Buber, 1958, p. 25); and in contacting an Other in their fullest self is the only way we can learn to become our fullest self.

Client case study "Charlotte": working with Borderline Personality Adaptation

In my experience, work with clients who present with Borderline Personality Adaptation (BPA) can be the most challenging yet rewarding. Typically, BPA is a pervasive pattern of instability of interpersonal relationships, self-image, and affects (American Psychiatric Association, 2013). Clients who have adapted to their childhood in this way tend to create a 'storm' in our consulting rooms, and the first challenge in these cases is holding steady. Essentially, BPA is an attempt to avoid real or imagined abandonment. There is a patterning of extremes between idealisation and devaluation of others in their life (including the therapist) along with an unstable sense of their own self. Marked impulsivity can be quite dramatic and may include self-damaging behaviour. Other experiences might include a reactivity of mood, periods of intense anger, and transient paranoia.

BPA is one where a client has failed to separate and individuate fully from the mother or father; leaving it hard to function effectively as an independent adult. Again, it can be useful to look at the object relations model to understand how the client came to adapt in this way. First, there is a splitting into 'good' and 'bad': the 'good' unit includes a good self and a good object; the 'bad' is composed of the bad self and the bad unit. In the good (sometimes labelled 'rewarding') side of the split, the self-representation is of a passive and compliant child linked to the object-representation who is approving of behaviour that keeps the bond tight. Essentially, the child is rewarded for staying loyal with sustained love, feeding, and care. In the bad (or 'withdrawing') side of the split, the object-representation attacks and is angry at any attempt for separation; the self-representation is therefore one of feeling bad, inadequate, and defective. If you spend any amount of time with clients who exhibit such an adaptation, you will come to know their oscillation of affect between feeling good (being fed) and that of rage, hopelessness, and helplessness (feeling empty). Other aspects I have witnessed include moments of panic and guilt associated with how they view their behaviour after an intense reaction within relationship. The earlier in life our clients experience these ruptures, the more marked the adaptation will be.

The humanistic take on this adaptation honours human nature's adaptive capacity. Greenberg (2016) explains that this is "a healthy adaptation to an unhealthy home situation" needed by the infant in order to survive (p. 155). Greenberg describes the affect storm as 'splash', conveying the sense of a child needing to keep their head above water, even if from the outside it seems inefficient and chaotic. Yontef remarks that any perceived "crazy, dangerous, unbelievable" behaviour (1993, p. 457) is entirely appropriate given what they were exposed to as infants. Gestalt relational modelling as movement towards and away from contact provides an excellent fit with exploring the threat the client with BPA feels whether separated or close to the Other, and to generate compassion towards that wounding. If the main objective in NPA is praise, the BPA client seeks love (Greenberg, 2016); and we can think of love as union – of self and Other, and of the split object relations.

Dialectical behavioural therapy (DBT), a mindfulness-based approach developed for BPA, is our entry into why a Buddhism-informed approach might be particularly effective in these types of client cases. In the case presentation of "Charlotte", I hope to illustrate this with reference to specific *Dharma* teachings brought into our work: the six psychological realms (as introduced in Chapter 4); the integration of opposites (form and emptiness); awareness (not just as moment-to-moment monitoring of experience but as an ever-present and healing witness); and relatedly, the Four Immeasurables (as a framework for cultivating love).

Charlotte, a personal trainer in her twenties, arrived at my consulting room seemingly excited and eager to get started. Charlotte explained she had benefitted a lot from previous therapy and was now coming to see me regarding her current relationship issues. My spiritual approach and being LGBT affirmative was important to her. I remember being immediately struck by her enthusiasm and apparent psychological awareness. It was only when we started running through my entry questionnaire that I realised there was much more to this effervescence – on asking if she was on any medication, Charlotte opened her bag and said "I thought you might ask, my psychiatrist suggested I bring this along to give you" while handing a list of current medication including mood stabilisers and anti-psychotics. I was taken aback, and Charlotte saw. "Quite a list, eh?" Charlotte offered. "Sure is!" I replied, "how does it feel to reveal this to me today, our first meeting?" Charlotte paused. "You're my last hope, Doc". There was something incredibly revealing in that moment – not quite a 'splash', but the idealising demand of this tall, athletic woman had certainly left a ripple in our relational field.

Over the coming weeks, Charlotte described what was going on at home. Charlotte lived with her girlfriend of three years, Sarah. The first 18 months had been "fun and full of intimacy", but more recently, Charlotte had become increasingly disturbed by a fear that she was making the wrong life decisions, including whether Sarah was the "right one" to the point of questioning her sexuality. Charlotte went on to describe how one moment she would be raging at Sarah and "wanting out"; and the next, full of guilt and panic that she was pushing Sarah away. She felt incredibly lonely. I asked if she was able to confide in her family and friends and find some support. "Let's just say it's a bit complicated with my Mum and Dad". I suggested we use a genogram to help her unravel some of that complication. Perhaps I was sensing the need for the shared activity as an anchor for our alliance anticipating some turbulent terrain.

Charlotte's mother was diagnosed with postpartum bipolar shortly after Charlotte was born. Recalling her toddler years, Charlotte remembers her mother swinging from depression to mania. "I can't explain how confusing it was for me, one minute she was all love and cuddles, and the next she would be sobbing and screaming". There were also periods where Charlotte's mother would spend days in bed, locked away and not answering the door. I felt a curiosity about her father, and Charlotte explained he was often away on business, but she did wonder if that was conveniently escaping her mother's swings. The genogram revealed the most stable relationship to be with her grandmother; the primary caregiver when Charlotte's mother withdrew or needed to be under psychiatric care. Early on in our work, Charlotte gained a good understanding of how her mother's illness set up a cycle of abandonment and smothering. Charlotte became her mother's way to manage depression and anger; a companion rather than a child that needed love. As Charlotte folded up the A3 sheet of paper with the completed genogram she sighed "I sometimes feel that Sarah treats me like a companion rather than her lover". In that statement the repetition-compulsion is found – finding a partner who elicits similar responses as a way of 'working through'. I sensed a current of something dread-like in my stomach, might I soon be added to the list of people who had failed her?

So far, except for denigration of previous therapists and criticism of Sarah, Charlotte had been presenting her 'good' self in the room. She was a compliant, hardworking client who complimented me and my "wisdom". Intellectually, I knew Charlotte's way of being was indicating aspects of BPA, as was her medication. Paying heed to my gut-sense, I expected and readied myself for the flip side to come. I didn't have to wait too long. Having been away on retreat, Charlotte and I had not seen each other for a few weeks. During our first session back, Charlotte came in reporting how she had walked out on Sarah and had been staying with a friend. A double wounding was the friend didn't seem to understand Charlotte's leaving either. As her story unfolded, her intensity of speech built – and as many therapists will relay, when BPA is present there is a sense of a rapidly building storm in the room. My gut was right, I was now receiving the full brunt of Charlotte's rage "and to cap it all, you weren't here for me". I had gone from being the 'all good nurturing mother' to the 'abandoning mother'. This was no time – nor little point – to remind Charlotte the last time we met just a few weeks ago she had cried while expressing her appreciation for all my support. A feature of working with BPA is the lack of 'object constancy', and Charlotte was unable to hold a memory of our relationship other than the one she was experiencing in her reality now.

In some ways, the rage is not the most challenging aspect of working with the BPA client. Rather, following sessions like this there would be guilt and panic that she was too much for me and she did not deserve my care. Charlotte was terrified of her "craziness" and that her rage might destroy me. I felt the pull deep in my solar plexus, but I had learnt through previous clients that empathy and care can be as triggering as disappointment. A flag to be mindful was in feeling her attempt to pull me back into favour by talking about her work achievements – being a personal trainer, Charlotte sought alliance with me as a "fellow well-being professional". Although this was needing my regard, often it felt edged with competition and a push-back against me. I developed a radar so that any kind of intensity building – negative or positive – was a reminder to hold my seat and ground.

Working with BPA can feel like walking a tightrope. Fears of abandonment lead to clinging and excessive demands for love and support; fears of engulfment lead to emotional or physical distancing, and the therapist gets seen as the needy mother who demands confluence. Week-by-week I was required to remain stable and offer my presence as support during Charlotte's volatility. This stoic position allowed me a vantage point from which I could get familiar with Charlotte's patterns; it also afforded me some protection from the emotional drain that can accompany work of this nature. Charlotte also benefitted from seeing this "anchored" Helen, and she grew curious as to finding her own 'steady state'. Some clients with BPA presentations that I have worked with often share they feel their emotional thermostat is broken. Charlotte preferred a different metaphor, that of a "wonky weathervane". "Sometimes it's an icy wind from the north, other times a hot wind from the South. I wish I could know which direction it's going to hit me and when!" I asked if it would be okay for me to offer when I see it coming; that she could piggy-back off my internal sense until she could recalibrate the weathervane of her childhood. Having gained sufficient confidence that I could track and predict Charlotte's cycles, in the weeks when there was enough stability in the working alliance, we went through some meditation-like exercises with the aim of helping Charlotte to get better at noticing and soothing the emotions and feelings when activated.

About a year into our work, Charlotte was still experiencing moments of "falling through a trapdoor" but she could minimise the scale and the length of time in her emotional storm. We needed to get to this point before Charlotte could take any challenge to her behaviour. Only clarification of her beliefs would help the reclaiming of her projections and to see how she split into 'all good' and 'all bad'. Some of my attempts to do this were too early in the work and resulted in temporary ruptures leaving an imprint that the trap was ready to spring. I stayed mindful. Given how often I found myself 'bracing against the storm' to come, with time I learnt to use recognition of 'bracing' to visit the polarity of 'open' and deliberately place attention there in my experiencing. Typically, my back body would volunteer, and my chest area would follow. Charlotte seemed to sense this opening presence in me, and she was able to meet me in the challenge rather than defend/attack. The trickiest times were those when Charlotte would bring a story from her week about a row with Sarah that took her to go stay with her mother (saviour), who only the previous week had been condemned (demon) for expecting Charlotte to pay for a dinner out. To allow her mother to be BOTH good and bad was the only way to help Charlotte finally break the contract made as a child: 'I will give you the emotional support you need instead of directing that to myself, and in return you will be able to function as a mother to me'. Charlotte once described a time as a nine-year-old when her mother demanded a hug. Even though she felt like screaming inside, she feared to deny would drive her Mum crazy and she would be left an orphan.

I said I would expand upon how the *Dharma* can help with the BPA. Charlotte was able to grasp how she split the world and people into good/bad. It was perhaps harder for her to lean into how that also played out in her experience of 'self'. In our meditation practices together in the therapy room, I invited a noticing of places in her that were still, places that were moving, and how these were appearing simultaneously. Likewise, she looked for places in her body that felt pleasurable, other places that felt unpleasurable. If asked to stay with one of these experiences, Charlotte started to recognise that while they were appearing, they weren't enduring nor made of any substance – or as the Buddhist teachings describe it, there is both form AND emptiness. Her growing confidence in experience during meditation also allowed her to become more aware of how things interconnected – how a thought or belief could lead to a sensation in her body and an emotion could grow. Undoubtedly, it was these practices that allowed her to recognise the dynamics within were also manifesting outside in relationship to others. One day she noticed how an unkind remark to Sarah arose from a belief that she was about to be let down. "And surprise . . . it came true! I got what I deserved, *karma* right?" I didn't point out the slightly oversimplified definition of *karma*! I smiled in acknowledgement that she was grasping interdependence – one thing leads to another, and we plant and receive seeds all the time. This flow also gave Charlotte a foothold on the movement between separation and connection.

Charlotte grew more curious about Buddhism during our work together; and one day she showed me a photo of the Wheel of Life (see p. 56) on her phone. With some 'synchronicity' Charlotte was exposed to this image whilst attending a workshop and had remembered the version hanging on the wall of my practice room. She was ready to receive a key message – that her experience of quickly changing moods was ultimately something that she could choose to keep perpetuating (and go round the wheel again), or she could move her attention away from blaming others and point the finger back towards her own choices. An explanation of the 'jealous god realm' resonated with Charlotte, recognising the paranoia and competitiveness that came up regularly with others. This acted as an opening to talk about how that came up between us in the therapy room. Not surprisingly, as someone who had experienced a long history of disordered eating, Charlotte particularly related to the 'hungry ghost realm' and trying to fill an insatiable need inside. At first, she laughed at the little figures with their big bellies and long necks, but as she connected more viscerally with the life in this realm, she cried and shared the terror of feeling so empty and starved.

The starvation was of love. Having never received a steady and reliable diet of love when she was young, she was confused how to experience it. For a time, she became less confident in her love for Sarah, worrying it was only a physical connection as surrogate for what she really craved. I asked if she would be interested in trying out another type of meditation practice – one that might help her come into a more satisfying connection with others. With her "yes", I introduced her to the practices associated with the 'Four Immeasurables', the attitudes of lovingkindness, compassion, joy, and equanimity. My own experience of practising with these wishes for others is that they also penetrate the relationship towards self. Indeed, many teachers suggest we start the round of wishes to be safe, healthy, happy, and live with ease towards ourselves before moving on to loved ones, strangers, and the difficult people in our life. This was also the case for Charlotte who started to see her own distress not as a failing but as a call for love; a love that she could bring to herself through the gentle witnessing presence of slowing down and turning within.

As I sit and write about my time with Charlotte, I feel a sense of fulfilment – which somehow feels an appropriate word to use in connection to a case study detailing BPA, where abuse and neglect have led to deep malnourishment. If you were to ask Charlotte how therapy helped her, she would probably start with a description of "still feeling the highs and lows but learning to surf the waves". I would add her growing ability to identify with the ocean itself: it was from that depth of experiencing that Charlotte became better at noticing her internal state before it tipped, and she came to trust herself in voicing her moment-by-moment experience too. I was particularly pleased to see this, as it seemed to convert her competitiveness into a wisdom that incorporated vulnerability. In becoming more capable of owning her feelings and voicing them to Sarah, their relational intimacy deepened.

Client case study "Frank": working with trauma and the Schizoid Personality Adaptation

In the final stop of our personality adaptations tour we come to the presentation of Schizoid Personality Adaptation (SPA): the pervasive pattern of detachment from social relationships and a restricted range in the expression of emotions in interpersonal settings (American Psychiatric Association, 2013). What is distinct in SPA is the profound indifference to connection – even with NPA and BPA, the person believes there is a route to communication with others. Such was the breach in the initial holding environment, the SPA client suffers extreme anxiety (often paranoia) with a catalyst to withdraw. Any shocking experience can retrigger a return to the transmarginal state. I have been struck in my work with such clients how centred around 'terror' the personality has become. It is no wonder this presentation has been regarded as an ontological wounding (Madison, 2000).

Let us again turn to object relations theory. The intrapsychic structure comprises two split defensive units. Firstly, we have the master/slave part-unit made up of a maternal part-object that is manipulative and uses the self, and a part-self who is the dependent and provides a function to the object. As we will come to learn through "Frank" in the following case study, the experience is of imprisonment yet at least being safe. Secondly, we have the sadistic/in-exile part-unit. Here the maternal part-object is dangerous, depriving, and abandoning. The associated part-self is alienated, isolated, and self-reliant. In this position, the affect is rage, fear, and aloneness of a cosmic scale.

When I was training to be a psychotherapist, many clients coming to the consultancy where I was completing my clinical placement seemed to carry shades of SPA. However, there was a lack of literature I could turn to in supporting my understanding and work in the room. I have since started to make sense of this paradox; mainly through an understanding of my own relationship with the 'separateness-connection dilemma' and coming to realise this as a "fundamental problem for all human beings" (Madison, 2000, p. 125). Writing this mid-Covid-19 pandemic, I have witnessed many – family, friends as well as clients – negotiate aloneness and altered modes of connection. There can be a transient Schizoid reaction (as many experienced in the pandemic), or a more disturbed and enduring mentality with considerably less 'self' to invest in being-with-others.

I believe the humanistic tradition has much to offer the therapist and client working through SPA. The underpinning of existentialism opens us to the angst that impacts our ability to live in the world-of-others. Furthermore, the phenomenological thrust of the approach reminds us to align with the reality of our client. Greenberg (2016) sees the main aim of the SPA client as 'security', and we must come to appreciate how important maintaining the bubble-like reality is for the client. However, it would be too simplistic to assume that the SPA client is experiencing 'death anxiety'. This runs deeper; as a client once explained to me when I asked about what they are trying to achieve, "I'm trying to get safely to the finish line". It might seem paradoxical that reaching death would bring long-lasting relief, but those with ontological insecurity are not concerned with death because they are not yet convinced of life (Madison, 2000).

To exist, or not to exist, that is the question; and one that I have explored deeply thanks to the views of existentialism. Many of us will have experienced differing magnitudes of feeling empty from time to time. As Welwood (2002) points out, existentialism extends a powerful call for heroism to counter the existential terror as we face the uncertainty and 'void' inherent in life. Yet when Sartre and others wrote about 'no-thingness' they viewed the human being as destined to feel our spaciousness and non-solidity as a deficiency, something to be filled up or nailed down. However, the Buddhist *Dharma* and practice of meditation reframes such emptiness and non-solidity from a terrifying deficiency to a powerful clarity and presence. It is here we meet "Frank", a client who knew the deep despair of cosmic aloneness but through his courage came to see this not as the ultimate condition but rather a process within a larger journey of transformation.

In our first meeting Frank described himself as a person who the outside world would consider as "successful, sorted even". A journalist, he got to travel the world and meet interesting people. Yet this job allowed a "facade" within which a "hidden self" was contained. Frank knew himself to be intelligent but considered himself "a walking head". "My life looks good but living it is a different matter" he told me. "I feel like I am living in a bubble. Life all feels so unreal. And inside I feel empty and lost, living in greyscale". Since getting a promotion, he was now spending more time living at home, "but it doesn't feel like home . . . I don't think I have ever felt 'at home' anywhere". Frank had often found sanctuary in churches when he was young and was pleased to find a therapist who was familiar with meditation. When he reminisced about "sitting quietly", I got the sense it allowed him to leave-rather than experience a being-with-his world.

Life took on some colour when Frank met his girlfriend on a travel piece he was writing in Italy; however, he struggled to allow himself to fall in love with Clarissa. What started as a long-distance relationship was about to change as Clarissa had just found a job in the UK and would be moving to England imminently. He knew he was challenged by the intimacy of an everyday relationship to come. Interestingly, and in a rather telling way, he quickly added. "I'm scared to be here, starting all of this, the quicksand swallowing me up". Over the first few weeks, Frank revealed a childhood history that explained the existence and threat of the quicksand. With alcoholic parents, Frank often felt like a utility, someone who could do the shopping, clean the house, and look after his two younger brothers. Whilst he "didn't really have a relationship with Dad, [as] he was always on the edge of oblivion" due to his drinking, Frank was able to describe his Mum as "intrusive and unreliable". In her sober moments, Frank found his Mum to be "overly attentive" in a way that he felt she was trying to "absolve her sins". Frank and his two brothers were often packed up to spend time with relatives, and while well-meaning, he didn't find any sense of warmth from family or 'home'.

I found myself very fond of Frank from early on in our work. Between our sessions, he would enter my thoughts quite a lot, and I would look forward to our sessions to find out how he was getting on. Although not that much younger than me, Frank felt like a young boy. He would sit in his chair and swing his feet, almost with a sense he was rocking himself for soothing. There was a curious 'both/and, neither/nor' quality for me being with this 'young boy' (I aged him at about six years old). There was a maternal-like pull to look after him, yet an awareness of needing to move quietly and carefully, almost as if not to frighten him. It felt akin to finding a baby animal in the back garden, a strong desire to coax it out from under the bush, to know it is okay; yet what that animal needs to be okay is for us to stand back, not startle it. I also became attuned to Frank's struggle with transitions into and out of our sessions. He would watch me carefully as he entered, and he would leave with a paradoxical hesitant-scurry. He was always incredibly polite and compliant – I could see how he had become so successful even if his social awkwardness was evident. Frank would never be a problem to anyone; yet I felt the "ghost" that he would describe himself as.

I got used to Frank's 'shell-encased-terror' self. I trusted the sense I needed to tread slowly and quietly; metaphorically, and literally (getting up to turn on a table lamp visibly scared him one session). One week, I came to understand what he had meant by 'quicksand' when I had referred to his father. Frank went deathly pale, and a tremor started in his legs. I could see Frank was 'falling' somewhere, and he needed to find solid ground. At first, I felt the 'whoosh' downward too, but I had enough contact with ground to direct him (us, more probably) to visual cues in the room to anchor him back to the present time. After some 15 minutes he was able to explain that it had been him who had found his father dead. "I don't think it was suicide, I think he was so drunk he didn't know what he was doing anymore". Frank was six at the time. There was now an understanding that trauma added to an already complicated childhood development for Frank.

Those of you who have spent some time looking at the literature on trauma will know the importance of helping our clients regulate during dramatic affect. I relied heavily on my meditative awareness to attune and facilitate co-regulation, and I came to know his patterns of connection and disconnection even on a very subtle level. Like the baby animal I described earlier, we need great patience to let such clients come out to meet us rather than us moving toward. I relied heavily on my own awareness to begin with, as Frank's own body was not a trustworthy resource for him. We spent a lot of time building 'scaffolding'[5] so he felt reassured he could navigate and survive the quicksand again. However, reassurance can be a trap with SPA clients, given caregivers have offered and failed to deliver, repeatedly. There can be a desperate wish in the countertransference to offer "it's okay" to the SPA client, but it is clearly NOT okay for them. It is key in this presentation to honour their reality and experiencing – as this is exactly what is missed by the parents in their 'objectification' of the child. With trainees, I often quote Brene Brown "No one reaches out to you for compassion or empathy so you can teach them how to be better. They reach out to us because they believe in our capacity to know our darkness well enough to sit in the dark with them" (2012).

With Frank, the imperative was for me to move my reality alongside, not to replace his. Staying in contact with his experiences helped me appreciate how he was falling – not just when encountering the quicksand, but as he went about his normal life. This awareness of the present-day environment was the first layer of scaffolding to give him ground in the groundlessness; with confidence, he could find himself back there. Frank was then ready to go inward, learning awareness of his internal world and of his micro reactions to relational disconnects between us. I would share when I experienced him move away (eye contact, bodily gestures) and would ask him "what did I do then that you marked with that movement?" We would do Gestalt experiments like changing the chair position and distance, dialogue with eyes closed/open – anything that might help him explore closeness-separation as felt in his experience. He came to know his breath as an anchor when I wasn't present to assist his grounding. In keeping with the paradoxical theory of change, the focus was on awareness of what is, and honouring any resistance to contact as the way he had survived such relational uncertainty.

Frank, like all the clients with SPA I have worked with, was incredibly compliant. With the progress we were making, and belief in the stability of the therapeutic alliance, at one point I became complacent and lost sight of what the compliance hid. I was experiencing issues with room bookings at the clinic and the management of caseload alongside other commitments was getting on top of me. When I met Frank that week, I had asked if I could move his session time. This was the second time I had asked him to move in a month but true to form, he said obligingly "of course". Relieved I had overcome a conundrum, I didn't stay adequately attuned to him for the rest of that session. The following week he came to his session, entering more carefully than he had done of late. I sensed something foreboding in my stomach. He slowly explained how "used" he felt; with a build in anger, he explained how he had only said "yes" to keep me happy. I had often seen Frank deathly pale; I was now experiencing immense colour – his face became alive in a way I had never seen and something quite electric sparked between us. The SPA literature will tell us that this is good news – that a shift from terror to rage comes as the self-re-embodies. It would have been easy for me in avoidance of my own affect to encourage re-grounding, but I knew my role was to continue a consistent validation of his experience and support the anger he needed to feel and communicate.

What followed was a testing time for Frank – both inside and outside of the therapy room. Opening himself to experience and express anger with me allowed an awareness of his burning rage. He deeply felt the push-pull of the rejecting and needy self; so much so that he could no longer maintain his routine of visiting churches to sit, the quiet feeling too much to tolerate. In the room, we turned our attention to practising sitting quietly together. The terror of not existing would become figural in his body affect, along with a knowing that it was holding back intense rage. Thankfully, the scaffolding we had built held him. He had been falling since infanthood, and he was rageful that his parents had not been there to catch him. It was during this phase I shared with him my all-time favourite quote from Tibetan meditation master Chögyam Trungpa "The bad news is you are falling, a million miles an hour, no parachute. The good news, there is no ground". At first Frank learnt to endure the free fall. As we sat together, he would sometimes break the silence to tell me what was going on inside; I would gently remind him to feel his feet on the floor as well as the falling. With time he could sit for longer periods, noticing the coming and going of the sensations, the waves of terror and rage alternating. He gained confidence that there was not a moment he would "crash" to the ground, no moment he would be annihilated.

The work with Frank lasted over three years during which time he learned to trust the connection he had made to his internal world, and with that he became more available to others. I experienced a more authentic presence in which he was visibly slowing down, allowing himself to lean into the moment-by-moment process. No longer a "walking head", he came to be "better at taking in all of me before I speak". Frank shared there wasn't as much dread ahead of meeting with me each week, and this paralleled changes outside the therapy room – still very "shy", he was learning to sense his own needs and make more conscious decisions whether he wanted to be alone or with others. He and Clarissa's relationship strengthened but Frank was able to explain to her that for now, he preferred they still had their own places. Like me, Clarissa understood the need to be patient and let Frank dictate the pace towards contact. In all of this, Frank was also able to bring up the topic of ending therapy, which we worked towards over a couple of months. I supported Frank in finding a community with whom he could share 'sitting quietly', a local Quaker practice group.

As one of my first long-term clients, Frank and I accompanied each other on a huge journey of learning. For me, he epitomised the 'dance of intimacy' that is psychotherapy. Whilst the SPA compromise of 'in-and-out' is bigger in magnitude, movement along the continuum between separation and closeness is something we all need to learn to do more fluidly. Maybe it is for this reason that our own Schizoid development has been proffered to make us better psychotherapists. "In order to empathise with a Schizoid patient, the analyst must have experienced similar disappointment and withdrawal" (Madison, 2000, p. 134). I recognise much of the fascination in my work with Frank was because I related to the 'terror of being'.

As we close the story of Frank, I would like to emphasise two points that I have learned in my work with this type of adaptation. Firstly, to note that in Frank's case there was both trauma and the early arrest in development. This is not to suggest that trauma leads to SPA, nor to say a traumatic event is needed to cause adaptation in this way. There are, however, some commonalities in the approach: the slow 'titration' of gaining awareness; the time to prepare the client to make that journey; the patience of the therapist to stand back and simply offer an outreached hand; and the care needed to lessen the likelihood of re-triggering dramatic affect. A second point is how well-equipped a Buddhism-informed approach is in acknowledging birth as the first trauma we encounter in life (followed by ageing, sickness, and death in the classical *sutra* texts). The 'thrownness' of our entry to this world from the safety of the mother's womb might be all that is needed to seed SPA. In some ways, this helps us understand the huge burden on the parents to be omniscient rather than 'good enough'. We cannot NOT fail one another in relationship; but we can better adapt to 'the fall'.

How working with complex presentations shaped my human being

There is something very humbling sitting across the room with people deep in distress yet able to maintain functioning in their everyday life. As I said in the introduction to this section on complex presentations, we all have the potential for sanity and madness, and it is only thanks to our circumstances that we remain 'sane'. Working with the likes of Frank, Charlotte, and Simon, I have come to realise the moments of my fragility; how close we *all* are to falling into madness. And yet society denies this. It takes human being and makes it a clinical, medical 'condition'; a failing. I am learning not to be embarrassed of my vulnerability; and these clients have been great teachers.

It is a double-edged sword, however. As well as deep compassion for such personality adaptations, the other edge – a learning edge – has been to find my authority faced with power and control. Particularly with BPA and NPA I have had to learn to keep my shape, to trust my experience when boundaries are being pushed and poked. At times I have had a deep knowing that a client is pushing at contact boundary in order that I push back and provide them shape. It is a challenge to find personal power whilst not taking the bait in a power-struggle. This is where, as a newly-qualified counsellor, I particularly appreciated continuing onto a training in psychotherapy and preparing for these more challenging encounters: to have an opportunity to learn the theory as a 'map', to hear from the explorers of that territory and learn and gain confidence from their experiences. To be warned of 'the storm' ahead of its arrival (BPA), to know the 'bubble' is fragile and risks bursting (SPA), to know the invitation to 'hold up the mirror' (NPA). To bring a parallel from my practice as a Tibetan Buddhist, it is as if the lineage of psychotherapists and psychiatrists 'have my back'. The task is then to transform the knowledge into wisdom; to integrate, to assimilate, and throw out what doesn't hold true in my embodied experience. It is a continuing practice, and one that remains at the forefront as I consider what it is to be an 'elder', and transition from 'mother to crone' on the journey of the feminine.

Notes

1 We could insert *karma* here.
2 I have chosen to append 'Personality Adaptation' in preference to the traditional phrasing of these diagnoses. Hence Borderline will be referred to as BPA; Narcissism as NPA; Schizoid as SPA, even if not used in the literature cited.
3 This can sound quite mystical, but the language of nadi (channel), prana (wind), and bindu (essence) is not very different to that of neurons, current, and cells, respectively.
4 Abstract or unchanging concepts such as 'justice', or 'goodness'.
5 Readers familiar with polyvagal theory might link this with learning to reside in ventral vagal (Dana, 2018).

References

American Psychiatric Association. (2013). *Diagnostic and Statistical Manual of Mental Disorders (DSM-5®)*. Washington, DC: American Psychiatric Pub.
Brown, B. (2012). *The Power of Vulnerability. Teachings on Authenticity, Connection and Courage*. Boulder, CO: Sounds True.
Buber, M. (1958). *I and Thou*. Edinburgh: T. & T. Clark.
Dana, D. (2018). *The Polyvagal Theory in Therapy: Engaging the Rhythm of Regulation* (Norton Series on Interpersonal Neurobiology). New York, NY: W.W. Norton & Company.
Greenberg, E. (2004). The Masterson Approach: Defining the Terms. In A. Lieberman & J. Masterson (Eds.), *A Therapist's Guide to the Personality Disorders. The Masterson Approach. A Handbook and Workbook*. Phoenix, AZ: Zeig, Tucker & Theisen.
Greenberg, E. (2016). *Borderline, Narcissistic, and Schizoid Adaptations. The Pursuit of Love, Admiration, and Safety*. New York, NY: Greenbrooke Press.
Kohut, H. (2013). *The Analysis of the Self. A Systematic Approach to the Psychoanalytic Treatment of Narcissistic Personality Disorders*. Chicago, IL: University of Chicago Press.
Madison, G. (2000). Existential, not Pathological: Proposing a Normal Schizoid State. *Journal of the Society for Existential Analysis, 11*(2), 124–138.
Preece, R. (2011). *Preparing for Tantra. Creating the Psychological Ground for Practice*. Boston, MA: Shambhala.
Ray, R. (2018). *The Practice of Pure Awareness: Somatic Meditation for Awakening the Sacred*. Boulder, CO: Shambhala.

Spira, R. (2019). *Trauma is a Trace Left in the Body Mind*. Retrieved from www. youtube.com/watch?v=N7xz2GB89Oc.

Welwood, J. (2002). *Toward a Psychology of Awakening: Buddhism, Psychotherapy, and the Path of Personal and Spiritual Transformation*. Boston, MA: Shambhala.

Yontef, G. (1993). *Awareness, Dialogue & Process: Essays on Gestalt Therapy*. Gouldsboro, ME: Gestalt Journal Press.

Chapter 10

Benefits of an integrated path

Bringing together heaven and earth

My training to become a humanistic therapist prepared me well for the encounters of the consulting room; often, a client struggling to live authentically tangled up in the 'should' introjects. The gap between what is being lived (the 'false self') and that yearned for (the 'true self') generates distress. Moreover, I found affinity with the Gestalt frame's view of 'selfing': not a fixed 'self' to locate at the centre of layers we peel back, but rather a process, always in formation, emerging and updating based on new experiences and moments of meeting others. This evolving self comes to be in distress when it is blocked; the adjustments that once brought safety in early life become solidified into fixed gestalts. Therapy becomes the act of freeing up the fixed and outdated ways of being. This process towards authenticity is ongoing, never ending. For some, the anxiety arising from the unpredictability of this journey is too much to bear, and a choice is made to stay in a fixed identity as a false self rather than proceed.

As I describe earlier in the book, my initial exploration of meditation came from a place of wanting more from my life than 'project identity'. I had started to see that what I did was not who I was. There was a sense that life held a bigger perspective than "me", bigger than my individual 'self'. At the time, this was framed as 'finding the spiritual' in my life. This was my first foray beyond self towards 'spirit', and the realm of the transpersonal. Meditation and Buddhist *Dharma* exposed me to the teachings on non-self. The 'finding myself' journey I thought I had set out on had shifted not only to 'beyond self' but now to disassembly of 'self'. On some level at least, I have come to find stability and comfort within the ultimate direction of my path (although at times it is terrifying for the 'construct' that is Helen to experience its annihilation). However, of late I have come across another complication to this evolution. I have always enjoyed reading across psychotherapeutic modality theories; and even when coming across theories that are difficult to reconcile with my humanistic training (e.g., Freud's structural

DOI: 10.4324/9781003383710-10

model of Ego, Id, Superego and the unconscious), I have found them to expand my understanding and empower my practice as a therapist. This was very much the case when I started to explore the work of Carl Jung. In fact, his work has impacted me to the extent I chose a therapist who is a Jungian. Exploration into Jungian depth psychology has had me encounter terms such as soul, psyche, Self (with the 's' capitalisation), and individuation: foreign language to a humanistic (and indeed Buddhistic) practitioner. Perhaps my relative ease with the Western and Eastern, the psychological and spiritual, the humanistic and psychodynamic, the psychotherapeutic and Buddhism, and the professional and personal, until now, has been thanks to a subtle compartmentalising. And yet, as I come to this stage of the book where I am making a case for an integrated path, reconciliation is being called for.

It was a very specific moment recently that inspired me to adapt this section of the book and spend more time with what could appear to be semantics. As I write this, we are a year into the Covid-19 pandemic. As many of my colleagues in practice will understand, the task of being a psychotherapist has been an onerous one. Working with clients always places a demand and emotional load on the therapist; yet when we too are living through the same experience (albeit with nuances) the load has been incredibly challenging to hold. As well as being in the same river, therapists are working online often for many hours a day. At the end of the day, socialising is also online (or choosing not to but then forgoing much needed connection to friends and family). This has been a challenging time. Personally, I have found the past 12 months exhausting. When I came across depth psychologist Matt Licata's expression of 'soul exhaustion' (Licata, 2017), a place deep in me sighed "yes"! This started a deep contemplation: How can a humanistic psychotherapist and Buddhist have gained so much relief when 'soul' doesn't exist?

A meeting of souls

I could have chosen to leave this experience aside, to continue compartmentalising to not muddy the water of my writing project. However, I always wanted this book to be 'experience-near', and a second experience in the same week confirmed I needed to address 'soul exhaustion' and all the different and seemingly incompatible aspects of the psyche and self. One morning, as I entered the Zoom room, my first client of the day unexpectedly asked, "how are you, Helen?" I was thrown, not so much by the question but the way in which it was asked and my felt response to it. On giving an authentic disclosure, the client and I explored what was passing between us. This client, normally so reticent within intimacy, shared her own exhaustion had been mirrored in me, speaking of the moment of connection as "one from soul-to-soul".

This section is therefore an (regretfully brief) attempt to reconcile some of the terminology a therapist might encounter. How can a humanistic therapist look to bridge the psychological and spiritual whilst ensuring they stay View-compatible and 'experience-near'? Before starting, I urge the reader to hold these ideas very loosely – the idea is to help organise experience archetypally rather than define objective entities.

The ground of psychotherapy

Whether trained in the psychodynamic or the humanistic tradition, we psychotherapists are working in the realm of 'psyche'. As a humanistic practitioner, this is the inter-psychic; for my psychodynamic colleagues, the intrapsychic. Jung described 'psyche' as the totality of all processes of mind, both conscious and unconscious. If psyche is the totality, ego refers to those processes that are conscious. Our sense of personal identity, the ego is the organiser of our thoughts, feelings, and sensations. It is ego that functions as the continuity across our life span, the 'me, my, mine' operation.

Self and self

Across the psychotherapeutic modalities we see numerous meanings and definitions ascribed to the word 'self'. In humanistic psychology, the self is considered the wholeness of the person, and as introduced earlier, one might consider the process of therapy as being one that allows authentic or 'true' expression of this wholeness rather than living as a socially conditioned 'false self'. A couple of aspects of this 'self' from the humanistic position are worth keeping in mind. Firstly, the self as defined in humanistic theory speaks to overturning the Cartesian split; the self is embodied-mind, it is lived experienced. Secondly, self is dynamic, created and found in the boundary of contact with Other (Philippson, 2009). Self is not a 'thing' with a defined essence but rather an experience. Definitions from the psychodynamic literature might also speak to 'self' as a totality, yet there is greater emphasis on the structural than the experiential, a self that encompasses the persona, an ego, and the unconscious.

We can think of Self (capitalised 'S') as the totality of both our being and of our potentiality; thus, it is transcendent, not defined by nor contained within the psyche (psychodynamic) and even beyond the whole self (humanistic). The Self is therefore paradoxically not one's 'self', but rather forms the ground of commonality between the personal self, the world, and the structures of being. In Jungian language, Self is a blueprint from which the personal self emerges. This blueprint or archetype includes the ability to perceive and experience the numinous (felt-sense of divinity or spirituality); it is what drives us to make meaning of our existence and the world around us. Self exists from the beginning of life and is from which the self and ego emerge during separation of the infant from caregiver.[1]

There are two terms in psychotherapy to make mention of here: actualisation and individuation. In the humanistic model, we speak of 'self-actualisation' – which self is this referring to? Maslow (1943) proposed that self-actualisation is the final level of psychological development, or as he states, "what a [wo]man can be, [s]he must be". In this process 'true self' comes forth, its potentialities being individual, highly unique, and varying from person to person. In his later writing, Maslow (1969) refers to self-transcendence, where through peak experiences the individual becomes 'fused' with the world. The latter appears to have much more in common with Jung's notion of individuation[2] – the task to unify the ego with the unconscious (the individual and the collective), becoming what you already are in potentiality, but now more deeply and consciously. From self to Self.

Soul and spirit

To write about soul, one must acknowledge the vastness of collective human experiences across time that have led to a quite complex and multifaceted concept. Soul is the dark and dank depths of human experience (Hillman, 1976). Terms like soul mate, soul music, soul food all evoke the blood and emotion of what it is to be human. When I shared my experience of 'soul exhaustion' with a colleague she concurred "yep, it's like a bad cold that chills to our bones". Soul is the animating force within life, creativity, imagination, relationship; an experience that enriches and broadens our personhood. Contacting soul takes us deeper into self, a turning inward to the depths of our being (Wellings, 2000).

If soul is the valley, spirit is the 'peak' or the high places (Hillman, 1976). Consider the word 'inspiration', a quality of the uplifted. We look to spirit for transcendence. If soul is about ego expansion, spirit is ego dissolution; if soul is the nitty gritty of life, spirit is the vast, the non-personal, the bigger picture (Wellings, 2000). Personally, I am coming to know soul as the moist and warm; spirit as cool and airy. Jung came to describe soul as anima, spirit as animus. Animus – the masculine – loves logic, reason, abstraction, independence. Anima – the feminine – is the basis of playfulness, creativity, receptivity, interdependence. If, as Jung proposed, Self is the outcome of individuation, it necessitates soul-making and spirit animation. In trying to conjure a metaphor, I think back to my time as a sport scientist. We intuitively know that if we want to jump high (say like a basketball player, or a high jumper) we first bend our knees deep – we know to get high we must go low. Biomechanics' principle of 'Ground reaction force' explains how pushing into the ground we can reach higher into the air. Likewise, we need to explore the depths of soul in order to leave the ground through spirit. Additionally, without soul, any experience of spirit might become 'top heavy' (as we will come to explore through the case study of "Jim"). Each requires the other for self to be whole, and for Self to be realised.

From self to non-self?

In Jung's eyes this realisation of Self was the pinnacle of the journey, the result of the love affair between self and the divine. Through this lens, the transpersonal is a noun. Elsewhere, Self is described in the realm of experiencing, an expansion of consciousness beyond the usual ego boundaries and the limitations of time and space (Grof, 1989). Thus, the transpersonal becomes an adjective towards an outcome that is post or supra-personal. If you are still following the nuances, you might see a continuum or spectrum of consciousness (Wilber, 2002).

- An existential level – which is the state of consciousness/awareness that psychologically mature adults possess, and one we come to expand towards wholeness within psychotherapy (self)
- A transpersonal experience – a disidentification with the contents of ego and development of a compassionate 'witness' (Self). You will note that this still contains a subject/object dualism
- A supra-personal or transcendent unitary consciousness – where no separate self-sense remains (non-self)

We visited something similar earlier in the book presented by Rupert Spira (the 'Known, Knower, Knowing', p. 37). Welwood (1977) in his writings from a Buddhist perspective agrees with this spectrum, speaking of the transpersonal as a "transitional phase between totally open, unconditional awareness and a separate self-sense" (p. 164).

From this, we also glean an arc for the healing task: the existential, as covered in the humanistic psychotherapeutic paradigm; the transpersonal, in which a Buddhism-informed psychotherapy can reside; and finally, the transcendent as associated with the teachings and practices of wisdom traditions. One might note that much of the work described in this book brings Buddhist ideas and practices that have helped clients develop the compassionate witnessing of (and disidentification from) their stream of consciousness. Buddhism as a path outside of the therapy room goes further, especially those practices found in Tibetan *Mahamudra* and *Dzogchen* lineages, where the supra-personal or ground of being is described as *rigpa* or pure awareness. Jung spoke of the goal of individuation as ego returning consciously back to the Self; whereas Buddhism understands ultimate realisation (or enlightenment) as immediate presence before it becomes differentiated into form and subject-object duality; i.e., non-self.

Joining heaven and earth

You will remember the three *kleshas* are the three impulses that obscure our pure nature (or immediate presence as just described): pushing away (what is unwanted); grasping (for what is pleasant); and ignorance (of not seeing reality as it is). Welwood (2002) has translated these energies that make up the human condition into pitfalls along our developmental arc. Spiritual bypassing is the avoidance of what is difficult in life by recruiting the spiritual path to transcend what it is to be human and escape (we will explore spiritual bypassing in more detail shortly with the case study of "Jim"). Ego-centric absorption is the opposite trap. It is the fixation on going inward, delving into feelings, archetypes, dreams and essentially turning down a solipsistic dead-end! The third, desensitisation, is one we see so frequently today – we might look at use of social media, consumerism, and other Western addictions; all ways to numb out and avoid the rawness of being fully alive. Welwood, in a turn towards Chinese philosophy, explains that

> because our feet are rooted to the ground, there is no other choice than to be right here, right where we are (Earth). At the same time, our head is oriented toward the open sky above and all around where we can see far off things and the vast context of space (Heaven). Bringing both together is the human, standing with upright head and shoulders and feet rooted in the ground exposes the whole front body and our heart to the world (Human).
>
> (2002, p. 14)

He concludes to not honour any one of these three leads to a distorted, imbalanced life.

Psychotherapy is thus a force that can help our grounding. By coming into form and strengthening the ego, we become embodied on this earth and avoid the trap of living with 'our head in the clouds'. In the context of the transpersonal developmental arc, this is a form of soul-work. Soul-making is a journey of inward and down, a deep experiencing of individual meaning, purpose, aliveness. Spiritual work is a journey of surrender and letting go of form or being 'stuck in the mud'. Even when we are 'fully functioning' (using the language of the humanistic tradition) there is still a sense of holding onto ourselves. We might feel nervousness in encountering space – for example, notice how you experience the gaps of silence. Joining heaven and earth is the position of the incarnate human and an invitation to awaken the heart. In therapeutic dialogue, listening to the client and connecting to the reality of their problems is in the realm of Earth and form; in the realm of Heaven, offering spaciousness and letting go of form allows a spark of creativity.[3] The therapist opens to both at the level of the heart, sitting with the reality of the suffering yet not being overwhelmed in the burden, a quality of tenderness or "the genuine heart of sadness" (Trungpa Rinpoche, 2009, p. 27).

Karma and the eight consciousnesses

When teaching on the phenomenological approach to working with trauma on the MSc psychotherapy, I invite a discussion on the conceptualisation and model of mind. We are 'psyche'-therapists after all – how do we explain the mechanism by which an adverse experience lays down an imprint in the bodymind? How does the experience get recalled with as much, if not more, vividness after the event? I believe it is important to reflect upon this given it will inform the interventions we use as we facilitate a path to healing and integration. One of the critiques levelled at the humanistic tradition of counselling and psychotherapy is its lack of developmental theory (Mahrer, 1978); instead, practitioners must reach over to another modality for ideas and consider how they might dovetail into humanistic practice. Without a theory of development, we can lose a vital window in the overall 'arc' of the human, particularly the mind as it emerges. For myself as a trainee, I found synergy with the writing of Donald Winnicott. More recently, I have come to appreciate the work of two Daniels: Daniel Stern and his Gestalt-compatible ideas on intersubjectivity; and the Daniel we met in Chapter 6 when exploring 'PART' (Siegel, 2010). In "Mind" (2016), Siegel offers a definition of mind that I have found helpful, "An embodied and relational, self-organising emergent process that regulates the flow of energy and information" (2016, p. 37). Perhaps from what I have described so far in this book, you can pick out some keywords in this definition that align with the experience-near approach of Buddhism. However, I wanted to take this a little deeper and present the Buddhist theory of mind – not only to address the importance of understanding how experience gets laid down, stored, and recalled but also then how it can be worked with through the Buddhist lens and interventions.

In the Buddhist *Dharma*, the mind is described as 'eight collections of consciousness', each of which has its distinct characteristics. The first five are well known to us: the five senses each have a consciousness associated with the sense organ or 'gate' through which it perceives (i.e., visual, auditory, olfactory, gustatory, tactile). The sixth is mental consciousness. The five sense consciousnesses are said to be 'thought-free' because they merely perceive their specific object without any kind of conceptualisation. The five sense consciousnesses merely perceive, while it is the mental or sixth consciousness that assimilates the perception – we may say it is the busiest of the consciousnesses! The sixth consciousness involves thoughts. Unlike the five sense consciousnesses, it doesn't have a sense faculty so comes into being immediately after a sense consciousness; i.e., it needs phenomena to become manifest. It is also important when we talk about meditation – as it is the mental consciousness that meditates. All these six consciousnesses apprehend objects: the first five apprehend their respective objects directly, whereas the mental consciousness apprehends these indirectly (and therefore more vaguely) and allows thoughts to arise.

The first six consciousnesses are categorised as 'unstable' as they come to arise and vanish depending on an object to perceive. The final two consciousnesses, however, are said to be 'stable', as they are continuously present and functioning. Before describing the seventh, we will leap down to the eighth, or 'all-base' consciousness, described as such because it is the basis for the whole mind. It is also known as the 'storehouse consciousness' because one role of the eighth consciousness is to capture all the imprints from the activity of the sense consciousnesses and from the mental activity of the sixth. Since the six consciousnesses are unstable, a second role of the eighth consciousness is to allow the re-collecting or re-awakening of the stored imprints so that the mind can experience them afresh. Thrangu Rinpoche offers the analogy of "the all-base consciousness working like a savings bank. Continuously money is paid into the bank and continuously it is taken out again" (2011, p. 37). This is how we might have an experience one day, say an angry encounter, and yet it can appear in the mind the next day. I know from personal experience that this is a savings account with interest – often recollecting the experience is more vivid than the actual event! In this working model of the mind, we also get to appreciate how 'states become traits', as through its capturing and recollecting role (Thrangu Rinpoche, 2011, p. 38), the eighth can be viewed as a kind of filter that influences the sense consciousnesses. Now hang in with me here – an important aspect of the Buddhist view to keep hold of is that appearances are NOT as inherently real as they appear.[4] The humanistic tradition's phenomenological and intersubjective approach goes some way in recognising this. The Buddhist model of mind explains that when an object appears to the sense organs, it is actually experienced at the level of the matching sense consciousness, NOT at the organ itself. Try this experimentally – close your eyes and reach out your hand to touch an object. Where do you register the sensation of touch? If you still think it is the hand, listen out for a sound and ask yourself: are the sound and the sensation of touch experienced in different places? With time, a meditator might come to appreciate that 'objects' arise in the mind, and in that way our actual experience of an object is not 'out there' but rather 'in here' (in mind). Go easy on yourself – this can be mind-blowing, as Thrangu Rinpoche explains "we have a hard time understanding that the sense objects appear as an image of the mind" (2011, p. 36) So, the imprints (or *karma*) from past experience as held in the eighth, rise up and modulate how we experience the sense object in the here-and-now.

Let us retrace our steps to the seventh consciousness, the level for the function of abstract thought and discernment of our inner world. Like all the other consciousnesses, it too has an object – the eighth consciousness. In its subtle, yet continuous thinking activity of turning inward and focusing on the eighth (which is expressing itself through *karma*), the eighth takes the form of self, or "I". The "I" formation itself is not a problem, it is needed for our functioning in the world (e.g., self-regulation). However, when ego activity mistakes the patterning originating in *karmic* seeds for a substantial self, this sets up the sticky clinging to the "I" (as described in the second of the Four Noble Truths). The rigid and inflexible sense of "I" is why the alternate name of the seventh consciousness is the 'afflicted mind' consciousness. The seventh consciousness is the level of mind that creates the sense that our thoughts are our own; and that we look out at the world from inside our bodies. Interested readers might like to look at Robert Wright's book *Why Buddhism is True* (2017), in which he discusses 'the default mode network'. An interacting web connecting brain regions, the 'DMN' appears to explain why our mind wanders when we aren't externally focused out into the world as in meditation. The DMN could be involved in the persistent sense of self, one that creates a thread from past through to future via the present in which we are trying to meditate and encounter a waterfall of what feel to be very personal thoughts, or the perpetuating sense of "Me, My, Mine".

Figure 10.1 depicts this stacked model of the eight consciousnesses; it is compatible with the emergent flow of energy mentioned in Siegel's definition of mind. At this point, you might have some questions around definitions, including: how do we differentiate mind, cognition, and consciousness? In this model, the mind is the all-base or ground consciousness (eighth), cognition is the afflicted mind (seventh), and consciousness refers to the five sense consciousnesses and the mental consciousness. Some Buddhist philosophical schools add a ninth consciousness – seen in the figure as the bottom square: this equates to a primordial ground, or pure awareness without reference point (what we have been referring to as *buddhanature*). Some schools fold this into the eighth in its transformed, 'pristine' state.

Vignette: how meditation transforms mind

It is important to understand that both the seventh and eighth consciousnesses are themselves 'neutral', they are localised spaces holding information and allowing process within – if this were not the case, we would be looking to rid ourselves of them rather than work with their contents. With the seventh consciousness, there is nothing inherently wrong, it is just the space where the obscuring *klesha* arises – the task is to know intimately how it is manifesting in each moment. Connelly (2016) outlines a two-stage process

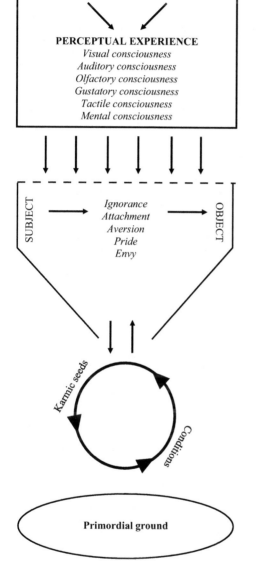

SENSE ORGAN   SENSE OBJECT

PERCEPTUAL EXPERIENCE
Visual consciousness
Auditory consciousness
Olfactory consciousness
Gustatory consciousness
Tactile consciousness
Mental consciousness

SUBJECT

Ignorance
Attachment
Aversion
Pride
Envy

OBJECT

Karmic seeds

Conditions

Primordial ground

Five Sense Consciousnesses
(plus Sixth mental consciousness)

Perceptual experiences arising as
sight, sound, smell, taste, touch,
thought

Seventh Consciousness

Data from six consciousnesses are
filtered through subject-object duality;
sets up rigid/evaluative relationships
to objects and individuals (i.e., five
kleshas)

Eighth Consciousness or Alaya
vijnana

Current experiences are organised
based upon past experiences and then
retained so shaping future experiences
(perpetuating behaviours and
interpretations, i.e., karma)

Figure 10.1 Buddhism's presentation of mind as eight consciousnesses

for working with the seventh consciousness: firstly, softening the afflictive emotions that arise here loosens the hold they take; and then secondly, letting go of the sense of self, itself. This leads to transformation of the afflicted mind *into* the wisdom of equanimity.

The eighth consciousness is a repository for *karmic* seeds planted over past times. Through training of ethics, wisdom, and meditation we can transmute at 'the root'. This model of a layered consciousness might help us understand why sitting in meditation practice allows repressed material to come to the surface. It is said in the ancient texts that this is the reason yogis would sit in full-lotus position – to bind themselves in meditation so they could not act on the *karma* arising and therefore prevent further seeds being planted in the eighth consciousness. The eighth consciousness has been equated to the unconscious by some writers.

Let me try and illustrate how the eight consciousnesses model comes to life in meditation. Let's say I am meditating in 'open awareness': this is a practice without a specific object upon which to bring attention to and rather is allowing awareness to simply notice what appears in the present moment experience. In practice like this, the sixth consciousness relaxes, but is still functioning. As I sit, a sound arises – a dog barking. The vibration hits the sense organ of the ear, and it registers in my auditory consciousness. My mental consciousness labels "dog". As I have no bad past experiences with "dog" (or no *karmic* imprints held in the eighth), the sound arises as 'neutral' and subsides without much ripple. Some minutes later, the sound of a siren appears. This time, the mental consciousness labels this "ambulance" surging into the seventh consciousness because I filter this experience through *karmic* seeds (arising up from the eighth) around 'loss'. The ripple in the seventh is one of 'anxiety' from the perceived threat, and my embodied reaction is to contract and congeal around what "I" will lose. This reaction might initiate a whole cascade of activity in the seventh consciousness, ricocheting into the sixth and a proliferation of thoughts – typically around how I can prevent 'loss'. We can see how a sound without inherent meaning can powerfully ignite the bodymind.

What if I can just hear the siren as a sound (without a label?)

What if I do label "ambulance" but can see the thoughts that arise and can cut them?

What if I open enough of a gap to feel into the embodied response and open to the anxiety?

What if, ultimately, I can rest in all the arising and falling in this experience – and through it, see the nature of mind manifesting in the eight levels?

A powerful analogy offered in the Tibetan Buddhist texts is that of the ocean and waves. One can compare the mind consciousness to waves and the all-base consciousness to the ocean. In the same way that the waves arise from the ocean, the mind consciousness emerges from the all-base. When the waves collapse and smoothen out, the ocean becomes quiet. This corresponds to the relaxed abiding of the mind consciousness within the all-base. Resting in the ocean and not letting the waves disturb the resting enables transformation of the habitually confused mind into wisdom mind in three aspects:

- The ripening of *karma*: coming to know our stories and habitual patterns and rather than being tossed around in the resultant waves, in the light of awareness, *karmic* seeds can be seen, known, and not acted upon.
- Consciousness of self: seeing how the *karmic* patterning causes us to separate experience into self and other, and therefore defend and reify what is "I", project onto other and 'it'.
- Through the imagery of sense objects: being with experience as process in the present moment as it arises through the five senses and mental activity.

Transformation of confusion (or neurosis in Western psychological terms) into wisdom (or complete freedom) is 'waking up'. The ultimate, pristine state of the mind comes when all six senses are still operating, but without projecting the content of perception as being self or other, and without any afflictive emotions arising from its own *karma*. The Buddhist texts, especially the Tibetan schools, emphasise this is not some special, lofty accomplishment, but in fact very mundane or ordinary. In other words, *nirvana* is not a heavenly abode to get to but rather, is right here now, where we are in this body.

The *alaya-vijnana* (the eighth consciousness) is referred to in the *lojong* or mind-training teachings of the *Mahayana* vehicle (I mention these in the opening 'Vignette' of Chapter 6, p. 80). The slogan "rest in the nature of *alaya*, the essence" is the invitation to rest in fundamental openness and enjoy the display of whatever arises without making it a big deal. "You begin to feel that sight, smell, sound, and everything else is just a production of home ground, or headquarters. You recognize them and then come back to headquarters, where those productions begin to manifest. The idea is to return to home-sweet-home" (Trungpa Rinpoche, 2005, p. 31).

Shuttling between insight and experience

As described earlier in this chapter, psychotherapy invites a fuller sense of self by paying attention to the connection with soul and earthly being. The spiritual dimension of a Buddhism-informed therapy offers dissolution of a separate self, opening the connection to the totality found in Self, and ultimately, non-self. How might that look in practice?

To get myself started with this book, I went on a writing retreat. I remember going over teaching material from Buddhist teacher and writer Susan Piver, who commented upon the value of "only teach what you know is true based on YOUR own experience" (2019). That remark became a key organising principle for this book: to distinguish between knowledge and wisdom. Furthermore, it underscored what I know through my work: insight as to what caused us to become the person we are is useful, but ultimately it is in *experiencing* we find healing. Depth psychologist Matt Licata explains the wound must open and be tended to in a new way for the revelation to filter down into our lives (2021). We can't heal a closed wound. I would argue that a Buddhism-informed psychotherapy offers clients the conditions for shuttling between insight and experiencing, both in sessions and between.

The role of the therapist is to facilitate this back and forth: accessing insight through dialogue, and the awareness of how that story is being experienced in the moment. We have already looked in some detail 'How meditation may help the therapeutic journey' (p. 102), and this all applies to the sequences of direct experiencing in the room. Meditation has a stabilising quality to both cognition and soma, thus allowing a familiarity to narrative and experiences whilst under less threat felt in our nervous system. A safe nervous system is open to new possibilities found in empathic, attuned dialogue. There is also a 'therapeutic split' into the 'knower and known' allowing the client to become a compassionate witness to the rapidly changing nature of experience. Witnessing may also allow formerly repressed material out from the shadow and into awareness for processing in therapy. With more material accessible, sets of psychological contents previously separate and unrelated can be connected in the exploratory dialogue and digested. If we conceptualise (as research has) meditation as a temporary and controlled regression, we might see how this develops a sense of basic trust and permits the therapy situation to 'titrate' the re-experiencing and re-configuring of trauma. At first, the client needs prompts, encouragement, and holding of their process. Overtime, a bit like a child growing out of the need for stabilisers on a bike, clients develop the capacity to guide themselves, whether in a therapy session, or in processing material independently between sessions.

I would like to stress the process of shuttling between insight and experience. I have found clients (and meditators in general) tend to conflate the two when they try practices at home between sessions. I therefore find it helpful to explain to clients how we relate to our thinking 'on the cushion'. In the classical meditation instructions for '*shamatha*' (p. 100), we provide the mind with an object to attend to, e.g., the breath. When (not if) the mind strays, we 'touch and go', acknowledging but not entertaining the contents of the thinking. I once had a client ask if it might be useful to have a notepad by their side when meditating so they could note any valuable insight. As Chögyam Trungpa would say "there are no VIP thoughts", all are treated the same. To investigate the content in meditation risks rumination and therefore perpetuating the narrative. Rather than 'why', we bring emphasis to the 'how', shifting interest towards our relationship to the experience. It can be helpful to use a label that describes the type of thinking or feeling, such as 'obsessing', or 'planning', and to then feel into the bodily sensation of how and where that experience resides.

Licata (2021) frames this in the context of layered narratives. We have the layer of our verbal narratives (our thinking, beliefs, stories about our life), our somatic narratives (where the stories have been deeply held, often for years), and finally, our neuroception (how our nervous system reacts to our held stories in the present). Meditative awareness allows us to get below the story (verbal), locate the holding (somatic), and tune into any felt-sense of threat (neuroceptive). Feeling unsafe and being unsafe are not the same thing. Meditation offers a holding environment in which we can KNOW we are safe (probably not many tigers nearby) and yet may PERCEIVE we are in danger. Rather than becoming overwhelmed, the holding environment of meditation helps practice self-regulation (particularly effective in the room with the therapist) offering a degree of refuge. Holding safety and threat simultaneously is what Jung (1939) called the union of opposites in which 'the new third', a transcendent function, emerges. In other words, we begin to rewrite our narrative from the bottom up.

The practices of Buddhism are therefore compatible and reinforcing for therapy, helping a therapist, the client, and the therapeutic process at various stages in the work. However, as we have seen in the case study examples of this book, the power of a Buddhism-informed psychotherapy is not just from the practices. The *Dharma* provides a frame through which clients can understand and scaffold their experience. For example, the Four Noble Truths provide a context to the direct witnessing of suffering in meditation. In recognising the felt-sense of fear in the body, we can link this to a narrative of grasping for certainty in a fluid world.

In summary, through the lens of the Buddhist View, meditation can quiet and focus the mind, facilitating surrender into direct experience and holding of emotions connected to pain and past trauma. Meditation can bring forth new material to the therapeutic process: past narratives and roots of distress can be explored more freely and empathically under the meditative 'light'. This is a reiterative process, one I have found well-described as a spiral; each moment of insight being taken deeper into experience, opened to, and in turn bringing more material into awareness for subsequent understanding.

Client case study "Jim": working with spiritual bypassing

Engaging with spirituality, like any adjunct to our work, requires critical thinking and consideration of a possible shadow. One such aspect is 'spiritual bypassing' (p. 17), a concept coined by psychotherapist John Welwood in the mid-1980s when observing Westerners using Eastern spiritual ideas to sidestep unresolved emotional issues, psychological wounds, and unfinished developmental tasks (1984). 'Bypassing' features a premature transcendence to rise above the raw and messy side of humanness, but "if we really want the light, we cannot afford to flee the heat" (Masters, 2010, p. 3). In spiritual bypassing there is a conceptual, one-sided kind of spirituality where the absolute truths are favoured at the expense of the relative: the impersonal over the personal, transcendence over embodiment, and detachment over feeling. In bypassing, there is hope that investment in spiritual work may deliver from the 'illusion' of psychological suffering (a distortion of the absolute truth teachings). With the demise in organised religion and simultaneous increase in spiritual seeking, we are now more likely to welcome searchers to our therapy rooms. It is important therefore that we understand how spiritual bypassing might come to derail the psychotherapeutic work.

"Jim", a man in his late 50s, exhibited some characteristic traits of spiritual bypassing.[5] Having started out on the path to ameliorate feelings of pain and emptiness, he displayed a disconnected and disembodied relationship to his experience, thereby denying the wisdom contained within. He also carried a subtle superiority and desire to only mix with "spiritual" people. Before detailing the work, some context might prove useful. Firstly, Jim was one of my first private practice clients, and was to become the case study fulfilling the requirement of my psychotherapy training; relatedly, you might recall I was using this training to explore how I might develop a Buddhism-informed style of practice; and finally, someone I held in high regard referred Jim to me. As I sit here now years later with fresh eyes, more experience as a therapist, and a deeper understanding of the Buddhist path, this revisit presents a valuable opportunity for critical thinking and elucidating a working methodology.

When Jim first met with me, he explained he wanted a therapist who understood his spiritual path, and with whom he could reference the *Dharma*. He had been a Buddhist for over ten years, having explored a spiritual life to help him through the distressing estrangement from his twin brother, adding "I started meditating because I hoped it would help me with the pain". Jim explained he was coming to therapy because of the dissatisfaction in his relationship with his partner, Louise, whose depression had worsened since she and Jim moved in together one year ago. In the struggle "to bring Louise to life", Jim felt he was losing himself. Initially, we contracted with the aim to consider the role he was playing in the relationship, and to regain a sense-of-self within it. I was struck by Jim's forward leaning and wide-eyed stare, and his 'jovial' character.

In listening to Jim's descriptions of home life during our initial meetings, figural for me was Jim's preoccupation-with and taking responsibility-for Louise. It struck me that it was Jim coming to therapy while it was Louise who was "struggling with depression and needed help". He conveyed a general inequality of effort towards the relationship, manifesting in mundane arguments about household chores. Jim explained "she's not seeing my efforts, and I'm getting annoyed". Jim's investment in the relationship and effort to find a solution was reminiscent of what the Transactional Analysis modality might call 'try harder' driver behaviour. At the same time, despite his accounts of loneliness and feeling hurt, Jim remained focused and insistent on the need to give Louise space and not "push it". This became a familiar pattern I saw in our dialogue. I would feel great sadness when Jim detailed scenarios such as Louise's coming home from work and going straight to bed day-after-day. Yet when I encouraged Jim to share what it was like to have the door shut on him, Jim would deflect from his actual experience to talk about how he 'should' be. He would often make mention of specific *Dharma* teachings that underlined his "unskilful behaviour" in aggravating the situation, and that he "should be able to work with this difficulty as a practice". Jim was distorting the Buddhist teachings and introjecting them as 'shoulds'. I could hear one part-of-self who was longing for contact and intimacy with Louise, yet another part denying that experience, "I wish I was detached enough. I should be able to meet my own needs". In TA terms, the *Dharma* was being adopted as the language of Jim's Critical Parent.

I came to hold in mind 'spiritual bypassing' because Jim would intellectually acknowledge the global "there is suffering", *but* I held a strong sense he was denying the personal and direct experience of hurt and vulnerability and shortcutting to the pursuit of "being compassionate" to Louise. One week Jim shared "I need to be able to give her more space. I think Louise reckons I want to talk about it all too much . . . after all Helen, I am the one firing the second arrow"; referring to the *Dharma* teachings on 'the two arrows' (see 'Suffering', p. 32). Another example that exemplifies Jim's flight from feeling to the *Dharma* comes from our third session, when on arriving late, I invited him to tell me what he was aware of in that moment. Jim attempted to pinpoint *why* he was anxious. Recognising the intellectual effort in the 'try harder' driver, I offered Jim some scaffolding to go into unfamiliar territory going through the practice of Focusing to bring him into relationship with the felt-sense. Jim found it hard to stay with the sensation of his "heart being too big for the chest" and when I asked what had happened as he took a deep breath, Jim spoke of it helping "control the tension, helping it on its way". I encouraged him to come back to- and be with- the tension, offering it space. With only a brief pause, Jim offered it was "impermanent, like all phenomena", again, directly referencing the *Dharma*.

We might frame Jim's presentation as one where he has learnt to interrupt the contact of experiencing by deflecting away from pain and replacing it with an introject. Where did he form this introjection adaptation originally? In the first session, Jim spoke of his parents with great warmth, giving the impression of an especially close relationship with his mother. However, it felt significant that Jim hadn't revealed to her the estrangement from his twin brother Paul, who had moved to Saudi Arabia on account of that rift. Sometime into this work, I remember my supervisor asking me about Jim's childhood, and it struck me how little I knew, as if his mother was barely present. With the lack of parental guidance, children creatively find other sources of authority to introject as surrogate. When I invited Jim to share his early years, Jim explained in characteristic style, giggling "My mum is very much alive, *bless her*". I wondered about the contradiction of 'being alive but not there' and the relevance of Jim choosing a depressed partner. Jim often commented he was "waiting for Louise to get better", and this was "a practice for patience". Did this point to a repetition-compulsion; a re-living of a situation in which Jim is 'too much' and gets to experience the 'present-yet-absent' other who controls his psyche? We might recall that Jim came to therapy because he felt he was losing himself.

Much of the relational understanding presented here was overshadowed by my focus on Jim's spiritual bypassing. Paradoxically, the common ground of Buddhism we shared was experienced by me as a separator in our relationship and this distracted me from the underlying vulnerability Jim felt in relationship, including ours. There were a few times Jim hinted at this when we explored the relationship he had with Louise. "I'm happy in my own company", and it was only in relationship with others that he felt a "lack". The introspective practices of Buddhism might appeal when to encounter Other exposes relational wounds. My frustration with the '*Dharma* shield' was exacerbated in the middle-phase of the work when Jim's last-minute booking on retreat resulted in only two sessions in a six-week period. I found myself offering an appointment outside of my normal practice hours, yet simultaneously feeling confused why I had done so. Responding to my offer, "I really am very grateful Helen, *bless you*" was a clue of a 'hostile' undercurrent in our relationship. Jim often used this phrase with a passive-aggressive edge when describing situations with both his mother and Louise. I also became increasingly aware of Jim's rebuttal of any empathic observation made and his defence of Louise's behaviour. Reminiscent of the 'yes, but' game (Berne, 1973), Jim would ask for ideas to work with in his meditation practice, only to come back the following week detailing the reasons he did not complete them.

Interventions in the therapy

In supervision, I had expressed my concerns about Jim's use of the *Dharma* to avoid feeling his pain and how my own interest in spiritual working could have me collude. Having noticed Jim's persistent wide-eyed stare, which felt somewhat adulatory, I had come to ponder his 'swallowing-whole' and came to see how Jim's presentation was the type capable of hooking my latent 'expert' within. Excited to be working with "my first Buddhist client", feelings of pride in having received a referral, and Jim's historic introjection patterning were all in the field. Supervision allowed me to name the 'complementary' counter-transference: a function of the client's projections on the therapist to fulfil a role originally played by another significant individual (Racker, 1957). Accepting the invite to be the *Dharma* teacher risked another source of introjection in Jim's life. From here, I moved my focus towards side-stepping this invitation.

However, Jim and I were only to meet four more times, meetings imbued with a growing awareness of my own anger and Jim's oppositionality. Yet I remained unable to bring what I was feeling and observing into the relationship for processing together. At the end of session nine, upon realising he hadn't yet written out his cheque, Jim got up, walked to my desk, and on opening a drawer, helped himself to one of my pens. I was aware of the rush of anger within yet found myself colluding in the laughter whilst clocking my own internal commentary about "being a good Buddhist". After he left, I found it hard to shake the anger, compounded by not being "a good therapist" in failing to speak to it in the moment! Jim was taking up a lot of my psychological space and time in supervision, not unusual when there is a confusing blend of joviality and hostility (Joines & Stewart, 2002). My supervisor and I considered my inability to confront and challenge what was playing out in the relationship, and how it might be for me to 'blurt' rather than expressing overly considered observations (Houston, 2003). This was a call to become more courageous and trusting in the phenomenological reporting method.

Outcomes of the therapy

Reflecting on this case, it is hard to articulate 'outcomes' since, from my perspective at least, there was much 'unfinished business'. Prior to a scheduled tenth session, I received an email from Jim confirming our next two appointments and explaining that he wanted to bring therapy to an end. Jim felt he was coping better at home, and he wished to prioritise "time with people who understand me and take me higher" in a *Dharma* practice group to be held on the day we normally met. I was struck by the parallels between the relationship Jim had with me and the one with Louise – a flight into health achieved through increased self-sufficiency rather than interdependence (Welwood, 1984). He and Louise had become housemates rather than being in intimacy. Jim explained "Louise needs to get well, and she can't do that in relationship with me . . . so we are going to review things in six months". Jim was still finding it hard to challenge and ask for his own needs to be met because of the risk of losing Louise altogether. Jim was ending with me rather than ending with Louise.

Two days later, I received another email explaining he would miss our next session to visit his mother who had taken ill. In our final session, Jim arrived 25 minutes late. Seeming fragile and emotional, he explained away my attempts to explore his current experiencing with descriptions of his hectic week of travelling to and from his mother. I found myself at a 'choice point': what would be the best for Jim in the remaining 20 minutes? It felt incongruent to offer a round-up of our work simply to allow the client to leave 'on good terms'. So, invoking the Gestalt spirit of 'blurting', I shared my opinion that to leave therapy now was to leave with work not done. Jim started to interrupt with praise: "this has been such a useful space, and you are obviously very good at what you do . . . you've had to put up with my ramblings, *bless you*". Trusting that I had spotted a marker of Jim's underlying aggression, I explained I didn't see the therapist as a passive listener, and I had felt kept out. He interrupted again, this time more abruptly, "well, that is *your* reaction". Not being able to bear my different stance on our relationship, the hostility that broke through added energy to our work we had not attained previously.

J: I enjoy being separate, definitely.

H: It has been frustrating for me. I wish we had met as Helen and Jim, not two Buddhists, as I think the Dharma has kept us apart.

J: Well, come on in!

H: Is that a safe invitation to make now Jim, knowing you're ending therapy?

J: I can't be doing things five days a week. I'm sure there would always be more work to do Helen, and I'm sure I would be fascinated.

H: What is it like to hear you've not let me in?

J: Part of me says "Blimey, do I do that?", but another part of me knows "I do that". Even in the sangha I sit on the sidelines, I struggle with interconnectedness. I've always spent time on my own. Even as a kid I'd ride off on my bike, for miles, to get away from everything.

In that last five minutes together, despite feelings of discomfort in the edginess, I felt more connected to Jim than I had ever before. The aliveness was in sharp contrast to how he had been 'killing the therapy' with a series of patterns: the patronising praise, lateness, and consistent 'aboutism'. Whilst the predicted 'unfinished business' did manifest, my blurting at least pushed us into the relational field. When he left the room for the last time, I felt very sad, left with the image of Jim riding away, alone.

Discovering my learning edge

As with any therapeutic relationship where the client and therapist share common ground, one could easily imagine the risk of colluding in the commonality rather than leaning into the healing opportunity found in difference. In the case of Jim, such was my caution in this maiden voyage integrating Buddhist psychology within Gestalt working in NOT colluding, I polarised to judging Jim's *Dharma* defence, thus setting up oppositionality. Any assessment of a client's being can have us objectify. My locating the problem in Jim just as Jim was locating the problem in his partner is an obvious parallel. The 'I-it' attitude is not conducive to the relational conditions we know to be necessary.

Getting caught up in the content means we lose clarity as to our embodied experiencing of being in relationship with the client. I was able to recognise the complementary counter-transference that 'hooked' the teacher in me, and by naming it for myself I was able to side-step invitations from Jim to play that game. However, in not feeding this information back into the dyad and working at process level, we lost the opportunity to work through his contact modifications of introjection and projection. Readers with knowledge of Gestalt therapy will know the power of interventions for externalizing introjection, including 'empty chair' dialogues (Mann, 2010) and 'internalised-other' interviewing (Tomm, 1999). Through such experiments, Jim would have had the opportunity to explore this as a process learnt early in life, and now being recreated with the *Dharma* as the measuring stick feeding his 'try harder' attempts to cover over the felt-sense of not being good enough. Furthermore, Jim's 'jovial' manner and praise kept another dynamic out of my awareness: that of 'concordant' counter-transference (Racker, 1957). The playful, childlike appearance hid his hostility and held my awareness of frustration at bay, even though it was a key characteristic in my relationship with him. Not deciphering whether the emotion was my own or a projection from Jim blocked an appropriate empathy to his situation and his deeply held vulnerability. In short, I failed to put the transference back where it belonged – the basis for second-order change (Bott & Howard, 2012).

Working with Puer

Coming to explore and appreciate Jungian ideas as a bridge between the humanistic to the transpersonal, one archetypal paradigm I have considered with Jim's case is that of the 'puer aeternus': the child-god who remains an adolescent in their emotional life. The spirit of puer is uplifting, soaring into the realms of divine inspiration and optimism, and it carries a desire to transcend the mundanity of worldly life (Preece, 2010). In its extreme, we might see a Peter Pan. Seeking such shelter from the challenges of the real world 'out there' often comes from incomplete development or early trauma, both of which may handicap the capacity to cope with the normal existential anxiety of being an adult human. Jim and I didn't create the relational field to explore much of his childhood. I can only hypothesise Jim never found the 'heroic surge' needed to transit from 'child of fantasy' to 'reality-orientated adult'. In Jim's case, dependency was placed on the nurturing and containing environment of the Buddhist *Dharma*.

Much like other dichotomies explored in this book, visionary inspiration of the puer finds its opposite in the earthy pragmatism of the 'senex'. Puer/senex do not easily live alongside each other and yet to develop they need each other. When puer spirit and vision is out of relationship to the grounding pragmatic influence of senex it can lead to spiritual illusion, an idealism that is an avoidance of the necessities of incarnating in normal life. Jim's flight into the *Dharma* may seem like a form of renunciation (or taking Refuge in the Buddhist path) but it probably represented a disembodied flight away from the pain of daily life. Spirituality lived as ungrounded, 'heady' and idealistic can lead to a kind of unreal, inflated belief in being special and earthly demands must be transcended – I certainly felt something of this in Jim's prioritisation of spiritual community over continuing psychotherapy.

The puer disposition might also help us understand Jim's pattern of introjection. Where senex is not consciously balanced it may play out in a more shadowy way, becoming morally rigid, dogmatic, judgemental, and authoritarian. The introjection of *Dharma* as a 'should' was apparent, but there was also a childlike oppositionality confused for autonomy (Bott & Howard, 2012). Was this at the root of Jim's inability to stay for longer-term therapy, a possible defending against vulnerability out of fear of intimacy? Seeing Jim's case through the frame of puer/senex archetypal energies might point to a path of integration: the heights of spirituality combined with a "full blooded investigation of our core wounds" (Masters, 2010, p. 4). One way to get into the messiness of soul is to become more childlike, and as invited by the interventions of Transactional Analysis, entering my own Child ego-state, through humour and play, could have met Jim in his joviality. A move alongside being the very opposite of acting out the transferential invitation to be a teacher from a Critical Parent ego-state. Such an approach helps clients access their Child ego-state and experience the same intensity of thought, feeling, and behaviour that set up the scripts in the first place. This exemplifies a balancing between the puer energy of play with the therapeutic container of senex.

How this work shaped my human being

This case study, seen through the frame of an integrated practice, illustrates the importance of a balanced and grounded approach to spiritual and psychological work; how we need to attend to all aspects of the developmental arc, its full scope (as accessed through the spiritual/transpersonal), without shortcut (grounded in the ordinary and mundane). Professionally, I learnt a lesson in how the spiritual dimension, the spiritual bypassing content, presents a distractor from the process playing out in the relational field. The regret that I was unable to sufficiently attend to the here-and-now of our relationship serves as a reminder that only when a working alliance is established can meta-communication about the system begin. Personally, I learnt a lesson of equal measure through this work: to know the spiritual bypasser in me. I've come to face this dimension along my own path, to the extent that I have wondered if spiritual bypassing isn't only natural but necessary. Like Jim, I came to meditation to help me through my pain of stress. More recently during the Covid-19 pandemic, it can play out as the temptation to withdraw from the heat of life to focus on *Ngondro* practice and need of a conscious will instead to open to my vulnerability. Each time I spot my attempts to avoid the messiness that begets liberation I benefit in seeing the true nature of spiritual work. As explained by Robert Augustus Masters "The spiritual bypasser in us needs not censure nor shaming but rather to be caringly included in our awareness . . . to name it so that we might begin relating TO it rather than FROM it" (2010, p. 6).

Notes

1 The reader might find it interesting to go back to Chapter 9 and consider this description alongside the relationship between different aspects of mind portrayed in Figure 10.1.
2 I mentioned in the opening of this book how we might differentiate Roger's actualisation and self-actualisation (i.e., necessitating involvement of self in processes of integration and symbolisation).
3 Gestalt therapists might make a link to the notions of the fertile void and creative indifference.
4 Neuroscientists are catching up with Buddhist psychology through their constructs of 'predictive coding' and 'controlled hallucinations' (Seth, 2021).
5 For an interesting phenomenological exploration of bypassing, see the work of Picciotto *et al.* (2018).

References

Berne, E. (1973). *Games People Play: The Psychology of Human Relationships.* London: Penguin Books Limited.
Bott, D., & Howard, P. (2012). *The Therapeutic Encounter: A Cross-modality Approach.* London: Sage.

Connelly, B. (2016). *Inside Vasubandhu's Yogacara: A Practitioner's Guide*. Somerville, MA: Wisdom Publications.

Grof, S. (1989). *Spiritual Emergency: When Personal Transformation Becomes a Crisis*. New York, NY: Tarcher.

Hillman, J. (1976). Peaks and Vales. The Soul/Spirit Distinction as Basis for the Difference Between Psychotherapy and Spiritual Discipline. In J. Needleman & D. Lewis (Eds.), *On the Way to Self Knowledge* (pp. 114–141). New York: Alfred A. Knopf.

Houston, G. (2003). *Brief Gestalt Therapy*. London: Sage.

Joines, V., & Stewart, I. (2002). *Personality Adaptations: A New Guide to Human Understanding in Psychotherapy and Counselling*. Nottingham: Lifespace.

Jung, C. (1939). *Conscious, Unconscious, and Individuation* (Vol. Collected Works 1). Princeton, NJ: Princeton University Press.

Licata, M. (2017). *The Path Is Everywhere: Uncovering the Jewels Hidden within You*. Boulder, CO: Wandering Yogi Press.

Licata, M. (2021). *Resting Your Nervous System*. Retrieved from https://mattlicat-aphd.com/resting-your-nervous-system-welcome/.

Mahrer, A. (1978). *Experiencing: A Humanistic Theory of Psychology and Psychiatry*. New York, NY: Brunner/Mazel.

Mann, D. (2010). *Gestalt Therapy: 100 Key Points and Techniques*. London: Taylor & Francis.

Maslow, A. (1969). The Farther Reaches of Human Nature. *Journal of Transpersonal Psychology*, *1*(1), 1–9.

Maslow, A.H. (1943). A Theory of Human Motivation. *Psychological Review*, *50*(4), 370.

Masters, R. (2010). *Spiritual Bypassing: When Spirituality Disconnects Us from What Really Matters*. Berkeley, CA: North Atlantic Books.

Philippson, P. (2009). *The Emergent Self. An Existential-gestalt Approach*. London: Karnac.

Picciotto, G., Fox, J., & Neto, F. (2018). A Phenomenology of Spiritual Bypass: Causes, Consequences, and Implications. *Journal of Spirituality in Mental Health*, *20*(4), 333–354.

Piver, S. (2019). *Why We Need the Feminine*. Retrieved from www.thewisewoman summit.com/.

Preece, R. (2010). *The Wisdom of Imperfection: The Challenge of Individuation in Buddhist Life*. Boston, MA: Shambhala.

Racker, H. (1957). The Meaning and Uses of Countertransference. *The Psychoanalytic Quarterly*, *26*, 303–357.

Seth, A. (2021). *Being You: A New Science of Consciousness*. London: Faber and Faber.

Siegel, D.J. (2010). *The Mindful Therapist. A Clinician's Guide to Mindsight and Neural Integration*. New York, NY: W.W. Norton & Company.

Siegel, D.J. (2016). *Mind: A Journey to the Heart of Being Human*. New York, NY: W.W. Norton & Company.

Thrangu Rinpoche, K. (2011). *Everyday Consciousness and Primordial Awareness*. Boston, MA: Shambhala Publications.

Tomm, K. (1999). Co — Constructing Responsibility. In S. McNamee & K. Gergen (Eds.), *Relational Responsibility: Resources for Sustainable Dialogue*. Thousand Oaks, CA: Sage.

Trungpa Rinpoche, C. (2005). *Training the Mind & Cultivating Loving-kindness*. Boston, MA: Shambhala.

Trungpa Rinpoche, C. (2009). *Shambhala: The Sacred Path of the Warrior*. Boston, MA: Shambhala.

Wellings, N. (2000). *Transpersonal Psychotherapy*. London: Sage.

Welwood, J. (1977). Meditation and the Unconscious: A New Perspective. *Journal of Transpersonal Psychology, 9*(1), 1–26.

Welwood, J. (1984). Principles of Inner Work. *Journal of Transpersonal Psychology, 16*(1), 63–73.

Welwood, J. (2002). *Toward a Psychology of Awakening: Buddhism, Psychotherapy, and the Path of Personal and Spiritual Transformation*. Boston, MA: Shambhala.

Wilber, K. (2002). *The Spectrum of Consciousness*. New Delhi: Motilal Banarsidass Publ.

Wright, R. (2017). *Why Buddhism is True: The Science and Philosophy of Meditation and Enlightenment*. New York, NY: Simon and Schuster.

Chapter 11

Ground, path, fruition

The beginning of this chapter transitions into the ending of this book. Buddhism invites attention to such moments of transition, the *bardos* of birth, death, rebirth. The therapist and their client too lean into each beginning and ending as opportunities to inform their relational journey. Thus, my intention with the final chapter is to speak to the various transitions and cycles contained within the whole journey in becoming a Buddhism-informed practitioner. This chapter aims to provide both an overarching view of the aspects contained in the book and to give a sense of how I have travelled this arc. The chapter is also informed by the work I currently do educating trainees in counselling and psychotherapy as a witness of their unfolding.

As you delve into the literature on Buddhism and Western psychology, you may come across authors using the structure of 'threefold logic': ground, path, and fruition. Expressing this Tibetan Buddhist method in Western scientific language, threefold logic parallels the theoretical considerations, methodological considerations, and goals and implications (Watson, 1998). Ground is where we find ourselves today, fruition is where we want to get to, and path is what we must do to get from here to there. Another presentation you might see is view, meditation, and action.

Presented as ground, path, and fruition is the 'conditional presentation', based upon the situation we find ourselves and the conditions inherited from previous situations. To take a farming analogy: there is the state of the soil, the work the farmer must do to make the soil fertile, and finally the production of the food. In the context of the *Dharma*, the ground is the experience of suffering, the path is meditation, and the fruition is the stability of mind that allows the confusion that causes suffering to be seen. The Tibetan schools of Buddhism tend to favour a more 'unconditional' presentation, one less focused on our relative experience of life and expressing how things are based on the absolute nature of reality. In this way, ground becomes our inherent *buddhanature* that is merely obscured; the path of meditation removes the obscuration to that nature; and fruition is the revelation of

DOI: 10.4324/9781003383710-11

what already is, leading to its fullest expression. The benefit of this approach is that it grounds in immediate experience yet encourages a lifting of the gaze as to the ultimate destination. The threefold perspective helps us to remember when we view something like a work of art or a human body, we are viewing a process of appearance rather than an independent, fixed form (Trungpa Rinpoche, 2008b). We might link this to the notion of 'selfing' or 'presencing'. Like an M.C. Escher painting, this is on-going: any fruition feeds forward into the next ground.

As therapists, we sit with clients trusting their being as already whole with inherent wisdom; the work is removing the obstacles to this 'basic sanity', coming to truly know who they are beneath the patterns. This is a reiterative process as anyone who has been on the journey of therapeutic training will know – it is as if, layer by layer, we deconstruct who we thought we were to reveal another version beneath. Cycles of dying, becoming, being. It is my hope that by telling my own story, key points as to how we go with that deconstruction can be offered for the benefit of others wishing to develop their own path.

Ground: setting out on the journey

As I set about writing my own experience from aspirant, to becoming, and now being a therapist and educator of trainees, I think back over a decade and reconnect with the excitement. It was a time at which I had made the decision to leap – to give up my successful career as a sport and exercise scientist and retrain. At the time if felt like moving from body to mind (although I now know that to not be the case); 'mind' was my muse. In the same year I was to start my counselling training, I was also flying back and forth to New York City to complete my training as a meditation teacher. Being the year of the London Olympics seemed to amplify my experience somehow. I remember one evening sitting in a Manhattan bar with my new NYC friends watching Olympic basketball. I turned to my instructor on that programme, Ethan, and exclaimed "Do you know how surreal this is, watching my old realm back home, here across the Atlantic in my new world?" Thankfully, Ethan held a deep appreciation for Western psychology in his teaching of Buddhist meditation, and he encouraged me to keep in mind how I might one day fold the Buddhist and Western psychotherapeutic paths together. For the time being though, my main psychotherapeutic inspiration was humanistic – and I remember delighting in my summer reading pre-course. Carl Rogers' *On becoming a person* (1967) stimulated my mind and warmed my heart. Even now, I can feel that inspiration and how right it felt to be taking that leap.

In the field was both the relief of leaving a life that no longer stimulated me, and the excitement of making changes and what that might bring.

Furthermore, there was my experience as a coach to athletes – I came to know how deeply people suffer, and how many of the obstacles are self-generated. At the time, I saw the suffering in others and wanted to 'help'. What I have come to know is how my own childhood 'trained' me to be the helper, a common theme for those entering the helping professions – the continuation in adult life of a special responsibility for the emotional climate as learnt in the family of origin (Bott & Howard, 2012). As a 'wounded healer', the desire to help others was also an unconscious attempt to alleviate my own experience of suffering. At some point in our training, however, we come to see it is NOT about 'helping'. In fact, helping gets in the way of healing. This took some time for me to see and absorb.

In the early stages of my initial counselling training, I ate, swallowed, digested, and metabolised the various theories and philosophies I was encountering with much delight and passion. 'Taking in' knowledge was (and remains) a source of great excitement – I love being nourished in this way (as anyone seeing my bookshelves will attest). And now, I get to witness this process in others year-on-year as another cohort sit down to dine at the feast of the humanistic paradigm. I see their relish for more and more theory and philosophy as they grapple to find their way; in the struggle of becoming, they think they need more to hone the craft of therapy – confusing the symptoms of indigestion for a lack. At the same time, the theories we encounter in the training make us question the very nature of our being. In the humanistic tradition, we come to desire the authenticity spoken of by the existentialists and the simplicity of subjectivity offered by the phenomenologists. Slowly it dawns on us that we are not who we thought we were, and our current way of being – with all our protective strategies – is in fact preventing us from living fully. The act of 'becoming a person' is not gentle; it can feel like a deep shock to unravel. I remember sharing this experience of falling apart with one of my tutors at the end of the first year. She explained this often happens, and reassured me that "in the second year, we put you back together again". A decade later this former tutor and now dear friend confesses she always knew this was an empty promise!

The solution is to find a way to relate to this emptiness by being, and not doing more. The theory we encounter is not about taking on more – that would increase the layers of personality that take us away from authenticity. The training strips us back, helping us understand how the layers came to be added, and the invitation arises to take off this coat of who we think we should be. This is one way in which I have found meditation to enhance my deconstruction – sitting down and coming to witness the scripts arising deep from the mind and the consequent impulse to act. 'Therapist' is not a role we play, or a thing we do; indeed 'doing' therapy will be counterproductive. The helper organised by obligation to provide love and affection is potentially providing a toxic combination (to be resisted at all costs in some client presentations). I see varying degrees of this play out in the experiential workshops I facilitate: the therapist-in-training trying to help, metaphorically reaching in and over the midline of the relationship, their colleague withdrawing behind the lines doing their best to retreat from the intrusion. The journey is one of realising we can stop trying so hard to help. But that takes trusting what is underneath – the trust of our own being, and the trust that offering the presence of our being (with the attunement, resonance, and trust that follow) to an Other is enough.

Path: personal practice and training

The humanistic psychotherapeutic paradigm is, in my experience, a very powerful vehicle for healing. A relationship grounded in the philosophy of the existential-phenomenological traditions provides an environment in which an individual gets to develop a healthy sense of self. What some might label 'actualisation', we might also call generating an experience of greater expansiveness. All modalities under the humanistic umbrella (some more explicitly than others) broaden awareness of one's experiencing. In Transactional Analysis, one comes to know the various parts-of-self that have been running the show, and the mechanics of the underlying scripts and drivers. Similarly, in the various 'tribes' of the person-centred approach, the therapist holding helps illuminate and soften a way of being that is no longer optimal nor sustainable. It is in Gestalt that the power of awareness is most obviously placed at the centre of the working methodology, the therapist inviting moment-by-moment experiencing to become figural. Bringing awareness to the here-and-now allows contact with any self-imposed limiters and to 'experiment' with relaxing what was once protecting. The honouring of both the material in awareness and that outside of our awareness in a form of dynamic balance and wholeness is key to the humanistic approach.

At the beginning of Chapter 6 I made brief mention of the research into the 'common factors' that make therapy effective (Wampold, 2001). Regardless of the theoretical model adopted, it is the relational vehicle that dictates outcome. Given what we know about human growth and development of the infant, it makes total sense that we come to know who we are through relationship with others. Western psychotherapeutic training ensures that trainees get ample exposure to working in and through the interpersonal realm. In my own training, each week the entire afternoon would be dedicated to group work. The first element was that of the experiential workshop where we would have the opportunity to work with a peer in a 'fishbowl' dyad. Whether in the therapist-in-training chair, or being the one to share, both roles required opening and being vulnerable in the presence of colleagues and tutors. As I recollect that time in my training, a part of me winces at how defended I was. The 'consummate professional' always in control yet screaming with anxiety underneath. I was rigid; absented by my own story rather than present to my colleague in front of me. Of course, I now see how focused I was on finding a solution to make their problem go away because it was my suffering in the face of their suffering that was unbearable. After each dyad, I would feel the adrenalin and thrill of relief. The tutor feedback that would 'make or break' how I felt about my time in the therapist-in-training chair and how I felt about my-self. Conditions of worth located externally? You bet!

The 'process group', held directly after the workshop, was an even bigger learning ground for me. In workshops, I could 'do' therapy quite well – I had after all been in the 'people business' for a while and had become a polished performer. Process groups, on the other hand, called forth our being and there was nowhere to hide. My external conditions of worth, to 'please others' and to 'be strong', got exposed and stripped away. The facilitator saw with much clarity the role I played and invited me to bring more vulnerability to the group. At first, that was an increasingly unedited sharing of what was under the professional veneer. This is often the first step in breaking the injunction "I don't do vulnerability". Yet, 'doing' vulnerability can lead to purging and inevitable oversharing. Just as I would leave campus on a high or low depending on tutor feedback, I would also carry home the shame of saying too much and not being met with an adequate response. I was still needing to learn the dance of intimacy.

As part of my teaching role now, I facilitate an experiential weekend of Gestalt working. Over the years witnessing successive cohorts grapple with vulnerability, I have been able to bring a two-stage process to trainees' awareness. At the beginning of the weekend (which takes place a little over halfway into the two-year training), I get to see how the trainees 'do' their vulnerability – by this stage, they are quite open with each other about what has come to hurt them, to anger them, to scare them in their life. They speak this (what we in Gestalt might call) 'there-and-then' into the middle of the room. Over the weekend, my co-facilitator and I will bring this to the group's awareness, and we gently invite consideration of how that content might also be playing out in the 'here-and-now'. How is the group hurting them, angering them, scaring them? And can they (with support) speak directly to the person they perceive as the activator of their sadness, anger, or fear? All trainees of counselling and psychotherapy know the importance of 'congruence', but very few really understand its two separate components – to be aware of one's own internal experience, and then the transparency or willingness to communicate to the other what is going on within (Lietaer, 1993). Students tend to confuse 'purging' into the middle of the room as being congruent or genuine; how can they be genuine IN relationship and thereby develop intimacy.

This was a slow journey for me on my counselling training course. As with other groups in my life, I had found my way to 'fit in', which I confused with 'belonging', by playing a familiar role. I had attempted to change my recurrent script of the 'be strong' leader by deliberately not offering myself as the course rep; but this didn't stop me being the dependable Helen in other ways. I became the group repository of knowledge – whether it being the daily timetable and room information, or the best texts to use for the upcoming essay, or simply being cohort nerd and fountain of knowledge! So yes, I found a place in the group, but this wasn't fulfilling a deep need in me to be seen and to trust I belonged. I saw those who seemed to belong without performing a service or a function to the group – those I perceived as the 'cool gang' within the cohort – and, very familiar to me, I felt on the periphery and not central to the group.

Years later, when completing my group therapy training, I was finally able to articulate my fear in the group. Having had to leave early one training weekend, I came back the following week and shared my sense of hollowness as I had left; I knew the group would continue without me, and in fact it drained me to my boots to imagine the moment I left, my chair being removed, and I being forgotten. The facilitator at the time supported my process and asked me in my imagining who had removed the chair. I spoke my fantasy directly to the colleague I felt was the core threat – one of the group's 'cool gang' – and I cannot convey how much that has helped me see through my projections and resolve much of my challenge in the group scenario.

Back in my initial training, I hadn't reached that point. In my second year I found myself in a process group with ALL members of the 'cool gang' and I spent the whole year with an internal battle. In my experience attending the Gestalt weekend (that years later, I now co-facilitate), I was the student in the middle of the group sculpt[1] inviting others to "come in and join me", mistaking my position in the middle and alone as being the only one IN the group 'doing' the work. As I retell that story, I reconnect with the pain I felt at the time, and also the heartbreak that I feel now for Helen-of-back-then. I know the importance of going through that painful time; it is only in re-living the experience of isolation that I have come to heal the felt-sense of being different in my family of origin. What I did come to know, very intimately, is how I chose on some level to keep meeting isolation in groups.

What has the Buddhist frame done for us?

Pardon the Monty Python-esque parody as I attempt to underline the 'value-added' dimension Buddhism might bring through its view of 'basic sanity'. When formulating the training for the contemplative psychotherapy course at the Naropa Institute back in the mid 1970s, Chögyam Trungpa Rinpoche (2008a) critiqued Western psychotherapeutic trainings' bias towards theoretical knowledge. Furthermore, he postulated that this is one factor Western psychologists recognise and now look to Buddhism for its experiential mode. It would be a mistake, however, to simply present this as a need for all would-be therapists to meditate. Meditation is but one of the threefold trainings, and you might recall that the first of those is *sila*. This inherent discipline simplifies one's life and eliminates unnecessary complications. This isn't just removing the burden of our consciousness (e.g., not causing harm to purify *karma*) but rather to see how we continually fabricate reality and impose layers of preoccupation. If only we could relax and see our true nature. This is what *samadhi*, the second component of the threefold training, offers. Through the stilling practice of meditation, we develop an attitude of 'bare attention' and can witness our thoughts, feelings, and sensations as overlay to our basic being. If *sila* is the ground, *samadhi* is the path, the fruition is *prajna*; the insight as to how the mind functions, its mechanics and reflexes, moment to moment (the model of mind presented in '*Karma* and the Eight consciousnesses', p. 166). *Prajna* is unbiased knowledge of one's world and mind; it helps us to distinguish confusion and neurosis. It is also the basic inspiration for intellectual study because on seeing one's mind more clearly, there is a natural desire to articulate and clarify what one has experienced. This is a very similar process to what is being advocated in the 'shuttling between insight and experience' (p. 171) offered by a weaving of therapy and meditation.

The development of wisdom and insight is best coming from direct experience and not theory alone. Importantly, it is meditation that grounds the Buddhist teachings and stops it being adopted as another source of concepts. The experiential component is often well-addressed in traditional Western therapeutic training. Training within a contemplative frame (using the language of 'Wholeness, human being and becoming', p. 16) stresses becoming familiar in the 'vertical' dimension of our experience before embarking in the 'horizontal' of the interpersonal. This sequence of training offers students the opportunity to see the dynamics of their own mind and how this style works within others; that a mind is really two minds meeting together (Trungpa Rinpoche, 2008b).[2] In seeing the intrinsic health of 'mind' (our own, that of others) this becomes our orientation towards human nature. In the Buddhist teachings, this is how being 'empty' of a fixed self allows a natural upwelling of compassion. Letting go of the small mind and 'doing', we can practice therapy from the expanse of our being.

Having reaped the benefits of having a meditation practice alongside attending my therapeutic training, I try to convey the benefits of awareness and presence to the trainees I work with in the weekly experiential workshops. Each session, I start with an invitation to feel into the interiority of experiencing. In getting more familiar with the internal world of sensations, emotional energy, and mental activity (body, speech, and mind in the *Dharma* lexicon) the flow of experiencing can be seen. Trainees get to directly witness a process-orientated self. I am careful not to force my beliefs on any student (as with clients), and therefore don't even use the word 'meditation' when facilitating a gateway to presence through embodiment. Spending time 'arriving' before dyad practice or group work has, in my experience, helped trainees see they are not their thoughts, feelings, nor emotions but rather these are temporary and superficial obscurations. There is also an invitation to bring whatever is present into their work, as it is pre-occupation with the suppression of 'wrongness' that risks intimacy in the horizontal relating. Through embodied presence, the opportunity thus arises for new meaning to be brought to experiences and to 'rewrite' "who I am".

In summary, training in the humanistic paradigm offers an excellent place from which an aspiring Buddhism-informed therapist can launch. When trainees approach me with curiosity about such an approach, I encourage them to develop a comprehensive grounding in Western theory and philosophy. From this ground we have a further, higher reach. We need to know and deeply reflect upon the existential questions; and to cultivate the phenomenological approach. We might say we develop 'good form' before loosening and 'dissolving' into a more transpersonal approach. The view and practices of Buddhism offer a going beyond self, reconnecting to the true nature and the very root of our being. Knowing our own mind, we come to see our nature is no different to all sentient beings and life itself. Our mind, two minds, one mind . . . or just 'mind'. Neither the humanistic nor the Buddhistic paradigm shy away from shadow material, but whilst the humanistic tradition allows incorporation *en route* to wholeness (and the alleviation of distress), Buddhism sees the shadow as vital for uncovering our true wisdom nature (and complete liberation from suffering).

What next?

I am writing this section during the final teaching week of the academic year. Yesterday, my day was spent with students completing their counselling postgraduate diploma. In the morning session, I offered them time and space to consider their next steps towards practice. For many, this is an overwhelming transition – and it can draw parallels with 'leaving home'. They were keen to hear my experience of this time, and what I would recommend they consider. I explained the importance of starting with 'good form' (to be deliberate with approach and professional issues such as boundaries, contracting, and ethics), as this can be relaxed to a position of greater creativity, spontaneity, and reflexivity.

Students will often ask for guidance on how to further their training. For many, there is a curiosity as to how to cultivate a more embodied approach to psychotherapy; for some, there is a further refinement of how to bring mindfulness into their work; and there are a few each year who ask for more specific ideas as to how to bring their own Buddhist path into their work. At the end of the session with my students yesterday, one student asked me "Helen, if you could offer us one piece of advice, what would it be?" What a great question! I paused, settled, and reflected upon what I have come to learn on this path so far. I replied, "Is it okay that I offer you two?" I shared that a few years ago, I had listened to a podcast by the late Michael Stone, a teacher I very much admired. In this teaching he urges a trust "to know you are already a *Buddha*, so you can live your life as a *bodhisattva*". I explained to the group that for me, that speaks directly to how we practice humanistic psychotherapy: the importance of first knowing we are perfectly okay as we are. There is no need to push or prove and rather, we can relax in our work with others. The second thought – one that is becoming more evident to me on the path as a *Vajrayana* practitioner – is that there is no need to be embarrassed of our neuroses or tendencies for confusion. Moreover, the *Vajrayana* or *tantric* approach is "to develop immunity [by] judiciously eating the leaves of a [poisonous] plant" (Welwood, 2002, p. 18).

Fruition: becoming a Buddhism-informed practitioner

When I graduated with my counselling qualification and set about getting into private practice, I was terribly excited and equally anxious. I felt the pressure of recruiting clients, and then not losing them. I was overly busy 'trying to be useful' (an obvious reenactment of my childhood role). With time I became more aware of the sharp contrast between my intention (to be) and the actuality of my practice (to do). I also noticed how much I was rousing my energy ahead of my working days with clients. Even when we do this work well, it does have an emotional energy load, but when overly 'doing' and investing in the progress in our clients, it is exhausting and ultimately not sustainable.

The further I have gone along the Buddhist path, the more I have come to notice what ignites my 'doing' and to notice when I am in 'trance' – an expression used by meditation teacher Tara Brach to describe when we lose presence and get caught up in our beliefs and stories. Before starting my writing today, I sat outside on the bench at the front of my house. A beautiful early summer day, I watched the sun rise at the end of the street. I could ask for no more, yet I felt a familiar 'pull' to get going – to exchange this perfect 'as it is' moment of being and get to my desk for my day of writing. Thankfully these days, I can both see and feel what is going on and bring myself back to the openness in the moment 'as it is'. Some days it is easier to connect with the trust of this moment being enough 'as it is'; and that I am enough because I am of the same nature as the blue summer sky. Much of the time, it still takes effort.

With a growing trust of my 'okayness' I am less likely to fall into the trap of getting busy in the room with clients. Essentially, what I 'do' as a therapist is less separate from the ground of who I am. Rather than thinking my way through a session, any intervention is one that arises from the experiencing of being in relationship. I have come to know the felt-sense of any tightness – my shoulders scrunching inward, my forehead feeling tight, a slight holding in my stomach – and with this recognition, I can re-open. Recognising the onset of the tightness is useful information and I get curious as to what might have happened in the room for my body to react that way. In other words, the more present and open I am, the more sensitive to the relational field. Another benefit of practising from presence is that it encourages our clients to meet their own presence – so they too become more receptive to our relating. More recently in my educator role, the more I am teaching from a grounded presence, the more curious the trainees have become in my approach. This has been the fuel for this book.

The fruition of a path that integrates theoretical and experiential (interpersonal) training along with more awareness of our own being enables the dual process of vertical and horizontal relating. From a position of knowing our own experience, we have an opportunity for more authentic contact and relating with Other. We sit opposite as two human beings with all their inherent vulnerability and goodness. From my side, I have noticed a shift in responsibility: from taking responsibility FOR the relationship towards having responsibility TO the relationship. From the client's side, the co-emergence of vulnerability and power allows suffering to be seen not as a failure, but something that connects to Other. I see this in the clients I am currently working with; a greater willingness to recognise and accept experiences of pain – being with it 'as it is'. For me, this is what takes the work from empathy to compassion – opening to the raw and messy side of what it is to be human. Through that we can find contentment and maybe even joy.

Becoming a human being

"The Practice of Human Being" speaks not only to the integration of two wisdom paths – psychotherapy and Buddhism – but also the interplay of formal practice with the everyday; what is often referred to within the Buddhist tradition I practice as "post-meditation". It would feel like an omission to not share how the three threads of being a Buddhist, practising as a psychotherapist, and teaching this 'mysterious art' have manifested in a Helen-shaped human being. What does my practice look and feel like now? How does this come to life? As you might imagine, any 'snapshot' narrative can only be indicative: no two practice sessions look nor feel the same; and even in my daily life with all its routines, the more I pay attention to my experience, the less "same-y" it becomes. I'll start with the formal practice of sitting.

Practise, practise, practise

I wake. My bedside clock tells me its 5:40am. I stroke my cat, wiggle my toes, and remember my intention to practise. I slowly manoeuvre myself from under the duvet trying not to wake my wife nor my cat . . . it is rare I succeed in the latter. She jumps off the bed and trots behind me as I go to the bathroom to clean my teeth, wash my face. Freshening up is part of the ritual; part of the intention to 'wake up' in both the literal and aspirational sense. I am already honing my attention, noticing the tastes, smells, sensations in each action, in the transitions.

Back downstairs to my study. The room is dark in the early hours, so I turn on my SAD lamp. I plump up my zafu cushion, the buckwheat grains rustling, catching the attention of my cat. I light the two candles on my meditation shrine. I enjoy the sound of the match strike, and I catch the odour as it is newly lit. I remember the brand of matches as being the same we had at home in the family kitchen. The candles illuminate the practice space, flickering in the draught coming from the old Victorian fireplace that is the backdrop to the shrine. I remove a stick of incense from the box beside my meditation shrine and I light it using the right-hand candle. There is no special significance to this, it is just habit. I bring the lit incense stick to my head, throat, chest; a gesture that it is my intention to synchronise body, speech, and mind, for the benefit of all beings. I place the incense into its resting place of a sand-filled vase, a gift from close friends when I graduated with my PhD. I remind myself to clean out the old incense embers later.

As I rest back onto the zafu, the scent of the incense begins to register. I hear the buckwheat rustle again. My cat looks up briefly, but then resumes her nap, curled up on the chair in the corner of the study. I reach for the blanket, fold my legs in half-lotus, and open my chant book. I pause . . . and then strike the gong three times. I listen until the sound recedes, and I chant the Four Dharmas of Gampopa.

> *Grant your blessings so that my mind may be one with the Dharma.*
> *Grant your blessings so that Dharma may progress along the path.*
> *Grant your blessings so that the path may clarify confusion.*
> *Grant your blessings so that confusion may dawn as wisdom.*

On other days there are more chants, but today is a session of 'simply sitting'. I close my chant book, put it to one side and put on my glasses. Doing so brings the fine detail of the Victorian fireplace into focus. I haven't always needed glasses during practice, but I find it helps me relax my gaze and soften my face. I appreciate the wisps of smoke from the incense across the front of the fireplace. I begin to settle in my posture, feeling the length of my back, the openness in my chest. I bring my attention to the physicality of my being, riding the in- and out-breath for a few minutes. Connecting to the out-breath feels like dropping an anchor, each one taking that anchor deeper into my being, deeper into the Earth.

After five minutes or so, I ask myself "How am I?", and with this I generally move my attention to the chest area. I get a sense of the emotional weather present today. I rest here for a while, opening to what is. Some ten minutes on, I raise my gaze – I am now looking straight out. I sit in 'open awareness', no object in particular, just allowing my senses to open to sights, sounds, tastes, smells, physical sensations, and noticing where my attention goes. It is a process akin to the lens of a wide angled camera, awareness open to the full panorama, zooming in to whatever sense experience that becomes the object of attention. In just noticing, awareness returns. "Touch and go". This psychonaut[3] is fascinated by how mind works and does all this without "me" . . . if I let it! Of course, thoughts arise. Sometimes these thoughts are successful in their hijack, the "me" is taken on a cross-country jaunt, having exited the metaphorical highway of aware presence. Early on in my meditation career, the main practice was to come back to the breath; to return again . . . and again . . . and again. The muscle of mindfulness.

But these days, when a thought arises, it simply becomes part of the perceptual display. On noticing the thought, awareness turns back on itself and looks for the "me" that is thinking; "I" cannot find "me". Who is doing all this? No-thing! Nor can I find the experiencer of the sight, the sound, the taste, the smell. It isn't uncommon that this "looking and not finding" brings on a greater intensity of a companion I know well, a vibrancy in my heart and chest. But again, there is no experiencer to be found. In that recognition, I settle again into the back of the body, and resume resting in open awareness. I cannot help but indulge in a little of the story of how the relationship to that sensation in my chest used to be so much more judgemental. I take a moment of appreciating my practice and feeling gratitude in finding these teachings, and to the lineage of practitioners to which I belong; the ancient masters, my teachers and mentors, and my *sangha*. I am touched and moved, my heart opens in acknowledgement, and tears come from that tender spot.

Some 40 minutes pass – during which there are a multitude of experiences. An oft used metaphor is an ocean and waves. Awareness is the depth of the ocean; each sensory experience, each mental event, the waves. The *Dharma* teachings explain the waves are of the same essence as the ocean. Similarly, thoughts, feelings, emotions are no different from awareness. Each session brings a different set of waves; some sessions are stormier, some days calmer . . . but whether still or moving, awareness of experience remains untouched. My timer 'pings'. I ring the gong three times to close my practice for the day, and I dedicate any merit gained, giving it away to all sentient beings in hope it might benefit them. My cat stretches again, maybe in grateful receipt – or it might simply be the gong disturbed her.

If there is one phrase to describe how my meditation practice informs my human being ten years on from starting out on the path, it would be 'switching allegiance' from the contents of experience to the awareness of experiencing itself: rather than being caught in the waves, resting in the ocean. I am building faith that the depths are not affected, and this depth is always there, no matter how tempestuous life feels.

Postscript: transitioning off the cushion

Perhaps the ultimate psychonaut, could "practice, practice, practice" and wake up. Arguably humankind's first phenomenologist, *Siddhārtha Gautama*, did this very thing – he sat down under a tree and by resting in experience, recognised the nature of mind and its workings, thus becoming *Buddha*. I, like many others, have benefitted in the system of teachings developed since the *Buddha*. Standing up post-meditation, I am supported by that scaffold as I move into the world.

Since taking the vow to become a *Vajrayana* practitioner, I have been introduced to a loftier scaffold and a vaster View. One such teaching is that of the three *kayas*. Each *kaya* relates to an aspect of awakened being, and we might come across them in different presentations. For instance, in the highest of Buddhist teachings, *Dzogchen*:

Imagine a sky, empty, spacious, and pure from the beginning; its essence is like this.

- This is a description of the *dharmakaya*

Imagine a sun, luminous, clear, unobstructed, and spontaneously present; its nature is like this.

- This is a description of the *sambhogakaya*

Imagine that sun shining out impartially on us and all things, penetrating all directions; its energy, which is the manifestation of compassion, is like this: Nothing can obstruct it and it pervades everywhere.

- This is a description of the *nirmanakaya*

Like fractals in nature, these *kayas* or 'truth bodies' permeate everything. For example, when I light the incense ahead of practice and set my intention to synchronise body, speech, and mind, this is integrating *nirmanakaya*, *sambhogakaya*, and *dharmakaya*, respectively. And so now in my practice, I can recognise the essence of meditation as no experiencer, simply awareness itself (the *dharmakaya*); and yet even without a subject, there is still a quality or nature of knowing (the *nirmanakaya*); and because of this essence and nature, the energy of experiencing unfolds (the *sambhogakaya*).

Practise, practise, practise . . . enough of the rehearsal, when does the show start?

. . . an exclamation I once heard from Buddhist scholar and teacher Robert Thurman. It is one thing to recognise the waves of experience whilst sitting still, alone on the cushion; how does this transfer to the world?

As if "on demand", overnight my bodymind offered an opportunity so that I could present a fresh illustration. I woke at 1am. I visited the bathroom and then went back to bed. I settled, cuddled the cat . . . and then it occurred to me, "mmm, sleep is not coming back". No-thing on my mind, and no apparent thing waking me. I was simply awake. As I lay there, I could feel an impulse for the narrative to rev up; and an almost simultaneous bodily reaction – the inward pulsing in the chest, what I would label 'anxiety'. As the existentialists remind us, "anxiety strives to become fear" – the search for an object, the search to make some-thing out of no-thing. For me, this is where the rubber meets the road, an opportunity for 'switching allegiance' in everyday life situations.

I roll onto my back, still in contact with my cat, I stroke her, feeling her fur, enjoying the soft purr it rouses. It is as if that is the cue to follow my own breath – to hear it, to feel it, to become it. With each out-breath, I feel myself connect more deeply into the mattress. As I would on the meditation cushion, I let go of the breath and open to awareness. I feel my body expand, and simultaneously, notice the coursing sensations: the deep pulsing in my chest, the pulse in my stomach, a tightness in my neck. I remember the probe of Rupert Spira "if you close your eyes, how do you know you have a body?" I move attention from the solid form and connect only to the sensations as points, as if they were stars in the night sky. Again, it evokes the archetype of the psychonaut, a curious explorer of experience.

Yet there is NO explorer (subject) of experience (object). When allegiance switches to awareness, the duality collapses. There is only experiencing. It is not possible to separate out the act of exploring and the sensations – both reside in awareness, there is simply 'sensing'. This is what the Buddhist *Dharma* points to when it says reality 'out there' is an illusion. As a *Vajrayana* student of Buddhism, THIS is my practice; in fact, this is my life "mission" – to recognise moment by moment the illusion of a separate "me".

As I write these words, there is a flurry of snow falling outside. In moments of contentment and stillness such as these, it is somewhat easier to stay in connection with awareness and non-duality. Moving from the perception of the snowflakes to awareness that knows. It is harder when in the heat of an intense emotion, or a volatile/precarious life situation. But essentially the *Vajrayana* path is one of using experience to highlight and recognise the constant, ceaseless presence that is our true being. When "I am anxious", who is that "I"? Where is "she"? When there is recognition of not being a separate self, I feel interconnected or interdependent with the world. The *Vajrayana* teachings point to this connection as Sacred World: mind, body, and emotions, self and other, self and world as a harmonious whole.

"Seeing confusion as the four *kayas* is unsurpassable *shunyata* protection" is the 14th of the Buddhist *lojong* slogans. Not the easiest of the 59 slogans to penetrate. Confusion in this case would be pinning the experience "anxiety" on a separate "I" and making it a thing (rather than an energy, or *lung*). The slogan invites us to consider confusion as a composite – the four *kayas*. "Wait a minute Helen, you said there were THREE *kayas*?" I hear you ask . . . well spotted, there IS a fourth – *svabhavikakaya*. In the example of my sleeplessness, the totality of this experience (as viewed from the *Vajrayana* or ultimate truth) is a composite of

- *Dharmakaya* is the spacious presence or awareness that knows the experiencing
- *Nirmanakaya* – the physical body, feeling my weight in the mattress, the touch contact made with my cat (and all other sense gate experience). This is sometimes called the gross body.
- *Sambobhakaya* – the subtle, or energy body. Last night, this was a 'buzz' which was somewhat unidentifiable in location yet present.

Svabhavikakaya is the realisation that none of these are separate. All the three *kayas* are simultaneously present. But how is this 'protection'? What is this *'shunyata'* being protected?

Being with the totality, experiencing on the level of the four *kayas*, 'protects' by helping us stay open and receptive to the play of experience 'as it is'. Confusion, or ignorance of the way things are (as empty of inherent existence, or *shunyata*), is what causes suffering in the Buddhist view. "My" sleeplessness could be experienced as a failing, that there is something 'wrong'. This is NOT to say sleeplessness is pleasant, desirable, and something we invite – there is a difference between allowing and resignation. I continue to do what I can to enhance the causes and conditions to bring sleep. But to struggle is firing the second arrow (p. 33). Dropping the narrative and resistance to 'what is' helps dis-identify with the waves and drop into the ocean, and again, connect with the inherent sacred wholeness of life.

Adopting this View means these days there is less separation between formal practice and practice in the world – not quite a seamless transition from on the cushion/off the cushion, but I see a movement that way. I feel it pervading my clinical practice.[4] I feel it in my time with students in the training room. And, perhaps most intrinsic to my practice as human being, it is a View now pervading most of my waking hours . . . and not just the insomniac ones.

Don't shoot the messenger

A good many of those waking hours carry an experience of anxiety; one might say that is my *karma*. Anxiety isn't my *karma* per se. It is the signal, the alarm that my *karmic* patterning is in the field. If I hear the alarm, the first reactive narrative is "I must press on"; there is a felt urgency that activates the reactive patterning. I am familiar with two patterns I can fall into:

- The first is one of planning and controlling. I get busy creating structure, making sure I know what is ahead
- The second is in relationship. I reach out, making sure I know others are there.

Both patterns are seeking confirmation, validation that "I" exist. But both patterns are looking outside of me for my existence. There is a metaphor I find useful, one of reaching out to a handrail, for something to hold onto when I lose my footing. And, if I check in with the underlying felt-sense on hearing the signal of anxiety, there is a sense of 'toppling over'. When I am thinking of my week ahead, I can sense I am living in the front of my body, leaning into what is to come. In relationship to others, I feel my energy going 'up and out', a focus on the other, and I lose my-self.

Anxiety flags up when I have lost my connection to ground; and I get busy in my attempts to 'fix' the problem of 'too much' space. I am reminded of the imagery in the Wheel of Life, the hungry ghosts 'reaching out' to fill the emptiness. John Welwood explains that the emptiness itself is not the problem. The 'problem' is our interpretation of it. For me, space often feels like a void – this is the confused view, and the pattern is to try and find certainty, ground. Buddhism points to the emptiness, *shunyata*, as potential, as clarity and presence. This is the wisdom View, one of groundlessness.

The point is to not change my *karma*; nor to fix my anxiety. "Working it through" is to feel the suffering of my anxiety fully, and see the direction it is pointing to, a u-turn. On feeling my up and out, I sweep my body, recognising how I am holding, contracting into "I". In the immediacy of that knowing, I lean back, reconnecting to the verticality. Waking up and waking down, the joining of Heaven and Earth. Trust, courage, surrender. I can't tease these out into chronological steps; it is as though leaning back in the body they emerge simultaneously. It is the play of wisdom in the *Sambobhakaya*.

When I find this openness, space becomes spaciousness. I am present, less speedy, less defended, at ease . . . generally a nicer person to be around! But it is so much more than that. The confusion transmuted to wisdom. Using the language of the *Vajrayana*, anxiety is the ultimate pointing out of the nature of mind. In seeing it, shifting allegiance to the awareness that knows. Anxiety shows me the road back home to the groundless ground.

I have come to learn through study and practice of the *buddhadharma* that there are many paradoxes to face on the path. Perhaps the one most fundamental is the invitation to know suffering intimately: to experience it fully; AND simultaneously realise there is no existent knower of that suffering.

Notes

1 an exercise designed to give participants an experience of their position in the group, often a re-living of the original family unit
2 Those of you familiar with Daniel Stern's work will appreciate this very practical application of intersubjectivity and the dimensions of relatedness (Stern, 2004).
3 Please indulge my use of the label 'psychonaut': someone who explores altered states of consciousness. Ordinarily this is through hallucinatory drugs, but I believe it applies equally to any serious student and adventurer of 'mind'.
4 On the training courses for counselling and psychotherapy, we encourage the students to reflect upon the process in the therapy room across self, other, relationship. To me, these map onto the three *kayas* in the following way: The Self and Other of the therapist and client are the physical manifestation of the *Nirmanakaya*, I propose the relational aspect between as the *Dharmakaya* – a space without form, substance, or concept of any sort. We might equate the notion of the therapeutic container; and this space of potential allows the play of therapy, the *Sambobhakaya*. This model has helped me understand some of the mystery that emerges in therapy.

References

Bott, D., & Howard, P. (2012). *The Therapeutic Encounter: A Cross-modality Approach*. London: Sage.

Lietaer, G. (1993). Authenticity, Congruence and Transparency. In D. Brazier (Ed.), *Beyond Carl Rogers* (pp. 17–46). London: Constable.

Rogers, C.R. (1967). *On Becoming a Person*. London: Constable.

Stern, D.N. (2004). *The Present Moment in Psychotherapy and Everyday Life*. New York, NY: W.W. Norton & Company.

Trungpa Rinpoche, C. (2008a). The Meeting of Buddhist and Western Psychology. In F.J. Kaklauskas (Ed.), *Brilliant Sanity: Buddhist Approaches to Psychotherapy*. Colorado Springs, CO: University of Rockies Press.

Trungpa Rinpoche, C. (2008b). *True Perception: The Path of Dharma Art*. Boston, MA: Shambhala Publications.

Wampold, B.E. (2001). *The Great Psychotherapy Debate: Models, Methods, and Findings*. Mahwah, NJ: Lawrence Erlbaum Associates Publishers.

Watson, G. (1998). *The Resonance of Emptiness: A Buddhist Inspiration for a Contemporary Psychotherapy*. New Delhi: Motilal Banarsidass Publications.

Welwood, J. (2002). *Toward a Psychology of Awakening: Buddhism, Psychotherapy, and the Path of Personal and Spiritual Transformation*. Boston, MA: Shambhala.

Travelogue

I set out on this book writing journey four years ago, and what an adventure; venturing across new terrain, within and without. Four years ago, it was my intention to collate my learning on the paths of Buddhism and humanistic psychotherapy, and to document my experience of bringing them together. I recognise that four years ago was a juncture at which I was needing to formulate my ideas into a coherent practice frame. This, after all, is something I ask trainee counsellors to do as they prepare to 'leave home' and move into private practice. "Know your frame". Through this frame, the therapist sees the client, their struggle, and the healing task ahead. This book was, in effect, setting about to write my own therapy manual. My inspiration grew as students asked me how the Buddhist path informs my Gestalt approach to embodiment; and thus, an aspiration became that this project may be of benefit to others.

Four years ago, we had no idea of the pandemic to come. Like many of you, I imagine, without the usual routines my sense of milestones during the pandemic lessened, if not disappeared. Subsequently, there has been an apparent distortion of time: expanses of timelessness, other moments seemingly speed warped, sometimes standing still. Personally, living a smaller life, I would even say a more introverted and introspective life, has afforded me more time on my Buddhist practice and time on my writing. Therapists are known "CPD junkies", and I am guilty as charged. This period of pandemic has been a perfect storm of causes and conditions to indulge my "little professor" archetype.

Four years ago, I had not started out on the *Vajrayana* path. The deeper my engagement with Buddhism, the more I have come to appreciate that Buddhism is not one system of thought. Each *yana* presents a different View and emphasis; and even the *Vajrayana* varies within the four schools of Tibetan Buddhism. My intense period of practice and study these past four years have made me appreciate that the *Vajrayana* has more in common with alchemy than Buddhism presented in the original *sutras*.

DOI: 10.4324/9781003383710-12

All this to say: as life stood still, my ideas and experiences have not. Four years on, thoughts and feelings concerned with being a human have waxed and waned. Thoughts and feelings about therapy that ennobles human-being have metamorphosed as quickly as I have been writing about them. Undoubtedly, if I were to write this book from scratch, it would not look like it does now. That was apparent to me when I read over the first draft of the manuscript. I found myself encountering a familiar doubt; echoes of completing my PhD 25 years ago. Back then I felt incredibly despondent, even ashamed, that the thesis I submitted didn't reflect the ideas I held going into the viva examination. Understandable, given the positivist view of the world I held at that time. Fast forward to now, I am better equipped to *go with* the groundlessness. On re-reading the manuscript I noticed the pivots and turns in my thinking about therapy and henceforth tipping points in the trajectory of the book. I faced the dilemma of revising the text; but it occurred to me that to write a book that reveals a *truth* of how to do therapy is nonsensical. To start that pursuit might resemble an M.C. Escher painting, a never- ending loop. Instead, this book in and of itself reveals a "practice of human being".

I share this process not to serve as a disclaimer nor to undermine read-ers' confidence in anything I have written. I am far from 'ashamed' of the end-product this time. I understand that I had to write this book *in order* to evolve my ideas and master my practice as a Buddhism-informed practi-tioner. This is the underpinning of heuristics – a way of research and writing I am committed to. Indeed, the whole Buddhist path can be considered heuristic: a constant reflection of the practitioner proffered by the phenom-enal world.

Ultimately, I believe the book contains two significant offerings. Firstly, in line with my original intention, we have been on a tour of what the *Dharma* teachings may offer the therapist, the client, and the therapeutic work. At the time I took the *Bodhisattva* Vow, I was given the name *Champe Sampa*, or "Bridge of *maitri*". True to making this name a practice, I have attempted to translate the *Dharma* in a way that those new to Buddhism find the teachings and practices accessible. Accordingly, this work bridges across the Western and Eastern views in a way that I hope benefits. Sec-ondly, documenting my path is an invitation: not to trace my steps, but rather to give other 'baby *bodhisattvas*' the courage to make their own way. One of the biggest learning edges a therapist will encounter is to develop one's own craft – it may sound a cliché, but there really are as many thera-peutic approaches as practitioners. Once trained in finding good form; let go of the reins; follow the smoke of your fiery passion in this field.

It is perhaps only on writing this epilogue that I am encountering a reali-sation, a bodily "a-ha" tells me so. It is as if the book has also been a bridge for me too, or to use a metaphor presented in the *Dharma*, a raft. The

Buddha invited practitioners to discard the teachings once we have "crossed over to the other shore": no point in carrying a raft on dry land! Similarly, the point of the Buddhist path is not to be a Buddhist, but rather to 'wake up'. The parallel I am making with my journey towards a Buddhism-informed therapy is appreciating I am arriving on another shore; to regard Buddhism as one methodology that leads to knowing non-duality. Buddhism points to being, it is not to be confused with the only vehicle nor the destination itself.

In the context of my psychotherapy work, Buddhism has brought me to straddle a threshold, one between the humanistic and transpersonal. I represent the benevolent other, one who knows both 'lands' and holds the door ajar if the client (through *becoming*) grows more curious in a world beyond the conventional self (*being*). Maybe this is *me* letting go of the reins.

In the context of this book, the usefulness of exploring Buddhist teachings can be described using threefold logic of ground, path, and fruition (p. 185). The ground is that we human beings don't remember (or trust) our inherent brilliance. And so, we need a path. That path takes us through the foothills of not causing harm (the skilful means of preventing malevolence in the *Hinayana*) onto the steep slopes of being a *bodhisattva* and opening our hearts to others (the practices of benevolence in the *Mahayana*). The View at the top is vast and expansive: the *Vajrayana* could not be reached without the earlier training, but the so-called 'cosmic joke' is that we have arrived from where we departed. The path of human being is not a linear one, but rather a spiral, taking us back over previous ground but experiencing it in new ways. Back to the wisdom contained in an Escher painting, the journey and destination are no different. This description is relevant to becoming a therapist: we need a path to unlearn what we have come to believe and to arrive in a place where our mere presence is mysteriously[1] healing.

The trajectory taken through this book has led me into many therapeutic valleys and atop many spiritual peaks. There is much transpersonal and non-dual literature informing my work now, and I again see benefit in bringing this to the attention of Western trained psychotherapists in a way that doesn't necessitate them retraining or ditching their home paradigm. I find myself inspired to write more on a psychotherapy that addresses two paths: the horizontal actualisation and the vertical transcendence. The former illuminates the shadow and wounds that make up our personality, offering the reclamation of wholeness of the personal 'self'; the latter awakens us to the 'Self', a timeless and formless being.

As I close, a return to the choice in naming this final section. This being my first book, I turned to the Oxford dictionary for guidance on what makes an 'epilogue'. "A section or speech at the end of a book that serves as a comment on or a conclusion to what has happened". It goes on to add "the meaning of the book's title is revealed". When I chose "*The practice of human being*", it was a working title, one that over time I came to find quite beguiling. I now understand what my meditation mentor pointed out as my writing travels were entering their final moments – "a book teaches you what you don't know".

We come to know our being through our doing. And yet, the Buddhist view is an invitation to inverse our attention. All our 'doing' in the world is merely an expression of the unchanging being in the backdrop of experiencing. And that unchanging being remains untouched by our human suffering. Turning attention around and the recognition of *being* IS the practice. Ultimately, I offer this book as an invitation to recognise the co-emerging *movement in practice* with the *stillness of our being*.

> *Grant your blessings so that my mind may be one with the Dharma*
> *Grant your blessings so that Dharma may progress along the path*
> *Grant your blessings so that the path may clarify confusion*
> *Grant your blessings so that confusion may dawn as wisdom.*
> The Four Dharmas of Gampopa

Note

1 Theories remain, and we have terms such as co-regulation, attunement; and yet when we rest in our being, is what we experience two minds becoming one? Is there some kind of 'subterranean' mingling of our consciousnesses?

Appendix: Glossary

Abhidharma   the Buddhist psychology. One of the three main collections of texts of the Buddhist canon – alongside the monastic code and the *Sutras*. Lays out Buddhist systems theory, describing the nature, origin, and interaction of all psychological and material phenomena, including human consciousness itself.

Alaya-vijnana   the foundation or basis of all consciousness. Holds the impressions of all past actions. Often called the 'store-house' consciousness.

Bardo   intermediate state or transition. In the Tibetan Buddhist system, there are six traditional *bardos*: of this life, meditation, dream, dying, *dharmata*, and existence – but this term most commonly refers to the transition between death and being reborn. Used colloquially to point to 'gaps between'.

Bodhicitta   awakened heart-mind; the quality to which a *bodhisattva* aspires and the expression of emptiness (non-self) and compassion (interdependence).

Bodhisattva   an ordinary person who aspires to attain the mind of a *buddha*; a spiritual warrior that compassionately refrains from entering *nirvana* in order to alleviate the suffering of all beings. On the Buddhist path, a Vow is taken at the point of this commitment.

Buddha   literally "awakened one". Most often refers to the historical *Buddha*, Shakyamuni, who as Prince Siddhartha sat down under a *Bodhi* tree to meditate and attained enlightenment.

Buddhanature   the fundamental nature of all beings being awakened mind.

Dathun   (meaning 'month session') an extended meditation retreat with extended periods of sitting meditation (eight to ten hours per day) and other contemplative practices, e.g., eating oryoki, a Zen tradition of taking each meal in the shrine room with chanting and ritual.

Dharma   can vary in its definition depending on context: 1) as primordial, the underlying reality of life and the world, the ultimate fact of who and what we are, i.e., true nature; 2) as phenomena, the basis of our ordinary existence and its thoughts, perceptions, occurrences; 3) as path, how we respond; and 4) as the teachings delivered by the *Buddha*. Traditionally, one of Buddhism's "three jewels" in which a practitioner seeks refuge as they take the Vow to become a Buddhist.

Dukkha   usually translated as 'suffering', but some commentators prefer 'dissatisfaction' or 'distress' to point to its subtle manifestations in mind and body. Anything 'unpleasant', and can therefore be understood as the polarity of '*sukkha*'.

Dzogchen   'great perfection' or 'completeness' and the ultimate view within the *Nyingma* school. The teachings and practices help reveal the nature of mind as '*rigpa*'. Might be considered similar to the *Kagyu* lineage practice of *Mahamudra*.

Hinayana   the first and foundational vehicle (*yana*) of teachings in the three tier Tibetan system of Buddhism (see *Mahayana* and *Vajrayana*), but often equated to the Theravada school.

Kagyu   One of the four main schools of Buddhism (along with *Gelug*, *Nyingma*, *Sakya*). An oral lineage, its main focus is on practice, e.g., *Mahamudra*.

Kalyanamitra   a teacher or mentor at 'eye-level' with the practitioner; often referred to as a 'spiritual friend'; someone who works with you to understand the teachings and helps you process and integrate them.

Karma   action, cause, and effect. No action is inherently good or bad but is designated according to the results the action brings. *Karmic* seeds are said to be sowed and stored in consciousness (see *Alaya-vijnana*) and come to fruition at some later point (or some later life according to traditional teachings).

Kayas   commonly referred to in the set of three, or *trikaya*, three bodies or three modes of being of the *Buddha*: the *dharmakaya* (body of essence), the unmanifested mode, and the supreme state of absolute knowledge; the *sambhogakaya* (body of enjoyment), the heavenly mode; and the *nirmanakaya* (body of transformation), the earthly mode.

Klesha   afflictive mind state. The three 'root' *kleshas* (or poison) are attachment, aversion, and ignorance (the latter being a wrong-seeing that leads to the other two). Sometimes, the five *kleshas* are described with the addition of pride and envy.

Lojong   mind-training; a set of (normally) 59 slogans containing concise instructions of how to approach meditation and how to awaken in daily life; a key component of the *Mahayana* vehicle.

Lung   wind or air energy. Might also refer to an oral transmission of a teaching.

Mahamudra The ultimate teachings of the *Kagyu* lineage and practices that help a meditator see the nature of mind. See also *Dzogchen*.

Mahayana greater vehicle, originating in India and now the dominant Buddhist movement. Emphasises the teachings of emptiness (of self, or phenomena) and compassion; *Mahayana* practitioners take the *Bodhisattva* Vow and practice the six *Paramita* and *Lojong* slogans.

Maitri lovingkindness, benevolence, or friendliness. The first of the Four Immeasurable qualities (with compassion, sympathetic joy, equanimity).

Mandala a round symbol of a universe, used to represent a deeper meaning. Most often seen in the teachings of *tantra* or *Vajrayana*. Carl Jung had a deep curiosity towards the Eastern *mandala*, seeing it as an archetypal image signifying the wholeness of the Self.

Ngondro Tibetan Buddhism's preliminary, preparatory, or foundational practices or disciplines common to all four schools of Tibetan Buddhism. Practitioners commence these practices as they enter the *Vajrayana* by way of 'emptying and preparing the vessel' ahead of deity yoga.

Paramita perfections or transcendent actions that Buddhists strive to cultivate. Most commonly associated with the *Mahayana* and central to practice of those who have taken the *Bodhisattva* Vow.

Prajna best knowledge or best knowing. Associated with the highest form of wisdom.

Rigpa pristine awareness or primordial purity that is the fundamental ground of mind.

Samadhi concentration or one-pointedness.

Samsara to flow on. Refers to the cycle of birth, death, rebirth and therefore endless suffering and dissatisfaction (*dukkha*). Release from this cycle (its opposite) leads to *nirvana*.

Samskara conditioned mental formations, all constructs, good, bad, or indifferent: dispositions, tendencies, volitions, impulses, emotions, strivings, and reactions. The process by which reactive emotional patterns or habits are formed.

Sangha the Buddhist community of practitioners. Sometimes this refers just to ordained practitioners (monks, nuns) but most often includes laypeople who follow the teachings of the *Buddha*.

Shamatha peaceful or calm abiding. Colloquially called mindfulness or concentration meditation. Leads to the practice of *vipashyana*.

Shunyata emptiness, not meaning a void but rather not inherently existing or existing as we ordinarily think something does.

Sila discipline, ethics, morality. One of the threefold trainings located within the Noble Eightfold Path; a code of conduct that embraces a commitment to harmony and self-restraint with the principal motivation being nonviolence.

Skandha   group, aggregate, or heap. As a collection of five, constitutes the entirety of personality: form, sensation, perception, mental formations, and consciousness.

Sutra   string or thread. Records of the oral teachings of the *Buddha*.

Tangka   A Tibetan Buddhist painting on cotton or silk drape depicting a deity, scene, or *mandala*. The purpose of *tangka* is to convey a particular Buddhist teaching or as a centrepiece for a ritual, ceremony, or practice.

Tonglen   "taking and sending". Designed to reverse our usual logic of avoiding suffering and seeking pleasure. Visualising taking in the pain of others with every in-breath and sending out whatever will benefit them on the out-breath.

Upaya   skilful means that allows wisdom to be conveyed in a way it can be received or absorbed by the practitioner.

Vajrayana   the diamond or indestructible vehicle probably evolving from the same roots as the *Mahayana*. Often called Tibetan Buddhism because of its proliferation there. Offers the 'fast path' to awakening using rituals and symbolism for its advanced mind training.

Vedana   feeling tone, to include mental component, i.e., not just physical sensation; often categorised as pain, pleasure, or neutral.

Vipashyana   insight, extraordinary seeing. In meditation, to see things as they truly are.

Index